P9-CKC-530

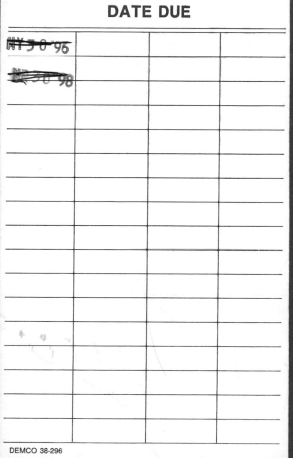

DATE DUE

BEATING JAPAN

FRANCIS McINERNEY AND SEAN WHITE

BEATING JAPAN

How Hundreds of American Companies Are
Beating Japan Now—and What *Your* Company
Can Learn From Their Strategies and Successes

TRUMAN TALLEY BOOKS/DUTTON
NEW YORK

TRUMAN TALLEY BOOKS/DUTTON
Published by the Penguin Group
Penguin Books USA Inc., 375 Hudson Street,
New York, New York 10014, U.S.A.
Penguin Books Ltd, 27 Wrights Lane, London W8 5TZ, England
Penguin Books Australia Ltd, Ringwood, Victoria, Australia
Penguin Books Canada Ltd, 10 Alcorn Avenue,
Toronto, Ontario, Canada M4V 3B2
Penguin Books (N.Z.) Ltd, 182-190 Wairau Road,
Auckland 10, New Zealand

Penguin Books Ltd, Registered Offices:
Harmondsworth, Middlesex, England

First published by Truman Talley Books/Dutton, an imprint of New American
Library, a division of Penguin Books USA Inc.
Distributed in Canada by McClelland & Stewart Inc.

First Printing, March, 1993
10 9 8 7 6 5 4 3 2

LIBRARY OF CONGRESS CATALOGING-IN-PUBLICATION DATA:

McInerney, Francis.
    Beating Japan : how hundreds of American companies are beating
  Japan now—and what your company can learn from their strategies and
  successes / Francis McInerney and Sean White.
       p. cm.
    ISBN 0-525-93577-0
    1. Industrial management—United States—Case studies.
  2. Industrial management—Japan—Case studies. 3. Success in
  business—United States. 4. Success in business—Japan.
  5. Competition, International. ·   I. White, Sean.   II. Title.
  HD70.U5M37   1993
  658—dc20   92-28313
                                                                  CIP

Printed in the United States of America
Set in Times Roman
Designed by Eve L. Kirch

To Katherine and Verna,
for love and loyalty over many years.

And to Ken Bosomworth,
for a start.

CONTENTS

BEATING JAPAN

INTRODUCTION

Cracks in the Facade

The Japanese Monolith Meets the 1990s

The idea for this book came to us during a trip to Japan in 1989. Accompanying our local distributor on a series of sales calls, we began to realize that the certainty of success we attribute to the Japanese was not shared by the people we were seeing. Many were alarmed at their performance outside Japan, even despairing.

At the time we were working for Northern Business Information, a publisher of research on the telecommunications industry, which we had founded in 1976 and sold to McGraw-Hill in 1988. Our biggest customers were in Japan, and we were there to find out how we could serve them better.

During the years we were building our business, the Japanese had come from nowhere to become serious contenders in the telecommunications market, particularly in the United States after the breakup of the Bell System in 1983. But by the mideighties it had become apparent that the Japanese companies we followed had been stopped nearly dead in their tracks. While Japan's reputation for invincibility grew, many competitors were quietly beating Japan at its own game. Outside Japan, stagnation and even decline followed early successes in telecom, a market specifically chosen by the Japanese government to begin Japan's "breakout" from cars and TVs.

Just as this Japanese invasion bogged down on the beaches, our own company went through a dramatic transition. A cottage industry of research boutiques tracking high-tech industries had boomed in the 1970s and was further fueled by the personal computer revolution and deregulation of communications in the early 1980s. NBI rode this boom, but by the mid-eighties, consolidation had set in with a vengeance: the easy years were over.

From 1985 to 1986, while the rest of the country prospered, two thirds of our competitors went out of business or contracted to one-man shops. We reeled from these blows and were on the verge of bankruptcy. After years of healthy growth, we had to lay off employees for the first time. It was a sobering experience. The rapid hemorrhaging of our cash reserves—we were down to cash advances on our credit cards—steeled us to the task.

We began cutting people and products in an effort to zero in on what our customers wanted most. In the process we realized our business, the mail-order sale of books, was isolated from customers. We had been dreaming up subjects we thought would be interesting to research, and hoped somebody would buy our work. A direct-mail machine sending out 75,000 or more pieces of junk mail per month had kept the orders coming in.

But now the orders were getting scarce. We were desperate, so we did the unthinkable: we talked to our customers. We hired a salesman. We dismantled the layers of organization between ourselves, the decision-makers, and our customers.

To our horror, we found out that our customers— incredibly—were not interested in our products. They had their own problems. While they valued the accuracy of our published research, they were looking for help in their daily activities, not for books to gather dust on their shelves. With our core product—research—virtually unchanged, we began to evolve into a service provider. Real live people, reachable at any time, solving real live problems. We were out of the book business.

Short lines of communications with our customers and high service levels led to two years of rapid, profitable growth—and to an unsolicited offer from McGraw-Hill to buy our business. With many "ship and forget" information subsidiaries, McGraw-Hill was anxious to convert to the service religion we were advocating.

As we traveled out of Tokyo in September 1989 to visit one of our customers, we realized that the Japanese companies we were studying and selling to were almost in a state of panic. Their position, which seemed so impregnable from the States, now seemed so vulnerable. What had gone wrong? Suddenly we saw the parallel between our own business and that of our Japanese customers.

Most big companies build barriers between themselves and their customers, but many Japanese have institutionalized these barriers. As we had done in publishing, our Japanese customers liked to dream up new products and then try to find a home for them. This had worked while computer markets were growing quickly; as soon as demand slowed and customers became more selective, the Japanese lost their momentum.

In the industries with which we were most familiar, we knew that we had discovered problems—ones seldom mentioned on TV or in newspaper editorials—that were creating a watershed in Japan's overseas expansion. We spent the next eighteen months studying other industries, and determined that in *every* market that the Japanese were attacking, the level of customer contact, not technology or capital, was determining market share. Japan's resounding success in cars and consumer electronics in particular has masked many of the problems that we have found, but it is precisely in these industries that Japanese companies are better integrated with their customers. In other words, these are the exceptions that prove the rule.

Selling is not easy. Nobody likes complaints; nobody wants

the brain damage that comes from customers who say no. In most companies, the higher-ups insulate themselves from customers so they don't have to sell. Selling is something done by underlings, like running machine presses or sweeping floors. The big Japanese electronics firms, such as Fujitsu, Hitachi, NEC, and Matsushita, have erected literally dozens of layers of management between real decision-makers and their overseas customers. The results are predictable: unacceptable performance in market after market.

Entrepreneurs—the ones that survive, anyway—know that their customers come first.[1] We learned this lesson the hard way. Pressed to the edge of bankruptcy, we were forced to examine our business from top to bottom. We had created a miniature version of the Bell System we published reports about, with half a dozen layers between ourselves and customers. We realized that anyone who does not talk to customers every day is doing a job better contracted out to someone else.

In the West, businesses tend to ossify as they grow. Japanese businesses do not—at least not in Japan. Big businesses in Japan are remarkably close to their Japanese customers. But the same structure that keeps management flexible in Japan insulates it from customers abroad. Simply put, Japanese management does not travel well. At least not yet. A new generation of postwar companies like Sony and Honda are more successful abroad than at home. These companies are experimenting with new management techniques that will undoubtedly be adopted by their Japanese competitors if they work.

To fuel its insatiable export machine, Japan has targeted information technology, especially computers and communications, for growth. The reason is not hard to find: electronics alone, only part of the information technology total, is the third-biggest industry in the United States and the fastest-growing of the top six. With some two million workers, electronics accounts for more exports than any other sector.[2] It is just as big and just as critical in Europe. Clearly, there is a lot of money at stake here. With fat profits from IT, Japan could bankroll expansion into ever more markets, high-tech or otherwise. But all has not gone according to plan. Japan is an also-ran in most IT markets, stuck as a producer of commodity hardware of ever declining value.

Recognizing the inherent weakness of Japan's export-driven strategies, we conceived this book as a way to provide specific, practical lessons on proven counterstrategies for Japan's competitors, while dispelling the myth of Japan's invincibility. These strategies are built on fifteen years of analyzing Japanese players in electronics and advising their American and European competitors, many of whom are beating Japan in key markets. We are not experts on Japan, but we do know about Japan's national champions in electronics and—most important—about their customers. Our advice is seasoned by the hands-on experience of building and running our own business.

You will find here no apologies for industrial failures in the West, no Japan-bashing, no self-pitying complaints about "unfair" advantages. If you are running a business, you have a job to do; we want to help you do it properly. Virtually *all* managers in *all* industries face a current or potential threat from Japanese competitors. If you are in any high-tech industry, that threat is particularly acute.

When we look at successful companies, we often ask, "What are they doing right?" More often than not, however, the right question is "What is everyone else doing wrong?" Few companies—and few people—do everything right. Many American, European, and Japanese companies follow some of the lessons in this book; none that we know of, including our own, follows them all. But like "zero defects" in production, quality management is something you strive for but never achieve. Come even close, and you won't have to worry about competition from Japan or anywhere else.

Japan has many strengths, to which its many successes bear ample witness. But Japan has not overrun the United States, and will not overrun Europe. Hysteria about the Japanese threat is energetically encouraged by the industries that benefit most from government protectionism. Chrysler here in America and Renault in France are only too happy to whip up the public support they seek for trade barriers. If you want to solve your own problems, however, start by serving your customers better.

If Americans and Europeans are to meet the challenges of the next generation, we believe, they must fundamentally rethink business strategy and completely restructure their organizations. Nothing short of a revolution in customer relations can save the West from industrial decline. In 1992, American-Japanese relations were strained when Japanese politicians said American workers are lazy. The Japanese are wrong if they think American workers are—but they are right to tell Americans not to blame others for their failures. The fact is, American management is coming up short not with the Japanese but with customers.

This book is about dismantling and rebuilding your business to make it truly competitive with Japan. It is about the concrete steps that you must take now, to change your thinking, to remold your company, to rebuild your own career. The lesson of this book is simple: to succeed, you must live and breathe your customers, no matter where in the world you may find them.

—1—

Facing the Threat

Competing Head-on with Japan

Sooner or later the Japanese are going to come after your company and your job. For Lee Iacocca, sooner is already here.

Today the Japanese set the agenda in cars, copiers, cameras, and consumer electronics. Honda, Nissan, and Toyota are not bigger than General Motors. But when Ford and GM talk about improvements, they talk about doing as good a job as the Japanese. Ever playing catch-up ball, the American auto industry continues to consolidate and lose market share.

As for consumer electronics, great American names like RCA-Victor and Stromberg-Carlson conjure only quaint images of families huddled around desktop radios listening to Mayor La Guardia reading the funnies. The industry that produced them is dead and gone.

Now established as part of the American landscape, Japan's industrial giants have new, more aggressive goals. First and foremost is IT—information technology—the huge and fast-growing market for computers, telephones, semiconductors, and other electronic products and services. Here a major assault appears well under way. Legions of computer chips, fax machines, laptop personal computers, and laser printers relentlessly pour into American homes and offices. According to industry accounts, the Japanese have already overrun these markets.[1] Decimation of Europe's electronics sector also seems well advanced.

The Japanese have other big targets: entertainment, construction, banking, real estate, retailing, aerospace, biotechnology, and agriculture. Japanese firms have bought Rockefeller Center, two of the biggest movie studios in the country, and dozens of cattle ranches, golf courses, and resorts. Already Japan controls 25 percent of the banking assets in California. Once its teeth are cut on America, Japan will turn to Europe for some more easy pickings in these new areas.

Unless you are employed by the government, you had better be thinking about your company's ability to meet its Japanese competitors. More important, you'd better evaluate your own job prospects. If you think you are safe, think again. Even if they don't kill your company, the Japanese may drop a product on the market that makes you, your department, or your division suddenly redundant. There are a lot of people at Westinghouse and General Electric who could find themselves on the unemployment line if the Japanese start selling cheap, durable, energy-efficient appliances in this country.

If your company can't compete, can you? Do you have the skills to meet a well-planned and well-financed threat to your business? The fact is, the Japanese want your lunch, and if you're not ready to fight for it, they'll get it.

Many companies respond to the Japanese threat by trying to imitate their greatest strengths: quality, cost reduction, fast product development, and motivation techniques, particularly for factory workers. While most simply talk a good game about learning from Japan, other companies have genuinely changed.

Detroit, for example, has made great strides in reducing automobile costs, improving quality, speeding up new product development, and motivating its workers. Unfortunately, its Japanese competitors have moved even faster, and Detroit continues to lag behind. From their conception in the 1980s, many of Detroit's new cars were designed to be as good as Japanese models. Unfortunately, "as good as the Japanese" in the 1980s does not do a company much good in the 1990s. Car buyers, of course, are looking for something better to justify switching their allegiance back to American products. "Just as good" just won't do.

GM, for all its efforts, saw its market share collapse during the 1980s, and by 1989 the best-selling car in America was made by Honda, not GM. The auto giant's retired CEO Roger Smith became the butt of a popular satirical film, *Roger and Me*. GM's fate awaits any company not ready to match its Japanese competitors, then go one better. Is your company one of those paying lip service to change? Does your company have a plan to outmaneuver the Japanese before the game is lost? If not, how long can your employer keep up the charade? And when will you have to begin looking for a new future?

Where Japan has done best, in cars, there has been a continuous and futile ceding of ground by competitors. Some firms once thought that if they gave up the low end of their business, the Japanese would be sated. This turned out to be naive. Detroit all but abandoned production of cheap, compact cars, only to find its Japanese competitors whittling away at everything from Chevrolets to Lincolns. Today, even posh European marques like Mercedes-Benz, Porsche, and BMW are feeling the heat, forced to do the unthinkable—compete on price—to slow the relentless push upmarket by Acura, Infiniti, and Lexus.

The scene has been replayed in industry after industry. Intel and Motorola ceded commodity memory chip sales to the Japanese, only to find them pressing ahead in microprocessors and semi-custom devices once considered too sophisticated for the Japanese to make. Xerox gave Minolta and Canon convenience copiers; now they are the innovators in color copiers, laser printers, and other turf Xerox once considered its own.

If you are a manager on the front line, the specter of Japanese competition is daunting. First, you must figure out how well your company is positioned to meet a serious and sustained Japanese threat to its business. Second, you must calculate what your company must do to be the best, not just "as good as the Japanese." Finally, you must assess the chances of your company implementing the changes needed to be the best. If the chances are poor, it's time to start looking for a new job or new career.

Japan Presses On

Any lingering doubts about Japan's intentions should be put to rest. Clearly the Japanese will not be satisfied with cars and consumer electronics. They will press on, for one simple reason: *they are desperate.*

Small and isolated, crowded and bereft of natural resources, Japan must export or die. Exports give Japan a sense of security and economic self-sufficiency in a hostile and capricious world. Indeed, exporting is synonymous with national security, and the motto of Japan Inc. could be "Exports R Us."

Japan Inc. has performed its task most admirably, but the need for exports becomes ever more voracious as Japan grows and ages. Japan is aggressively developing its service market opportunities overseas. But no amount of success in banking, real estate, and hotels will pay the bill: Japan must export.

And export it does. Japan sells America twice as much as it buys. But its balance of trade with the rest of the world is not so favorable. Indeed, Japan's surplus with the United States barely covers its fuel bill.[2] Without new markets, Japan will face a threat to its security and prosperity. Sixty years ago, such fear drove Japan to secure its sources of oil and other raw materials by military force.

Along with Japan's success has come an increasing propensity to consume. The postwar generation of savers and workers is being replaced by a new breed of consumers and relaxers—or so it seems to the old guard. In truth, the Japanese remain thrifty and diligent by world standards. Nevertheless, the Japanese are enjoying at least some of the rewards of their past efforts. They travel, spend more time with their families, drive new cars. As a result, less of the country's output is available for exports. This change comes at a time when Japan's long-term growth rate is declining.

Just as critically, Japan's population is aging rapidly. In the late 1980s, Japan had fewer retirees (as a proportion of its total population) than its big industrial competitors; but by 2025, it will have the most. From the turn of the century on, Japan will gray very quickly, and its population will decline. Japan needs to generate trade and government surpluses now to pay for these future pension costs.[3] But Tokyo has been pressured by the United States to shrink its trade surplus by increasing government outlays and boosting imports. The need for cash is made all the more acute by the financial reverses of the early 1990s.

Meanwhile, Japan's postwar success has drawn forth a host of copycats. Following a well-beaten path blazed by Japan, these competitors are producing ever cheaper shirts, ships, and chips.[4] The "Four Tigers"—Korea, Taiwan, Hong Kong, and Singapore—have been especially threatening. And the list of upwardly mobile countries grows. Indonesia, Malaysia, the Philippines, and Thailand are right behind the Four Tigers. India, Mexico, and Brazil will lead the third wave.

Japan is caught in an economic war on two fronts: battling the other industrialized economies for domination of new, high-tech markets, while fighting a rearguard action against the Asian Tigers. At home a declining and rapidly aging population will depress living standards markedly after the turn of the century, unless the export war is won. Japanese government and industrial leaders are acutely aware of these threats, all of which aggravate Japan's sense of *higaisha ishiki* (literally, "victim consciousness"; less generously, "paranoia"). Japan finds itself alone, against the world.[5]

Thus, Japan sees danger at every turn. Perhaps this is the

key to their success: the Japanese have done well because they are hungry. Too often Americans have fared poorly against the Japanese onslaught because they were fat and happy. Which are you?

What Comes After Cars?

Selectively, Japan Inc. has targeted overseas markets where the addition of advanced technology and better manufacturing has or will produce a strong competitive advantage. But there are remarkably few of these "targeted" markets. In many areas, Japan is a potential threat, but not now a leader.

In the United States, by far Japan's biggest export market, Japanese companies dominate one large market, cars, and several smaller ones, notably consumer electronics, cameras, and copiers. But these markets are maturing. In Japan's car industry, consolidation has already begun. Fuji (known as Subaru in the United States) has already been taken over by a competitor, and many more of Japan's eleven auto makers are headed for a fall. In 1992, Daihatsu withdrew from the United States. Nissan's and Toyota's overseas car sales have been flat since the mid-eighties, Honda's since the late eighties.[6]

Since the mid-eighties, production in Japan of each of the following products has declined or stopped growing: calculators, cameras, motorcycles, stereos, tape players, trucks, TVs, and VCRs. Passenger-car production expanded during this period, but exports from Japan fell. Consumer electronics—Japan's first real success—have been particularly hard hit, as the industry fragments. Giants Sony, Matsushita, and Sharp are spending enough on R&D to keep their lead, while the others (including such household names as JVC, Kenwood, Pioneer, and Sanyo) struggle to keep up. This is an industry in transition, to say the least.[7]

Worse yet, prices are falling, year in and year out, for many of the products on which Japan Inc.'s livelihood depends. VCRs that cost $771 in 1979 when introduced in the U.S. had fallen to $265 in 1990; from 1983, when they came on the market, to 1990, compact disk players fell from $1,000 to $350.[8] Prices continue to free-fall. The downward spiral is steepest for the components that go into these kinds of products.

In other words, Japan is coasting in the United States, after a home run and a couple of base hits early in the game. To maintain rapid growth, Japan needs another major success like cars. And the Japanese know it.

They Are Here to Stay

What else can we buy from Japan? Japanese suppliers have already captured a huge share of American consumer durable purchases—cars are the largest purchase a family makes, other than a house—and their market is simply played out. To grow, Japan must sell something else to Americans, or find new customers around the world, like Europeans.

The easiest future course for Japan is to keep exporting cars, TVs, and cameras to untapped markets outside North America. Mature industries or not, if Japan could sell consumer durables to others with the same gusto as it does in the United States, its growth in the next century would be assured. But the countries with the money to trade with Japan will not play ball.

Japan expanded its share of the European car market dramatically in the 1980s. But the European Community is now building as many administrative barriers as possible to keep the Japanese out and to undermine the success of those Japanese firms already there. Europeans look on Japan's success in the United States with horror and will not allow Japan to succeed in Europe, whatever the cost.

Japan currently faces automobile quotas and "voluntary restraints" in Britain, France, and Italy, among other countries. Toyota, Honda, and Nissan have decided to build cars in Britain

to get around these barriers, but Continental suppliers are pushing to raise "local content" rules to frustrate their plans.[9] Further
restrictions seem likely, despite pressure on the EC from the
United States (of all places) to open up to Japanese cars made in
America for export to Europe.

With a poetical allusion to "divine winds," or kamikaze, the
French industry minister stated in 1991 that the European market
should not become "a territory open to all winds."[10] Translation:
"Japan keep out." A whole new generation of industrial policy
for the electronics industry is in the planning stage at the EC's
Information Technology Directorate. One scheme calls for high
duties on Japanese electronics for a five-year "adjustment" period. The EC does little to hide its raise-the-drawbridge intentions toward the Japanese.[11]

In Asia, many of Japan's target markets have been part of a
forced Japanese coprosperity sphere once before, and these countries have little desire to repeat the experience. Asians want Japanese capital and jobs, but they don't want Japan's exports.

Japan recognizes these problems—and they believe high
technology is the antidote. That's why Japan graduates the most
engineers in the world, and why Japan is no longer a follower in
high tech. Japanese companies produce a rapidly growing share
of all the patents granted in the United States, and they will soon
become net exporters of technology after relying on foreign ideas
for decades. While their international competitors cut back, the
Japanese invest relentlessly in R&D to produce the next high-
tech breakthrough.[12]

Where will these new goodies be sold? In the United States,
which remains Japan's best hope for export growth, and in Europe, if at all possible. The Japanese are here to stay. If you think
some kind of equilibrium will develop between Japan and the
West, while the Japanese find greener pastures around the world,
you are very likely to be wrong. No other markets offer Japan
the same potential. We must learn to compete with the Japanese
or die.

Success Starts at Home

Americans love to hate the Japanese, the best excuse we have for failure. The fact is, we can blame only ourselves for our problems. If you want to succeed, forget about the Japanese and fix your own business.

The first response of many companies, however, to the threat of Japanese competition is to wrap themselves in the flag, plead for government protection, and hope for the best. Begging for government handouts and tariff barriers may be fine for Lee Iacocca of Chrysler. However, if you are a middle manager at a middle-size company, your options are considerably narrower. Governments will not help you with your mortgage payments when you're walking the pavement. Your flag may have sentimental value, but that's about all you can expect to get from it.

Many American journalists and intellectuals are enchanted with the state-managed *dirigiste* (centrally directed) model that they believe works so well for Japan. They yearn for legislated solutions for America. But in Europe and Canada, where *dirigisme* is the political philosophy of choice, "industrial policy" means bailing out terminally ill industries that rarely, if ever, recover. The Europeans have spent the equivalent of tens of billions of dollars[13] to keep commercial aircraft maker Airbus Industrie afloat, but the company has never made a profit and continues to be beaten thoroughly in the market by Boeing. The French car industry is little more than an expensive unemployment scheme funded by French taxpayers. The Canadian government has its fingers in virtually every industrial pie, the purpose of which is to keep the Great Satan (i.e., the Americans) at bay. The result: few Canadian companies that are world leaders, persistently high inflation and interest rates, and crushing burdens of taxation and government debt. Not much of a role model.

National and local governments everywhere battle fiercely for the right to underwrite Japan's overseas expansion. While our own big companies can also cash in on this largess—grants to

build new plants, free employee training, twenty-year tax concessions, and more—small companies, those that spearhead most
new advances in high tech, are left high and dry. If Tennessee
wants to bribe Nissan to build a plant there, why shouldn't the
Japanese take the money and run?

The Japanese are throwing money around in Washington,
where—no doubt about it—money talks. The lobbying for free
trade by the Japanese does America no harm—Americans get
better products for less. But the special protection American
business buys—"voluntary" car and machine tool restraints,
semiconductor price fixing, textile agreements, farm quotas—
does a great deal of harm. American competitiveness is under-
mined by special favors for the few. U.S. "voluntary restraints"
allowed our domestic car companies to get away with another ten
years of sloppy management. Machine tool import restrictions all
but guarantee Japan's market share at the expense of rival products from Korea and Taiwan.[14] Trade in semiconductors "managed" by the U.S. government was all that made memory chips
profitable for the Japanese in the mid-1980s. Tariffs and quotas
keep out Jamaican sugar and Indian textiles, and consequently
many countries have trouble servicing the debt held by American
banks.

U.S. and European governments squander taxpayer resources on useless research projects, from futuristic jet fighters
that don't work to multi-billion-dollar particle accelerators that
serve a limited and redundant purpose. For all its notoriety, the
Japanese government spends a fraction of what Western countries
lavish on R&D; Japan spends its R&D dollar privately, and
spends it smarter. Those Western companies not getting big government contracts are left holding the bag.

Clearly many Westerners blame Japanese chicanery for
problems of their own making. In the United States, government
management of the entertainment and broadcasting industry keeps
NBC from investing in a movie studio, but welcomes Sony and
Matsushita with open arms. Federal law tries to keep Citibank out

of California, but permits Japanese banks to take 25 percent of the market. The Japanese didn't create these rules and shouldn't be blamed for them. Many Americans are looking to the government to "fix" the trade problem with Japan. But in view of Uncle Sam's track record, more industrial policies don't seem like the solution. Americans ought to be wary of government fixes; they might wish for Japan, but end up with France. We believe that the United States should follow the high-growth, *laissez-faire* path taken by Hong Kong: let Americans solve their own business problems.[15] How to solve them is the point of this book.

You Can Run but You Can't Hide

Most Americans will probably face the Japanese sooner rather than later. If you are hoping its financial setbacks of the early 1990s will make Japan pull back, dream on. Such adversity is more likely to make the Japanese redouble their efforts. The Japanese want to follow up on their success in cars, and, one way or another, you've probably been targeted. If you are smart and act now, you can meet this challenge and come out on top. If not, chances are your company will take a dive, or even go out of business. And you will lose your job.

The purpose of this book is to tell you how to compete against the Japanese and win. It is not about survival. It is about winning. Americans think that Pearl Harbor was attacked by surprise; in fact, there were plenty of warning signs, but they were ignored. In thirty years of hard work developing their export markets, the Japanese have made their plans for industrial expansion crystal clear. To avoid being run over, you must act now.

Japan has made its biggest inroads in manufacturing, and manufactured exports will remain the cornerstone of Japan's expansion strategy. But services from credit cards to data communications are next on the agenda. When Takashimaya and Mitsukoshi, two of Japan's largest department stores, choose new locations up the street from Saks Fifth Avenue in New York, you can bet there is going to be lots of pressure on managers in the beleaguered retail industry.[16] Can an Isetan in every mall in America be far off? Any talk about services being "safe" from Japanese competition because Japan is a manufacturing power-house only is foolish. The Japanese see the future is in services as well as anyone. The question is, how well will they do? And how well will you respond?

Japan is not a monolith: its performance varies widely by industry and by company. Some Japanese companies do well, some poorly. If you understand how the good ones succeed and why the bad ones fail, you will be able to meet your Japanese competitors head-on, and even preempt them. You will be able to evaluate how your company stacks up against Japan. And if you find yourself considering a job with a Japanese company, this book will help you pick a winner.

To best your Japanese competitors, "keep the forces concentrated," as Clausewitz said, and attack them where they are weak, for "it is impossible to be too strong at the decisive point."[17] Japan's greatest successes and greatest failures are with its customers. Japanese companies that have best integrated customers into all aspects of design, production, and service have excelled. Those that have disregarded customers to pursue internal agendas have failed, often abysmally. This book will help you determine where and how the Japanese have failed, and what you can do to exploit their weaknesses.

We have identified four management characteristics—four fatal flaws—common to many Japanese companies. These flaws keep them removed from their customers, preventing what we call "customer integration," the key to business success for the next generation. These flaws are Japan's Achilles' heel. Attack there, and success is assured. But you must concentrate your efforts on the decisive point: your customer.

Our four fatal flaws all affect customer relations. Fatal Flaw One is that the Japanese are too vertically and horizontally integrated to respond quickly to changing customer needs. Their bloated industrial empires are too unwieldy to do what customers want. Fatal Flaw Two is that they are too centrally managed and bureaucratic to communicate effectively with overseas customers. Large management teams take months, even years, to ponder what should be decided in days. Fatal Flaw Three is that their decision-makers have little or no direct contact with overseas customers. Tokyo is far away from most of Japan's markets, and Japanese companies rarely devolve real power to overseas managers, Japanese *or* Americans. And Fatal Flaw Four is that the Japanese prefer to sell what they value most about themselves, usually their technology, rather than find solutions to their customers' problems. As a result, they prefer to sell through intermediaries (such as distributors and dealers) rather than face the music themselves. From our observation of how successful players meet the Japanese challenge, we have distilled four rules of counterstrategy.

Those Japanese companies—and their foreign competitors—that have done best are well focused. They are decentralized and unbureaucratic, and closely connected with their customers. They provide real solutions to real customer needs. In short, these companies give their customers what they want, or at least do so better than their foreign competitors. But customer integration is relative. In some markets Japan has gotten away with less than optimal customer relations because its competitors have been even worse. The Accord did not become the best-selling car in America because Honda meets its customers' needs in some absolute sense. Honda just meets these needs better than everyone else.

Customer integration requires far more than being "customer-oriented," or even than providing good service. Companies with a high level of customer integration live and breathe their customers, incorporating them into all activities and exposing virtually all employees to their whims. There is no magic formula: this is hard work.

You can't ignore Japan's strengths. You must produce and sell quality products at the best price, of course. But you could bankrupt your company trying to outdo the Japanese on product quality. Instead, you should take advantage of Japan's weaknesses, rather than trying to imitate them and doing a poor job of it. Zero in on customer relations, where many Japanese companies do poorly. Be the best where it counts: with your customers. The car industry will turn the tide on Japan not by doing mediocre imitations of Honda and Toyota, but by taking advantage of the four fatal flaws, and doing more for customers than the Japanese do. This book will show you how, with four management principles, each based on years of real-life experience and keyed to one of Japan Inc.'s four fatal flaws.

Two pillars support Japan Inc.: a strong manufacturing culture and near-complete domination of the Japanese market. Our four fatal flaws are integral to the structure of these pillars. As we will explain, the Japanese cannot respond to threats at their weak points without undermining the pillars of their success. By following our guidelines, you can attack your Japanese competitors with impunity and—most important—move the game onto home ground. The advantage always goes to the home team.

That is not to say that Japan will not respond to better customer integration on your part. Firms founded in the postwar era by maverick entrepreneurs, like Akio Morita of Sony and Soichiro Honda of Honda Motor, have already recognized the flaws and are actively trying to change their ways. The biggest threat may be yet to come, when the next generation of entrepreneurs, the Konosuke Matsushitas of the twenty-first century, begin to pour it on. If real change occurs, Japan's overseas expansion before the 1990s will seem a mere prelude. The combination of advanced technology and strong customer integration will prove unstoppable in market after market. You must apply our lessons without delay. Once the inertia that prevents correction of the four fatal flaws is set in motion, its force will be irresistible.

It Can Be Done

"I keep hearing all this talk about 'level playing fields' in world trading relationships. Frankly I couldn't care less. Just show me a market, let me figure out the rules of the game, and I'll play on the field, level or not."

So we were told in 1990 by Hugh Hamilton, a marketing vice president at Northern Telecom, a Canadian supplier of telecommunications equipment. This wasn't bravado. Northern Telecom has done what Fujitsu, Hitachi, and NEC tried and failed to do in the United States in the 1980s: come from nowhere to become the country's number one supplier of computerized telecommunications products. Northern was smaller than its Japanese rivals and shared many handicaps with them. In the 1970s, when its market assault was conceived, Northern had a small domestic market, subsidized R&D, and mediocre products.

What did Northern do right? It followed our four rules. Northern abandoned vertical and horizontal integration, decentralized control from Canada, turned the entire company into a sales organization, and focused on customer needs. Was it easy? Not easy at all. It took fifteen years, and many mistakes were made along the way. Northern still has problems, of course, but Japanese competition is not one of them. If General Motors could say the same, America would be a far more competitive nation today.

Northern has also done what few of its American rivals have accomplished: cracked the Japanese market. For years it was the only foreign company with contracts of any magnitude with Nippon Telegraph and Telephone, one of the world's largest companies. What Northern sells in Japan is made in the U.S.A. How did Northern do it? By solving its customer's biggest problem: enormous government pressure to buy American. Once in, Northern fought hard to stay there. One disconsolate Japanese competitor told us, "NTT learned about service from Northern Telecom."

Despite well-publicized political and financial scandals, an aura of invincibility still surrounds the Japanese. In preparing this book, we have encountered a nearly universal belief that Japan will dominate every market it enters. As a result, we are told by everyone, Japan now has America on the run and is about to roll over Europe. Japan still has momentum, no question. But the Japanese industrial juggernaut can be stopped and, in fact, *is* being stopped by many U.S. companies and industries cited later in the book. We are offering in this book practical, proven steps that can be and are being used to meet the Japanese on any field, level or otherwise.

The fact is, this book is not about Japan. Rather, it is about understanding the behavior of Japanese companies outside of Japan. It is about the fundamental flaws that are frustrating many Japanese companies in many markets, and that may cause the Japanese export juggernaut to run out of steam sooner rather than later. It is about the steps you must take to drive a wedge between your customers and your Japanese competitors, whether strong or shaky.

Japan Inc.'s export drive has undergone a number of recent setbacks. But, nowhere have these failures been more conspicuous than in information technology. Despite thirty years of heavy government subsidies and dogged determination to engineer a "breakout" from Japan Inc.'s beachhead in cars and TVs, Japan's electronic giants, including Fujitsu, Hitachi, NEC, and Toshiba, have a few stunning victories and many expensive losses to show for their efforts in computers and telecommunications—the leading-edge industry in any advanced country's arsenal of modern high-tech muscle. It is in information technology that the four fatal flaws are most conspicuously at work.

Chapter 2 considers the reality of Japan's performance in information technology, debunking the widely held belief that Japan dominates the world's computers and telecommunications markets.

Chapters 3 through 6 examine Japan's four fatal flaws, one

at a time. Then in chapters 7 through 10, we show how each of our rules of counterstrategy works, and how successful competitors are exploiting Japan's flaws to advantage:

Japan's fatal flaw	Rule of counterstrategy
Chapter 3: Vertical and horizontal integration	*Chapter 7:* Disintegrate!
Chapter 4: Centralized management	*Chapter 8:* Decentralize!
Chapter 5: No customer contact	*Chapter 9:* Maximize customer contact!
Chapter 6: Technology driven	*Chapter 10:* Sell peace of mind!

In the final four chapters, we discuss Japan's prospects in the new markets it has targeted for future growth, provide an action plan for putting our four rules to work, describe the ideal, "customer-integrated" company, and predict the challenges to American business that loom beyond Japan.

The Information Technology Fiasco

Japan's Export Failure

Despite unquestioned and well-deserved achievements in cars and consumer electronics, Japan's export strategy has flaws, and these are particularly apparent in information technology. Thirty years and billions of dollars of government and private investment have made Japan the Saudi Arabia of memory chips—and little else. Japan is also strong in a few other commodity hardware markets, such as fax machines, laptop computers, printers, and disk drives, but prices for these products go nowhere but down, and competitive pressures from Korea and Taiwan (not to mention the United States) are relentless. In more complex products, like workstations and communications systems, which account for the bulk of the market, Japan's role is marginal. At home, a program of rigorous import substitution has guaranteed a big and protected information technology market for Japan's electronics giants, but exports pale in comparison. In services and software, high-growth areas that bind suppliers to their customers, Japan is nowhere.

Go Where the Money Is

Japanese business leaders understand that information will dominate the world economy in the twenty-first century. As the first industrial revolution substituted mechanical power for manual labor, the second will substitute information for mechanical effort. This structural shift in the economic order will require a massive investment in information infrastructure, which is now underway. So Japan has developed a simple strategy to maintain growth. Go where the money is: information technology.

Japan has targeted information technology as the engine of future prosperity. To maximize the information content of all its exports, Japan is computerizing everything from bread makers to stereos to robots. Selling information-intensive products has many benefits for Japan. Of primary importance, demand is growing quickly, and information does not use natural resources Japan does not have. Based on its early success in semiconductors, Japan feels confident that it has a comparative advantage in information technology which can be exploited. Furthermore, as computer and communications products are "consumerized," Japan's clear edge in consumer electronics can be put to work. Finally, Japan's advanced manufacturing facilities are the perfect laboratories for such information-intensive activities as computer-aided design and manufacturing, and robotics. In short, IT is a natural for Japan—or so Japan believes.

To hedge its bets, Japan is developing many other markets as well. Some, like financial services and aerospace, are large and mature; others, like biotechnology and new materials, are just emerging from the labs. But none of these offer the scale and export potential of information technology, which is already nearly twice the size of the car market, and growing many times as fast.

The chart below plots Japan's performance in a number of markets, representing relative market size, market growth rates, and market share for Japan Inc. outside Japan. We have chosen

Japan's Export Performance

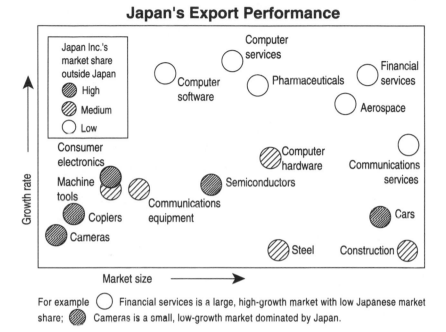

For example ◯ Financial services is a large, high-growth market with low Japanese market share; ▨ Cameras is a small, low-growth market dominated by Japan.

some of the key markets on Japan's "wish list," excluding new areas like superconductors and biotechnology, for which significant demand has not yet developed. Many, from steel to construction, in which Japan has become a significant player are small, slow-growth, or both. In the high-growth, high-tech target industries (many of which may be included in information technology), Japan remains a minor player on the world stage.

Many, misled by naive reporting and protectionist lobbies, believe Japan's control of computers is already a done deal. Plenty of terrifying statistics exist. For example, during the past two decades, computer exports from Japan alone grew an astounding 200-fold.[1] Expansion like this is remarkable, to be sure, but you must remember that this growth rate is measured from a tiny base figure, from a time when Japan's computer industry was just getting on its feet. Furthermore, these exports overwhelmingly represent low-value components and peripherals. The growth of the Japanese computer industry has far more to do with a rapid increase in demand at home and an aggressive program of import substitution than with any of Japan's international achievements.

There is no denying Japan's many accomplishments—and denying them is not the purpose here. The purpose is rather to put these accomplishments in perspective. Japan has had a string of successes, but is now running into problems in high tech, particularly IT. By understanding Japan's weaknesses, you can act now to strengthen your own position, to raise the stakes by binding yourself to your customers.

"Climb Mount Niitaka"

According to leading lights in Japanese business, IT markets will be driven by the confluence of three technologies: computers, integrated circuits, and communications. This belief was eloquently expressed by NEC chairman emeritus Koji Kobayashi in his seminal work *Computers and Communications,* published in 1985.[2] He outlines in considerable detail the evolution of information technology from its origins in the nineteenth century to an epochal point some time around the millennium when all electronic hardware forms will converge. This vision was widely popular in the 1970s and early 1980s and was adopted as a strategy by all of Japan's electronic giants. Fujitsu, Hitachi, NEC, and Toshiba staked out their territory in communications, computers, and semiconductors. Western competitors like AT&T, IBM, and Siemens followed the same path. There is some truth to this vision from a technical point of view. As telephones have been "digitized" (i.e., converted to the 1's and 0's of computer languages) they have become in some respects indistinguishable from computer hardware. And of course all such devices are built on integrated circuits.

To realize their plans, NEC and the other national champions employed a three-pronged attack. First, establish preeminence in semiconductors. The idea was "make the chips and the rest will fall in place" (or more ominously, "control the chips, and control everything else"). Second, attack the mainframe computer market to undermine IBM's core business and primary money-maker. And third, take a lead in computerized communications systems, the cornerstone of the telecommunications network. This attack was driven by ferocious competition at home, aggressive investment in technology, and careful guidance by the Japanese government.

At home and abroad, Japan's national champions are relentless competitors. For Fujitsu to take the lead over NEC in a major market like communications systems, for example, is considered a great disgrace for NEC. Competitive analysis is taken seriously in Japan; rivals are studied endlessly for new ideas and performance benchmarks. If Toshiba introduces a new memory chip at a given price and performance level, Hitachi's goal is to go one better. Competition between industrial groups, or *keiretsu,* is fierce, influencing nearly all strategic decisions.

The investment in research has been enormous. For the engineers who run Japan Inc., technology is the font of all wealth, past and future, with an almost mythical ability to solve problems. Naturally, investment in R&D takes a top priority for Japanese companies. In 1991, NEC spent 17 percent of its revenues on R&D, a remarkable sum (IBM, no slouch in this area, spent 9.5 percent of its revenues on R&D in the same year).[3] Once Toshiba decided it wanted to be on top in semiconductors, the company poured it on; between 1983 and 1988, $2.9 billion was spent to propel Toshiba into the front ranks, 40 percent more than its nearest competitor spent.[4]

Several key official programs have also been important catalysts. The Japanese government spearheaded the initial assault on information technology, principally through the Ministry of International Trade and Industry (MITI) and Nippon Telegraph and Telephone (NTT), the semipublic telephone company. Japan has invested more public funds in IT than in any other industry.

During the seventies and early eighties, critical years for Japan's infant industry, the government paid for most of Japan's investment in computer and telecom research, plant, and equipment (maybe even more than 100 percent of this investment, depending on how you count low interest loans).[5] And protectionist measures kept imports at bay.

While the tariff barriers came down in the 1980s, government spending continued. The "Fifth-Generation" artificial intelligence project, initiated in the mid-1980s, was an attempt to leapfrog American software development, but is now considered something of a dud.[6] In 1990, MITI proposed a $1 billion "intelligent manufacturing" program (to include foreign and Japanese companies) to combine production and computer technologies.[7] Then, also in 1990, a "Sixth-Generation" computing project was conceived to reverse the lead enjoyed by American suppliers in parallel computing, a radically different technique for building computers; in 1991, foreign companies were invited to join the ten-year, $300 million program. While government cash now pales in comparison to company investment, the MITI masterminds keep their eyes on the ball.

Unfortunately, the synergy once expected between computers, communications, and semiconductors has not been realized. A number of Japanese managers have confessed to us that these businesses are poorly coordinated—impossible to coordinate, in fact—and are run separately, their advertising copy about the wonders of integrated information technologies notwithstanding. This vision has fallen short for Japan's competitors as well: IBM entered and withdrew from the communications equipment market in the 1980s; AT&T and Siemens have stuck it out at extraordinary expense. Although a viable industry has been created at home, Japan's IT performance internationally has fallen short of MITI's goals. Success in semiconductors has not been matched in computer and communications systems. Telecommunications has been an outright failure.

For Japan, these failures are ominous. If Japan's leadership believes that IT is key to the country's sustained growth well into the twenty-first century, and if Japan cannot succeed there, a crisis of titanic proportions is brewing.

The chart below shows how Japan's IT suppliers fared at home and abroad in 1990 (further detail is given in the Appendix). By commanding a remarkable 80 percent of their home market, these companies boosted their world market share to 20

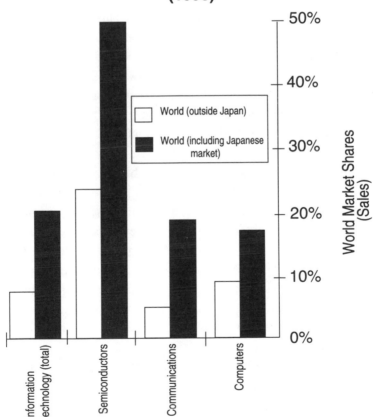

Japan's Information Technology Market Share (1990)

percent. Outside Japan, however, they held only 7 percent of all sales. A respectable performance, perhaps, but not a great deal to show for thirty years of effort and billions of dollars of investment.

Chips Ahoy

Japan has invested heavily in semiconductors, and for its efforts has become, as we have said, the Saudi Arabia of the computer business, pumping out more than half the world's supply of commodity memory chips. But in so doing, Japan has no more "cored out" American industry than Saudi Arabia has. And like the Saudis, the Japanese are easy prey for anyone else who can turn up capacity and slash prices. At least in the oil business, prices sometimes go up. DRAM prices always go down. By 1991, the Koreans had already taken 10 percent of the 1MB and 4MB memory chip market from Japan.[8] The pressure from the industrializing Third World will be relentless.

Yes, Japan now dominates DRAMs, the memory chips that store information in a computer. But in high-end microprocessor chips, American companies like Intel and Motorola reign supreme. Japanese suppliers must buy from these outside sources, or if they are lucky, obtain licensing agreements. Customers want standard processors, like the Intel 486 and the Motorola 68040, and no amount of effort by Japanese vendors has convinced them otherwise. That's why the United States turned a surplus in semiconductor trade in 1990.[9] Only in Japan itself can proprietary Japanese microprocessors, of which there are many, be foisted on the market.

The battle between Japanese and American suppliers for IC leadership will continue. Americans seem to hold all the cards in RISC chips (a powerful new generation of microprocessors), although alliances between U.S. suppliers and their Japanese competitors make score-keeping arbitrary, to say the least. Similarly, alliances between LSI Logic, Motorola, and Texas Instruments and the Japanese to make signal processors for high-definition television muddy the waters. Americans supply crucial technology to the Japanese for the manufacture of liquid crystal displays (which the U.S. International Trade Commission hit with a 63 percent duty in 1991).[10] And Intel was an early leader in a new generation of memory devices called "flash" memories, but formed an alliance in 1992 with Sharp to bring them to market.[11] Are these companies reasserting America's leadership in semiconductors, or selling their souls to the devil? The answer depends on your perspective.

Japan's gains in memory circuits—important as they are— have not been transferred to other areas MITI covets. Japan has not become a leading supplier of the products into which its DRAMs are incorporated, like personal computers and communications systems. On the contrary, Japan's electronic giants are ever more dependent on Americans for microprocessors and on the software that they run to create demand for Japanese DRAMs. What's more, American chips go into Japanese camcorders, cameras, and cars as well.[12]

DRAMs are a tough business. After spending nearly $10 billion to develop and ramp up production of 4-megabit memory chips, Japan Inc. saw the price of these devices fall so fast in 1991 that costs will probably never be recovered.[13] A shakeout, starting with some of the marginal players, is probably inevitable.[14] As a result of their heavy dependence on commodity DRAMs, Japan's chip makers took a real beating during the recession of 1991–92.[15] The last time Japan's chip suppliers found themselves in such a mess, the U.S. government bailed them out by forcing them to raise prices. They may not be so fortunate this time.

Fool's Gold

When MITI stepped up its investment in computers in the 1970s, its goal was to challenge IBM's domination of computers. Since mainframe computers built IBM, selling big systems became Japan's obsession. For twenty years, Japan slugged it out in this arena, and now the number two and three players after IBM are Hitachi and Fujitsu. Unfortunately, large computers are the fool's gold of the information age, as computing power continues to shift to small desktop computers.

Mainframes traditionally accounted for half of IBM's profit, and Japan Inc. believed it could not seriously challenge Big Blue's preeminence without taking IBM on at the high end.[16] But by doggedly chasing IBM, Japan missed the minicomputer boom of the 1970s and early 1980s, the PC boom of the 1980s, and the workstation boom of the late 1980s and early 1990s, and may miss the parallel processing boom of the 1990s. What's worse, just as the Japanese established themselves in big systems (both mainframes and supercomputers), inexpensive powerful workstations and massively parallel processors began to reduce demand for large, expensive, conventionally designed computers—precisely what Japan had to sell. Maybe MITI picked the wrong company to imitate.

Japan's most notable success has been at home, where the government has done a good job of keeping foreign suppliers out. After thirty years of relentless pressure from MITI and billions of dollars of investment by its competitors, IBM was finally displaced by Fujitsu as the leading vendor of mainframes in Japan. But MITI's influence produced lopsided results: by 1991, Japanese companies had 94 percent of government mainframe sales, but only 59 percent of those to private companies.[17]

In world software markets, Japan sells neither operating systems nor applications. Programs like word processing, spreadsheets, and databases are what give computers value. Outside Japan, computer buyers demanded, and got, standard software that allowed them to mix and match their hardware inventory. This flexibility gave buyers more leverage and forced suppliers to drive down their costs and lower their prices. Inside Japan, however, Japanese computer suppliers remained wedded to proprietary software that is useless on competitive machines. Partly this is due to the nature of consumer loyalty in Japan: an "NEC man" may buy everything from NEC, always. But outside Japan, consumer pressure to standardize was overwhelming.

For mainframe and PC exports, Japan followed IBM standards, effectively surrendering control of their fate to American software developers. But the idea that some cultural flaw keeps the Japanese from writing software is nonsense. For the domestic market, there are half a dozen major suppliers all writing their own programs. In fact, Japan produces altogether too much software. The problem is that nobody outside Japan wants it. At the same time, because each has gone its own way, Japan's national champions have stretched their software resources to the limit.

Japan plays a big part in commodity segments of information technology. Of its $20 billion in exports in 1990, 85 percent was parts and peripherals.[18] In printers, displays, disk drives, and keyboards, Japan's solid manufacturing and miniaturization skills have paid off. Here Japanese companies are strong. But this is the low-tech—maybe no-tech—side of computers. And the newly industrialized third world upstarts are breathing down Japan's neck in most of these areas.

One key success has been laptop and notebook computers. Toshiba in particular applied its consumer electronic skills to make the PC portable, taking the world lead in this segment by 1990. It is important to remember that Toshiba's machines run American software on American microprocessors. Nevertheless, this is a critical computer market, and its loss should be cause for alarm among competitors. If other types of computers can be "consumerized," Japan will indeed have an advantage—and so will its third world competitors. In 1992, Toshiba quit the low end of the PC market, laying off 150 workers at a computer factory in California.[19]

Like climbing past the fifth station on Japan's Mount Fuji, it is in software and services that the tough going and real rewards lie. And it is here that the hearts and minds of customers are won. Through miscalculation and stubborn desire to export hardware, Japan is forgoing huge opportunities. As a result, their IT national champions are losers on the international playing field. Hardware manufacturing skills are essential to success in IT, to be sure. But manufacturers that do not add value—with better networks, service, and software—to their products will get battered remorselessly by customers. Japan has not reached the fifth station.

Sorry, Wrong Number

In telecommunications, as in all information technology, Japan is strong in terminals. But these are low-tech commodity markets, with little long-term potential. Japan sells look-alike faxes and answering machines on price, losing share to the Koreans and Taiwanese continuously.

In network systems and services, the vast bulk of the telecom market, Japan has not fared well. Japanese suppliers have not captured telephone company and corporate demand for large, complex systems in any major markets outside Japan. In most sectors of the U.S. market, Japan's share has been flat or falling since the mid-1980s. The Japanese seem unable—or unwilling—to engineer and support large networks.

Despite the liberalization and privatization of many communications markets around the world, Japanese carriers have not even addressed international opportunities in services, like long distance, cellular radio, and cable TV. Services cannot be exported, so MITI is not interested. NTT is in fact forbidden by its charter from operating overseas. The market, however, has a different view: services count.

NTT's goal for Japan's telecom equipment suppliers was to be the first team in computerized communications systems. Despite investment now running in the billions, however, performance outside Japan has been abysmal. Failure resulted largely from NTT's presumption that anything it designed for its local stable of suppliers they could sell overseas. But like MITI's efforts to dominate computers, NTT's plans proved futile.

Cheap Terminals

All in all, Japanese industry gambled badly in the early 1980s, betting that features and applications would be embedded in silicon "firmware." As envisioned by MITI in the 1970s, this change would have given producers enormous market power, complete control of information technology and its uses, and the opportunity to extract unprecedented monopoly rents. Instead, suppliers, driven by U.S. consumers, developed flexible, software-based systems, effectively sidestepping Japan's strategy. Customers, not Japan Inc., have appropriated for themselves control over the direction technology takes. The value of electronic systems is increasingly provided in software and communications networks, areas in which Japan Inc. plays virtually no role.

We can, of course, thank Japan for cheap, reliable telephones and facsimile machines. AT&T can thank them too: skyrocketing demand for new network features and better long-distance services enriches companies like AT&T, while Japanese hardware manufacturers beat each other's brains out selling cheaper and cheaper faxes. Japan loses twice: the value of features in terminals (such as fax and answering machines) has tumbled, but Japan has no position in foreign service and software markets. Thus, Japan has not benefited from the huge increases in expenditures for software and communications services that its terminals helped stimulate. This unfortunate irony has not been lost on Sony and Matsushita, proud owners of American movie studios and record companies, which realized that consumers spending $150 on a VCR or Walkman spend thousands on movies and tapes.

Applications programs such as Lotus 1-2-3, Microsoft Word, and Aldus Pagemaker have driven the PC revolution. The hardware running these programs is of far less concern to customers than the software. While PC prices continue to crash, software expenditures per site have risen quickly, from $162 in 1989 to $470 in 1991.[20] Software giant Microsoft, not Japan Inc., is the PC market winner of the past decade.

We have noted Japan's success in laptop and notebook personal computers. This success is undeniable and well deserved. But the notion that a strong showing in this niche can be leveraged into control of the computer market is absurd. Similarly, Japan's lock on faxes and answering machines does not translate into control of telecommunications. Western observers are confusing Japan's hope for the future with their rather less spectacular track record.

Where Is Japan Inc. in Networks?

While they bill themselves as "total system suppliers," as we have said, Japan's information technology giants are conspicuously absent from networking. While they can indeed provision many of the hardware components that make up computer and communications networks, they offer little in the way of software, service, and support to make those networks run. This, in turn, means forgoing additional hardware opportunities as well. And there's a lot at stake. By the mid-1990s, a third or more of all computer purchases may be for networking applications.[21]

The PC market alone has gone through three networking stages. In the early 1980s, people began buying computers and using them in isolation (connected only by "sneaker-nets," taking a disk out of one computer and walking or running it over to another). As PCs began to communicate, LANs were required. As LANs choked up with all the traffic between PCs, LAN servers were introduced. Japan Inc. (with some very limited exceptions) has missed the boat on all three occasions, and without a better understanding of why companies network their computers, Japan's PC players will not catch up at a later time.

Some networking applications are pure service—no hardware is needed. Communications carriers can offer their customers "virtual private networks," which range from small business systems called "Centrex" to global data communications capabilities. The common denominator is that the carrier's software makes its internal network look as if it belongs to customers, who buy little or no equipment of their own. If you don't sell to the carrier (and Japan has done poorly there), you are locked out of this opportunity. Cable TV carriers are about to do the same thing for home television, and Japan may get locked out of this market too.

Customer outlays for professional computing services are rising rapidly, and in the United States are expected to be double the size of the mainframe and minicomputer markets combined by 1995.[22] Similar growth is taking place in Europe.[23] Two of the fastest-growing services are systems integration (by which customers contract a third party to purchase and assemble their computer operations) and outsourcing (by which customers turn over their entire computer or communications operations to a third party). In 1990, the top ten systems integrators (including Anderson Consulting, DEC, EDS, and IBM) accounted for more than 50 percent of sales worldwide. *This list did not include a single Japanese company.*[24] The story is the same in outsourcing.[25]

Computer applications—graphic computing and data communications in particular—are already placing extraordinary demands on the networks that connect computers, and on the computers that run the networks. Capacity requirements for controlling and monitoring such systems grow even faster. For example, a one-page graph contains ten times the information of a page of text, requiring an order-of-magnitude increase in power on the computer that stores it and the network that transports it. A simple color photograph consumes thirty to forty times the amount of space required to store all the pages of this book. Sending a color image from one PC to another today can tie up both systems for an inordinate amount of time.

We call this the "MIPS meltdown," when the processing power (measured in millions of instructions per second, or MIPS) required to run the network itself starts to overwhelm the capacity of the computers attached to the network. Network management requirements are growing faster than processing power. This condition creates enormous aftermarket demand for equipment. Access to such demand is the difference between rising and falling hardware sales for suppliers in the United States. While Japanese terminals, particularly faxes, are helping to fuel the MIPS meltdown, Japanese companies are missing out on most of the hardware sales opportunities that result.

High-Tech Image

The reason for Japan's mediocre performance in IT is immediately evident to any visitor to Japan: technology is not used in business outside its factories. Japan wants to sell America IT, while at home the standard office configuration is four battleship-gray desks butted together with a black rotary phone on a lazy Susan in the middle! Booming sales of laptops and notebooks are finally bringing computers to Japanese offices, but as recently as 1991, the United States had more than twice as many computers per capita as Japan.[26]

Even Japan's computer giants go shoeless while the cobbler exports his wares. On numerous visits to IT suppliers in Japan, we have been in offices completely devoid of PCs. And the way office systems are employed is also unsophisticated: generally, they are used for word processing and little else. While dedicated word processors have long since been replaced by fully functioning computers capable of a broad range of tasks, many Japanese still use their *"wapuro,"* oblivious of the changes that took place a decade ago. In the United States, multiple applications are the norm, and half of all software purchases are for spreadsheet and database purposes.[27] And compared to Americans, the Japanese connect only a tiny share of their PCs to networks.[28]

Too much Japanese information technology research has been driven by government procurement, not hands-on experience. Focused on everything but the customer, Japan's labs turn out high-performance products in search of a market. Some sell; most don't. There are two approaches to R&D: find out what customers need, then develop it; or, like MITI and NTT, develop something, then find a home for it. The first is almost certain to succeed; the second is almost certain to fail.

Information technology has received a big dose of government cash, with mediocre results. Most industries in which Japan has been truly successful have not enjoyed such largess. MITI claims that Japan finances with public funds only 3 percent of total industrial R&D, compared with 35 percent for the U.S. government.[29] Taxpayers of the world, take note!

Too Many Losers

Over fifteen years, we have observed two qualities that correlate highly with success in information technology. First, companies that are focused on a limited number of product areas bring to bear the energy needed to excel in this highly competitive area. Second, companies that generate more than half their sales from international sales have developed the capacity to reach out to their customers wherever they may be.

Too Many Losers

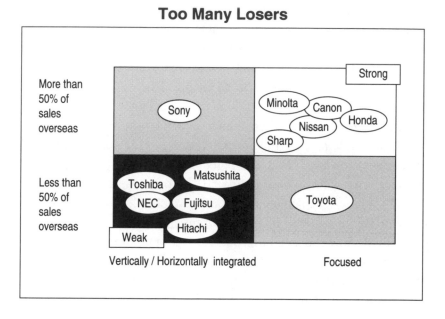

They invest in the markets in which they sell, and they turn over decision-making to those in the front lines, with the customers.

In the above chart, we have placed Japan's top electronics firms according to our two criteria. Most fall into the "weak" corner. These are the companies that Japan hopes will lead the challenge across a broad range of high-tech industries. Our analysis suggests their performance will be poor without substantial change in direction. We have also included on the chart Japan's top three car companies, to illustrate that they are focused and export-oriented.

For thirty years, Sony stuck to its knitting, and the results showed: a clear leader with a clear purpose, generating more than three-quarters of its sales outside Japan. But Sony is turning its back on its past, with ambitions that cover a vast number of areas, many of which are tangentially related, at best, to its core business. Sony may have seen its best days.

Two smaller and more flexible players fall into the "strong" box: Canon and Sharp. Canon, at heart a camera company, sells a relatively narrow portfolio of products, including copiers and fax machines. Sharp, probably best known for a broad range of "me-too" tape players and TVs, focused its efforts considerably over the past decade, with emphasis on highly differentiated optoelectronic and semiconductor products. This is a company to watch. Real threats from Japan in high tech are likely to come from competitors with clear objectives, and perhaps from up-and-coming entrepreneurs. Bloated, overprotected, overfunded industrial dinosaurs of the postwar era will not break out of Japan without radical change in their strategies.

Jack of All Trades and Master of None

Fatal Flaw No. 1: Everything to Everyone

Most people associate Sony with success. No one tops Sony when it comes to making audio and video equipment smaller and better. Indeed, the Sony name is synonymous with top-of-the-line home electronics, the Cadillac—no, make that the Mercedes—of its business. But this valuable reputation was earned in the 1960s and 1970s. Then Sony started coasting, living off past achievements; by the mid–1980s, times had turned tough.

During the boom years of the mid-eighties, Sony's total sales were stagnant and foreign sales were actually declining for several years. Heavily dependent on overseas markets, Sony was hit hard by the rapid appreciation of the yen, which made its products too expensive outside Japan.[1] But there was a bigger problem: the company had built its business on better ideas, and the well was running dry. Products like the Walkman portable cassette player had powered Sony sales in the early 1980s, but were quickly copied by others. And attempts to boost VCR sales with its Beta format were killed by an unholy alliance between Matsushita, Sony's archrival in Japan, and Dutch electronics giant Philips, an early backer of the VHS video system.

Then came the vision. Akio Morita, the charismatic founder of Sony, figured that introducing better technologies, like Beta, was no good if Sony could not control the movies and music they played. Instead of selling high-margined Beta VCRs built on its own technology, Sony was forced to sell me-too VHS players. The problem was that the movie companies abandoned Beta when it became clear that VHS was winning the battle for customers. Morita's solution: make the movies and the music. Then consumers would have to buy new Sony hardware if they wanted to hear and see their favorite entertainers.[2]

So Sony's leader engineered the acquisitions of CBS Records (in 1988) and Columbia Pictures (in 1989). CBS and Columbia would supply the software (i.e., music and movies) to make Sony's new hardware (Walkmen, VCRs, etc.) work—and sell. Sony had become the premier entertainment "hardware and software" company, integrated both horizontally and vertically. Sony was behind the power curve now—or so Morita thought.

First came the DAT fiasco. Sony engineers dreamed up a new recording technology—called DAT—that greatly improves the audio quality of audiocassettes, but requires consumers to buy new players and new tapes. Philips, Sony's Dutch rival, countered with DCC, which features DAT-like quality, but plays on machines that also accept the analog cassettes consumers now own. Sony decided to "reposition" DAT for "professional" users. Translation: DAT was dead.[3]

Sony tried again in 1992, with Mini Disc, a new, small CD that records as well as plays. But like DAT, the Mini Disc technology requires customers to buy new stereo equipment, because that's what Sony wants to sell. The recording industry, nervous about antagonizing customers by introducing new formats just when CDs have finally replaced the old LPs, doesn't like Sony's self-serving innovations. Nevertheless, both Sony and Philips have lined up record company endorsements for their formats. Sony's own music subsidiary tried without success to jump-start hardware sales for Sony by releasing its own records on DAT tapes, but decided to sign up with the Philip's DCC standard to hedge its bets. Matsushita also fell in behind Philips, licensing DCC for its own hardware products. It's too early to call this fight, but the outcome will have little to do with the availability of Sony Music on Mini Discs.[4]

While still reeling from its humiliation by Matsushita in VCRs, Sony introduced in 1986 a new 8mm format for video recorders. The 8mm tapes are much smaller than the VHS cartridges that are now standard, allowing Sony to introduce its tiny Handycam videocamera, a runaway success for home movies. But Sony's goal is bigger, to make 8mm the next generation for video, rendering the current VHS format obsolete. To boost sales for its hand-held Video Walkman, Sony has released some 8mm movies from Columbia's huge "software" library. But 8mm movies are not catching on. Who wants to junk their VCR? You can't play your Sony 8mm home movies on your existing VCR, but must wire up your Handycam to the TV each time you want to view them. Sony's customers seem willing to put up with this inconvenience to get a smaller video recorder, but there is little incentive to buy an 8mm player—least of all for a few 8mm Columbia movies.[5]

Sony spent over $7 billion to buy the software that would keep its hardware factories in Japan humming. So far, the plan is not working. To cover its software debt and cash requirements, Sony decided in 1991 that it needed to raise as much as $3 billion to stay in the movie and music game. At the same time, infighting between hardware and software groups became evident. As if the financial pressures weren't enough, Sony's movie and record producers were further saddled with pressure to supply their products in formats nobody wants to buy.[6] Customers who get stuck with tapes they cannot play and machines they cannot use will not be happy. So much for the "synergy" of vertical and horizontal integration: Sony may yet make money from its software business, but Columbia Pictures and CBS Records will not help the sales of Sony hardware nobody wants to buy.

The Do-It-Yourself Conglomerates

Many of Japan's biggest and most powerful companies remain true believers in old-style vertical and horizontal integration, once championed by the likes of Siemens, Ford, Royal Dutch Shell, and U.S. Steel. Supplying their own parts and making a wide variety of products give many advantages to Japan's industrial giants. But speed of response to customer needs is not one of them.

With vertical integration, in-house suppliers serve the interests of the organization, not its customers. Costs are built into the system, and flexibility is engineered out. There are huge risks associated with developing production machinery, components, and complete systems at once. Vertically integrated suppliers assume all of these, without necessarily adding value for their customers. With horizontal integration, managers lose touch with customers, and lose the visceral feel for a market that makes for winners. How can Jack Welch, who is the CEO of General Electric, have any sense of what makes his customers tick when they buy everything from jet engines to dishwashers from him? The answer is that he can't. Running your company without knowing your customers personally is running it blind.

One reason the Japanese have done so well in cars is that they are *less* vertically integrated than their foreign competitors. General Motors makes 70 percent of what goes into its cars, while Toyota makes only 27 percent.[7] On average, do-it-yourself parts account for 30 percent of Japanese cars, 40 percent of European cars, and 50 percent of American cars.[8] And while its American competitors have become mini-conglomerates, diversification for Honda means making lawn mowers and generators, all driven, like cars and motorcycles, by internal combustion engines.

In high technology, just as in cars, we have discovered that market share is inversely proportional to the level of integration: if you focus on what you do best, you can do well; if you try to do everything, you fail. Compaq's rise to the top in high-performance personal computers was due to focus: when this company stuck to its knitting, the results showed.

Henry Ford kept a sheep farm to grow wool for seat covers. Japan's electronics giants would appreciate this strategy. Says Takashi Kono, one of Sony's top engineers, "If you don't know how to make the parts, you don't know how to make the camera."[9] Yet in facsimile machines and laptop computers, where Japan has done especially well, key components come from American suppliers. Rockwell International sells the lion's share of crucial components for facsimile machines,[10] and Intel (or one of its licensees) makes every microcomputer chip that goes into Japan's IBM-compatible personal computers.

On plant tours in Japan we have been lectured on the merits of vertical integration by our Japanese customers. In the same plants, we've seen layouts as confusing as a New Jersey highway interchange, little old ladies hand-dipping computer parts into vats of solder the way chocolate is put on a Dairy Queen cone, rafter-high piles of inventory that made Canal Street sweatshops look well organized, and homemade production equipment held together with rubber bands. The Japanese do not have a lock on manufacturing know-how. The most efficient operations we have seen are at companies that avoid vertical integration religiously.

Added to these sins is Japan's almost heretical belief in horizontal integration, long since discredited by companies like GE, RCA, ITT, and United Technologies. Their desire to balance economic cycles by selling a broad range of products had nothing to do with the needs of customers, and their efforts failed. All of these companies have been forced to narrow their focus, some, like ITT, dramatically. ITT was the ultimate conglomerate, much akin to Japan's big *keiretsu*, selling an extraordinarily broad array of products and services. But ITT's once-admired strategy came unraveled. In the late 1970s and early 1980s, divestitures greatly reduced the size of this company. Once the proud alter ego of AT&T outside the United States, ITT sold its telecommunications operations to French rival Alcatel. Today, ITT is essentially a financial holding company, with interests in insurance, forestry, and industrial components.

American companies still cannot resist the siren call of diversification. While their Japanese rivals pounded away at their market share during the 1980s, the big three auto companies invested in unrelated markets. GM acquired Electronic Data Systems, a computer service bureau, and Hughes Aircraft, which makes satellites. Ford, not to be outdone by GM, bought its own aerospace company. Little Chrysler bought a corporate-jet maker—must have been fun for Lee. Great new businesses, but they did nothing for car customers, and they sapped scarce capital and management resources.[11] These are the same people whose advertisements—somehow all three make similar claims—proudly boast "the best-built cars in America." And since the Japanese now make their cars here, "the best cars designed and built in America." For the Japanese, this must be like shooting fish in a barrel.

Japan's electronics giants are horizontally integrated, often across many lines of business. Hitachi is a true conglomerate, making everything from refrigerators, pipes, and batteries to nuclear power plants, locomotives, and computers. NEC, Oki, and Toshiba make a broad range of electrical products. Sony and Matsushita have sprawled from consumer electronics to computers and communications and now to entertainment with their acquisitions of Hollywood studios. Fujitsu is unusual in that it is relatively focused, by Japanese standards, on one industry, information technology (which still covers a lot of ground).

Firms from smokestack industries are diversifying into high-tech markets, with mixed success at best. Kubota, which makes tractors and iron pipes, has a portfolio of U.S. investments, including Mips Computer, which makes advanced microcomputer devices, and Stardent, which made high-powered minicomputers. Stardent, formed out of two faltering Kubota companies, Ardent Computer Corp. and Stellar Computer Inc., folded in 1991.[12]

Kobe Steel has invested heavily in semiconductors, and in 1990 formed a joint venture with Texas Instruments.[13] In 1991, Kobe pulled the plug on another of its investments, PrairieTek, which made computer disk drives. A third Kobe investment, memory device producer Racet Computers, also went bust. Altogether, Japanese steel producers have started some five hundred new, mostly high-tech ventures. A large number have already been shut down as the steel companies refocus on their core businesses. Hoping to offset sales in declining, mature markets, these companies tried to do what America's conglomerates did in the 1960s and 1970s.[14] Can Japanese conglomerates do what ITT and the others could not? Are Japanese ambitions any different? The track record so far says no.

The War on Two Fronts

Your vertically and horizontally integrated Japanese competitors are competing on too many fronts at once. For every product they sell against you, to be successful, they must succeed in dozens of other markets as well. When Hitachi introduces a new computer, it must get the system right, of course. But if Hitachi wants a competitive product, it must excel at machine tools, computer chip design and manufacturing, disk drives, and process control, to name only a few of the products and services the company supplies to itself. At the same time, Hitachi may be launching new communications or medical systems, elevators, power plants, or ceramic devices.[15] In short, this company is all over the map. If Hitachi's biggest competitor in computers, IBM, focused on large computers alone, Hitachi would not stand a chance. Happily for Hitachi, IBM is all over the map too.

As if it did not have its hands full with movies and music, Sony has diversified into computers as well. After a string of failures in PCs, Sony shifted its efforts to several new product areas, including the Palmtop, a small computer operated with a pen instead of a keyboard; the Data Discman, a computerized reference book; and high-powered workstations. None of these has met with much success.[16] Now Sony is making laptop computers for Apple. Not a bad opportunity, perhaps, but quite a comedown for a company that prides itself on its original ideas. Not only does it risk failure in computers and entertainment, but Sony may also be vulnerable to more focused competitors in consumer electronics if underinvestment of capital and management time is the result of diversification. When Sony built its business, competitors like RCA were spread too thin. Sony is now repeating this mistake.

For NEC, as for many Japanese electronics companies, AT&T was the model for industrial organization. The old Bell System, completely integrated vertically, once dominated the American and world telecommunications stage. But since the U.S. Justice Department broke up the Bell System in 1984, AT&T has abandoned vertical integration, while its old pupil NEC still believes that there's only one way to do it right: do it yourself.

Not only does NEC make many of the components that go into its products, it also makes many of the machines that make these components (robots, as well as semiconductor manufacturing and test equipment, for example).[17] Like many of its domestic rivals, NEC steers 20+ percent of computer chip purchases to foreign companies, to ease trade frictions.[18] As a rule, however, NEC tries to keep business in the family. In effect, its designers are not free to draw on the best sources of supply in the world; rather, they must hope that what they buy internally will be up to scratch. Sometimes it is and sometimes it isn't.

Horizontal integration is as complete as vertical integration. NEC's product portfolio includes TVs, air conditioners, kitchen appliances, and video games. In electronics, NEC makes everything from faxes and answering machines to microprocessors and supercomputers. But NEC may be changing its ways. NEC boosted PC sales dramatically outside Japan when it abandoned proprietary designs for standard Intel chips. And in 1991, NEC started selling Stratus Computer systems to plug a gap in its own product line.[19] That was once heresy at NEC.

Ten short years ago, AT&T made virtually everything it used. Now microprocessors, memory chips, production equipment, and even software are outsourced. Ironically, AT&T gets components, including some semiconductor designs, from NEC, a company AT&T helped found in 1899.[20] AT&T is more focused now, although its determination to sell computers as well as communications products continues to sap cash flow.

AT&T insisted on reopening a second front for itself with the acquisition of computer maker NCR. A decade of failure surely proved that AT&T had no business in the computer market. Determination is a virtue to be admired, but AT&T has gone too far, throwing billions of good dollars after bad. Actually, AT&T has done a pretty good job investing in the stock market, making hefty profits on its Sun Microsystems and Olivetti stock sales. Our advice to Ma Bell: tart up NCR, sell it at a profit, and focus on long-distance communications. There are plenty of potential threats to AT&T's core business, including Japan's top two telephone utilities, NTT and KDD.

In personal computers, a market it created and still dominates, IBM showed the advantage of abandoning vertical integration. Big Blue does not make many of the parts that go into its best-selling PCs. But IBM may not have learned this lesson: in an effort to eliminate the inflexibility of vertical integration, the company is selling components to competitors.[21] IBM believes that the Japanese keep component divisions on their toes by exposing them to market pressures. It may work for the Japanese, but it will be a generation before IBM's culture of internal supply changes. Trying to out-Japan Japan could be a dangerous game for IBM.

IBM made the right decision in 1991 when it spun off its small laser printer, typewriter, and keyboard businesses into Lexmark International, a new company in which IBM retains a

10 percent interest.[22] IBM has enough on its plate defending its computer business without dissipating resources on such low-tech products. However, splitting its far-flung activities into half a dozen autonomous operating companies, as IBM decided to do late in 1991, will not solve the company's problems unless this restructuring is a prelude to selling off peripheral activities.[23]

Danger Sign No. 1

More than 5 percent of your purchasing expenditures flow to sources within your company.

The Cult of Manufacturing

Manufacturing is important to countries and companies. But serving customers is even more important. In Japan, a kind of macho competition exists between manufacturers. They believe that there is something degenerate, if not actually effeminate and distastefully American, about subcontracting. "Sissies sell services, real men make hardware" sums up this view. Indulging themselves like this may be a luxury your Japanese competitors can afford. You cannot. If you want to serve customers better, you must shift costs and associated risks to suppliers, thereby releasing financial, managerial, and creative resources to concentrate on customer needs.

If you are a retailer, do you really want to compete in a dozen related markets at the same time? That's what Mitsukoshi, one of Japan's biggest and oldest upscale department stores, is doing. Its big new store on Fifth Avenue in New York will be supplied with items popular in Japan and made by Mitsukoshi-owned or -controlled factories in China. Competitors like the Limited and Nordstrom that are unencumbered with factories they need to keep running and that really understand what their American customers want will eat these people alive if they try to move off Fifth Avenue. If your business is retailing, your energy is best spent on delivering the best merchandise and the best service to your customers. If your idea of service includes obsequious clerks bowing low at the front door, return to Tokyo.[24]

Chrysler can take credit for creating the minivan market in the United States, and is still the leader with its Dodge Caravan and Plymouth Voyager. In 1990, the company introduced a "new and improved" minivan incorporating many customer suggestions with considerable design flair. So far so good. However, imagining that it could improve the performance of its product with its own drive train, Chrysler developed an advanced four-speed automatic transmission, which it produced at its Kokimo plant.[25] When *Consumer Reports* panned the new models because the transmission didn't work properly, sales threatened to go into a tailspin. Vertical integration did not benefit this company's customers, to say the least. How many millions did Chrysler spend developing this component, tooling its plants to make it, fixing the ones that didn't work, and then patching up its reputation? Chrysler buys plenty of parts from outside suppliers, including the popular Mitsubishi V6 engines in its minivans, but made a bad call on the Ultradrive. Ever ready to get the government to help fix its mistakes, Chrysler later asked for protection against Japanese minivan imports.[26] Why the U.S. government would be interested in protecting sales of Chrysler minivans made in Canada with Japanese engines is baffling. Especially when it has trashed Honda Civics made in Canada with *American* engines!

Many Japanese managers will tell you that they are quite free to buy from outsiders, but conduct elaborate studies to prove to themselves that internal sources are the best. Such "freedom" is abstract, to say the least, and is not backed up by the facts. Internal sourcing is the preferred option. Most will not even look outside their own "family" unless forced to do so. They insist on making most of their own parts because they believe manufacturing is the "real" business of business.

The supplier with the best quality, cost, and delivery will get the order, so the party line goes. Nevertheless, Fujitsu makes its own state-of-the-art components, and goes outside for low-tech items like screens and memory chips.[27] Claims of "freedom to choose" outside suppliers echo similar contentions advanced by AT&T managers before the breakup of the Bell System. AT&T didn't mean it then, and the Japanese don't mean it now.

Under pressure from the United States, the Japanese government has forced its manufacturers to buy foreign semiconductors, breaking the stranglehold of Japanese chip suppliers on their home market. But purchases are carefully limited to the 20 percent range, the target set in trade negotiations. Government pressure will not so easily break Japan's preference to put internal interests before those of customers.

When the "not invented here" demon is cast out, Japanese companies do well. Toshiba, which took the lead in laptop PCs in 1990,[28] relies heavily on outsiders. Its personal computers use state-of-the-art Intel chips and Conner disk drives; in total, 64 percent of parts are outsourced.[29] Toshiba's energy is focused on building the best laptops, not the best components. You have to keep your eye on the ball if you want to succeed in a competitive business like PCs.

The "make and export" philosophy has other, real costs, especially in computers. By focusing on the technology alone and not its applications, Japanese companies are ceding services, the fastest-growing segment of the market, to their competitors. Few, perhaps, have suffered more from lost service opportunities than Fujitsu. Over several years in the mid-eighties, Fujitsu acquired GTE's communications systems operations, including GTE's large field service organization, or FSO. Field service had been booming because GTE was one of the few players that could support large Fortune 500 company networks built with products from dozens of different suppliers. On the hardware side, meanwhile, Fujitsu's communications products, designed in Japan and sold in the United States on their technical merits, were losing share to American rivals. Why not then drop the hardware and develop the field service business, capitalizing on customer contacts? Fujitsu management was not interested in services; it wanted hardware exports. A great business opportunity was squandered.[30]

Many Japanese companies are glad to buy designs from American companies, as long as they do the manufacturing themselves. Matsushita licensed Sun Microsystems technology for its own line of workstations, to be made in Matsushita plants in Japan.[31] Americans feel hard done by when foreign companies license American ideas, but the Japanese are smart to do so. If they were even smarter, they would also buy the components and save themselves a lot of trouble.

Danger Sign No. 2

You are doing studies to "prove" your own parts and services are better than those of others.

Total System Supplier

In a race against time, Japan's top electronics companies have filled all the gaps in their product lines. Fujitsu, Hitachi, and NEC all make everything from chips to supercomputers, from faxes to telephone exchanges. On multibillion-dollar shopping sprees, Sony and Matsushita have acquired the "software" to make their "hardware" run. You can't accuse Sony of being stingy—its record-breaking contract with Michael Jackson shows the company is willing to put its bets on the line.[32] But Sony brings nothing to the entertainment business but money. The notion that the customer who buys a Sony Music tape will prefer a Sony Walkman to play it on is simply bizarre. When people talk about "synergy" to justify outrageous prices for acquisitions, hang on to your wallet, for trouble lies ahead. The acquisition frenzies of U.S. conglomerates in the 1960s and 1970s were justified on such grounds. Most of these conglomerates are now mere shells of their former selves, having squandered billions to get there.

The sons are repeating the sins of the fathers. IBM and AT&T, at extraordinary expense, tried to become "total systems suppliers" during the 1980s. IBM bought telecommunications gear maker ROLM, while AT&T expanded aggressively into computers. Failure resulted. Incredibly, AT&T then acquired NCR in 1991. Commented an AT&T spokesman to the *Wall Street Journal,* "NEC, Fujitsu and Siemens are characterizing themselves as computer and communications companies. Why should AT&T, an American company, settle for something less? We're not going to settle for something less."[33] The performance of these three companies is not much for AT&T to aspire to.

During the 1980s, AT&T formed a strategic alliance with Olivetti to capitalize on the synergy between computers and communications. The idea was that Olivetti, a major European computer supplier, would sell AT&T communications products in a market where AT&T was weak. Conversely, AT&T would sell Olivetti computer products in America. The results of this "total systems" approach are well summarized by Olivetti's chairman Carlo De Benedetti to the *Wall Street Journal*: "What's the result today of putting together computers and telecommunications? A total failure, which everybody now realizes."[34]

Suppliers other than the Japanese continue to find the "total system" allure irresistible. Intel and Motorola, not content to dominate microprocessors, have introduced complete computer systems based on their own components.[35] These companies bring little to the table other than technology. Worst of all, they risk alienating chip customers, now also their competitors, in the process. Neither company has been particularly successful with its new products. Compaq, an important Intel chip customer, responded to this competition by investing $1 million in Nextgen Microsystems, which is developing a new chip to compete with Intel's PC components.[36] As for Motorola, its previous attempt to become a "total system supplier" with the acquisition in 1982 of Four-Phase Systems, a minicomputer maker, was a flop.[37]

The fallacy of the total system strategy is this: it serves your agenda, not your customer's. There is no reason for customers to buy your VCRs because they like your movies, or to buy your mainframe computers because they like your fax machines. In the computer market, if customers are looking for one-stop shopping, they don't look to hardware vendors, but rather to systems integrators. They know that the vendors have only one thing on their minds: hardware quotas!

In Japan, companies like to buy as much as they can from one manufacturer, preferably one with which they have close business ties both as a supplier and a customer. Many Japanese companies mistakenly assume that their foreign customers think the same way. Outside Japan, people like to pick and choose what they buy. Foreign customers are not members of a *keiretsu*.

Danger Sign No. 3

Your advertising talks about your company's vision of the future, promising everything to everyone.

Keiretsu: Golden Handcuffs

Most big Japanese companies are locked into vertical and horizontal integration. As part of vast industrial groups, or *keiretsu,* they are bound (by formal and informal ties) to customers, suppliers, distributors, banks, shippers, and labor unions. While benefits exist, the *keiretsu* have become golden handcuffs for many, tying Japan's best companies to self-defeating methods of competition.

American and European competitors see only the benefits of the *keiretsu* structure: lower costs of capital, labor, and components. They see long-term relationships that ensure sources of supply and guarantee quality. And while it is true that the Japanese have gone to great lengths to reduce the disadvantages of vertical integration, the bonds between *keiretsu* companies have nothing to do with customers outside of Japan. They have everything to do with internal interests and politics. In Japan, this system works because customers as well as suppliers are tied into the group. Outside Japan, such ties do not exist. And besides, in America at least, *keiretsu*-type bonds violate antitrust laws.

Breaking the bonds of the *keiretsu* means breaking the bonds that bind Japanese society together so tightly. Japanese management is based on personal relations, often reaching back to university days. As with any "old-boy network," concerns of the group come before those of outsiders. Foreign customers are outsiders. These are barriers that foreign competitors can easily exploit.

Signs indicating a breakdown in the *keiretsu* system are misleading. The Ministry of Finance may say that real estate and stock market strains are loosening the cross-holdings of banks and other institutions. No doubt examples can be found: in *Business Tokyo,* a Japanese business leader recounted confidentially how Matsushita did the unthinkable—poaching NEC's subcontractors to make a competing product.[38] But if you think anything has changed, just ask T. Boone Pickens, whose attempt to buy his way into the Toyota network of suppliers was dramatically rebuffed. *Keiretsu* cross-holdings barely changed during the 1980s.[39] And the big 1991 financial scandals, in which brokerage firms were found refunding the large trading losses of big customers, show that many relationships go well beyond the *keiretsu,* but are invisible to outsiders.

The *keiretsu* system is under political pressure from abroad. Americans and Europeans resent the way all purchases are kept in the family, particularly overseas. As the big Japanese car companies have set up plants in the United States, some 350 Japanese component manufacturers have rushed in to supply them.[40] And much of the electronics gear sold overseas is to other group members. Sumitomo group customers buy NEC computers in Japan, and take these preferences with them when they expand internationally.

The U.S. government is tackling the *keiretsu* problem under the "structural impediment initiative" talks with Japan. Should these family bonds actually give way, the task of competing against Japan will be far more difficult. Two of Japan's best performers in the postwar era are Honda and Sony, neither of which is part of a *keiretsu*. Both of these companies do better outside Japan than at home, because the lack of group ties hurts in Japan but helps internationally. The sheltered workshop, the inward-looking product development, the reliance on sister companies for sales overseas, may all go. But if the Japanese are forced to compete without these handicaps, they will really be dangerous.

Danger Sign No. 4

Your company is reorganizing itself into a Japanese-style conglomerate.

When Tokyo Calls the Shots, Japan Comes First

Fatal Flaw No. 2: The Neglected Customer

Koji Kobayashi, NEC's chairman emeritus, is one of Japan's great industrial entrepreneurs, the Alfred Sloan of his company. Starting as a salesman in the radio division in the 1930s, Kobayashi rose to the top of NEC after World War II, transforming the company from a small communications equipment manufacturer into a diversified electronics giant. But Kobayashi's dream was to turn NEC into one of the *world's* electronics leaders,[1] and in this he has failed.

To execute his globalization strategy, Kobayashi reshaped NEC from head to toe. He pushed hard to diversify beyond telecommunications to semiconductors and computers.[2] He instituted a rigorous policy of quality control; it was said at the time that he "raised the Z flag" at NEC (a reference to the Z flag used by Admiral Togo to signal attack on the Russian fleet at Tsushima in 1905, and again by Admiral Nagumo at Pearl Harbor in 1941). To manage the NEC he envisioned, Kobayashi developed an elaborate organizational strategy he called the "top theory," designed to balance corporate and customer requirements. He decentralized power to NEC's line groups, where senior executives were charged with reconciling the needs of their divisions with the needs of the company as a whole. Kobayashi visualized this structure as a spinning disk, or top, with himself at the center, and his group executives at the periphery. To further decentralize decision-making, Kobayashi dispersed NEC's manufacturing operations throughout Japan, making each plant an independent company with its own management structure. For these regional production subsidiaries, visualize a second disk mounted above the first. Finally, the top theory was applied to foreign operations, and a third disk, representing the overseas sales organizations, was mounted above the second. Each disk had its own management hierarchy.[3] NEC management might thus be represented by a jukebox with three record disks stacked up, each spinning around the center spindle, the corporate headquarters staff departments which hold the whole organization together. The top disk represents the line divisions (e.g., Computers and Industrial Electronics Systems); the second disk the regional manufacturing in Japan (e.g., the NEC Kofu Ltd. computer plant in Yamanashi Prefecture, about two hours from Tokyo by train); the third disk the country sales organization (e.g., NEC America, Inc.).

Sound complicated? It gets worse. Try applying this theory to NEC's computer business. NEC designs and manufactures laptop computers for sale outside Japan at NEC Technologies, Inc.,[4] headquartered near Chicago. While NEC Technologies formally reports to NEC America, on a day-to-day-basis U.S. managers might deal with their counterparts at the computer division in Tokyo regarding marketing and sales issues and with the regional production companies in Japan regarding engineering concerns. At the same time, they need to keep the North American sales group at NEC headquarters in Tokyo informed of key activities. Imagine a frontline employee—or worse, a customer—trying to move an idea through a bureaucracy like this. It's tough, to say the least.

Even when responsibility is decentralized, as it has been in personal computers, NEC's top theory structure makes everyone look to the "local" center before acting. And the local center looks to the three corporate centers (line, sales, and plants), not to mention the HQ staff group. Knowing where to look for action, therefore, is an art rather than a science. As a result, no matter how much product development is localized, the focus of the corporation is always elsewhere. With the spinning disk analogy, senior management is at the center, local management at the periphery; customers are off the disk altogether, somewhere in the outer darkness. There is always pressure on management to hold the organization together against the centrifugal forces created by the demands of customers. NEC always comes first, customers last.

The top theory adds a significant staff burden and slows down decision-making—NEC has far too many managers for each frontline employee dealing with customers. The total number of layers of management from a salesman in the field to a decision-maker in Japan is large, probably unknowable. Real authority in the NEC organization—littered with divisions, subdivisions, and subsidiaries—is hard to identify. Accountability is extremely diffused. Everyone claims to have the customer's interest at heart, but no one is directly accountable to customers, except for salesmen. And they have no authority, so accountability is meaningless to themselves and their customers. Because of these organizational complexities, field personnel are always in a wait state. And their customers are on hold forever. Top theory, not customers, drives NEC. It is not an exaggeration to say that the company's entire structure is designed to keep customers away from important decisions. Considering that Kobayashi first made his mark at NEC in sales, this is quite a state of affairs.

By centralizing control of the "top" in Japan, NEC pays the price in poor performance overseas (in Japan, physical proximity and personal relations have enabled NEC to overcome the limitations of its management organization). Despite Kobayashi's globalization strategy, NEC's international sales are a declining share of total revenues. In its 1991 fiscal year, foreign sales actually declined by 3 percent; in the same year, NEC suffered the indignity of withdrawing from the U.S. consumer electronics market.[5] NEC remains overwhelmingly a Japanese company, and Kobayashi's dream remains unrealized.

Leading From Behind

While many Japanese products are made in the United States and Europe, all important decisions are made in Japan. Japanese subsidiaries abroad are run by "straw men," locals nominally in charge but really controlled by Japanese nationals who must consult Tokyo at every turn. At headquarters, questions percolate up and down and between organizations until consensus is achieved. As a result, decision-making is slow and far removed from customers; responsiveness is impossible. Companies that do not empower those dealing directly with customers to make significant, on-the-spot decisions are sitting ducks for competitors willing to turn on a dime.

Already some 350,000 Americans work for Japanese companies; by the year 2000, an estimated three quarters of a million Americans will receive paychecks signed in Tokyo.[6] In the United Kingdom, where much of Japan's European investment is concentrated, an additional 400,000 will be employed by mid-decade.[7] Throughout the late eighties, Japanese direct investment flooded into the United States and Europe, appearing almost recession-proof. Indeed, foreign investment reached feeding-frenzy proportions, with Japan's blue-chip giants trying to outdo each other by "globalizing," that tired mantra of the eighties. In the United States, Japan initially bucked the recession trend, tapping its nest eggs at home to invest for the long term, even as its American competitors got cold feet.[8] In the early nineties, investment did slow down, particularly acquisitions, after a string of failures.[9] Nevertheless, Japan's investment in America has reached the point where in some industries, like TVs and cars,

Japanese products are more American than America's. Zenith, the last American-based TV manufacturer, decided to close its last American plant in 1991; Sony and Matsushita sets are made in the U.S.A.[10] Many "big three" cars have fewer domestically made parts than Hondas do.

Clearly, whatever reluctance Japan once had to setting up shop overseas seems to have been overcome. Despite the scale of their offshore operations, however, Japanese companies are reluctant to let go of control, to decentralize. Locals running Japanese subsidiaries are simply excluded from the consensus-building process at headquarters. In short, they are given their marching orders and have little or no say in the matter.

During the 1960s and 1970s, Japan built its markets through exports, with scarcely any local production. Overseas locations, the number of which was kept to an absolute minimum, served as sales offices and "listening posts," gathering competitive intelligence and market research. Trade pressures put a roadblock on this one-way street, so Japan started building plants to get behind the trade barriers. The objective of this investment was not to get closer to customers, but to solve a political problem. Tokyo remains firmly in the driver's seat.

A number of Japanese companies do realize the benefits of effective decentralization of control, and are experimenting with real decision-makers who are not Japanese. With few if any exceptions, these remain experiments. Agile competitors can exploit these long lines of control, but must do so soon. For Japan's lumbering giants—the ones that make it overseas—will inevitably decentralize their companies.

In our business we constantly encountered American employees of Japanese companies who were frustrated and cynical about their ability to have any effect on corporate direction. One young MBA we interviewed for a job told a remarkable story about a middle-size Japanese bank trying to crack the New York secondary commercial paper market. American salesmen were supported by American researchers who qualified leads. So far so good. But all loan approvals had to be made in Japan. Even the Japanese managers in New York—and all the managers were Japanese—could not approve loans. As a result, decisions took as long as three weeks; domestic competitors responded in twenty-four hours. The bank could only get business it was willing to buy by cutting margins razor-thin.

Our customers at Japanese companies were always recounting stories of advice not listened to and opportunities lost. One capable engineer at a Japanese electronics manufacturer spent a year researching the market for a new product, talking to customers, sizing up competitors, building a plan—in short, doing his homework, largely on his own initiative. The planners from Japan who visited the U.S. operation were not interested in the advice of our customer, who, not surprisingly, soon quit in frustration.

In one case, we made a presentation to a group of U.S. employees of a Japanese company before visiting their head office in Japan. These seasoned American managers, with years of experience with their customers, pleaded with us to take their case to Tokyo. They believed we had the ear of the top guy in Japan, while their views were not welcome. And indeed, the decision-makers we met in Tokyo were not the least bit interested in the opinions of their U.S. subordinates, whom they considered next to worthless.

Like American multinationals in the immediate postwar period, Japanese companies are reluctant to trust their local employees enough to make key decisions affecting everyday relations with customers. In *The House of Nomura,* Albert Alletzhauser quotes a Nomura executive who says to his American employees during a botched attempt to crack the New York equities market, "Remember, Nomura will always be a Japanese firm run by Japanese."[11] Giving foreigners control of customer relations means ceding to them control of corporate strategy and direction. American companies took twenty-five years after the war to change.[12] How long will it take Japan?

Hiroshi Yamauchi, head of Nintendo, the electronic game giant, considered moving the headquarters of his company from Tokyo to the United States, where most of his customers and employees are. The move makes sense: America is Nintendo's biggest market, and most of his programmers are there. Yamauchi told the *New York Times* that the only issue regarding the relocation was "whether the Japanese government would let me." The reaction from the Japanese powers that be was swift and definitive: no way! Nintendo started backtracking, announcing that decision-making for the game business would not be moving to the United States. The company claimed that Yamauchi was kidding when he said the headquarters would be moved.[13] If a small company like Nintendo gets so much flak for decentralizing, a real power shift from Japan to its markets is clearly some years off.

Enchanted as they are with Japanese technology, foreigners often overlook this fatal flaw in their Japanese competitors. It takes a lot of product quality—which Japan sometimes has—to cover up such structural weaknesses. As long as Japan Inc. wants to keep control in Tokyo, far removed from overseas customers, it is exceptionally vulnerable to decentralized competitors.

Carpetbaggers

Successful players in the global marketplace invest in the countries in which they sell because it brings them closer to customers. While Japan Inc. has dramatically increased local production and research in the last few years, it is playing catch-up ball. As recently as 1989, Japan manufactured locally a mere 4 percent of what it sold abroad, compared to 18 percent for the U.S. and more than 20 percent for the major European countries.[14]

Building local plants will close this gap statistically (and probably turn back the protectionist tide, as intended), but Japanese companies will fall short of their goals until they deal with the bias against local decision-making. The beneficial aspects of Japanese management philosophy, such as consensus-building and lifelong employment, are left behind in Japan, while the drawbacks, such as low pay, overwork, short holidays, and racial discrimination, are all too often imported wholesale. Many Japanese companies are trying to overcome this problem, but the process is a long one, as the experience of American and European multinationals has shown.

"Japanese and American management practices are 95 percent the same and differ in all important respects," said the late Takeo Fujisawa, the cofounder of Honda.[15] Amen! In Japan, employees are willing to exchange the positive for the negative, but outside Japan, employees are not given the same opportunity. Control, exerted from Tokyo, is effective and stifling. While Japan learns its lessons, problems with customer relations will be ongoing—and could permanently damage chances for success in many markets.

Even in Japan, those outside the group are excluded. Prejudice against individuals of the wrong background—and sex—is overt and seldom challenged. Before he joins a large company, an employee's "documents" and background are thoroughly checked. The ensuing "male bonding" that ties together managers is especially tough for outsiders to crack.[16] As for foreigners, their treatment can be particularly shoddy; until 1990, second- and third-generation Koreans, forcibly removed to Japan before and during World War II, were not eligible for citizenship unless they gave up their Korean names, and they had to be fingerprinted by the police annually.[17] No visitor to Japan can fail to notice the position of women in business. The "tea lady" is ubiquitous and obsequious; the female manager extremely rare. Over a number of years, visiting dozens of customers in Japan, we can recall only one young woman who seemed to be a manager (or at least a management trainee). During the course of a presentation to a small group, she would not make eye contact, but stared intently at her notebook.

The Japanese are, of course, entitled to retain their customs. The point is that those outside the sanctum sanctorum, whether customers or Korean-Japanese, are not involved in decisions that may affect them. You can exploit this systematic exclusion if you are willing to expose the inner workings of your company to customers, and those employees closest to them, whatever their nationality or position.

Senior managers of Japanese subsidiaries in America will often tell you they are given a lot of slack by their bosses in Japan—but they are paid to toe the party line. In the same breath, they will tell you that they talk to Japan every day. One Fujitsu executive told us that he worked late every night so he could talk to his boss in Japan.[18] In the *Wall Street Journal,* Clark J. Mathers II, president of 7-Eleven, said of his new owners, Ito-Yokado in Japan, "By the hour, they want to know what's going on."[19] If you delegate power to someone, he doesn't have to check with you on every decision he makes. Somebody checking with the boss at every turn is not making decisions—the boss is.

Employees don't like being kept on a short leash, and neither do customers. One of us had been a Sony customer since he had received his first Sony product, an AM pocket radio, at age nine. Over the years, he purchased many other Sony products; for nearly all consumer electronics needs, he went to Sony first. None of his Sonys ever failed—even that first radio still works after thirty years. Never failed, that is, until he bought a Sony Outback radio-tape player for his children in 1989. Everything went wrong with this machine—it was a lemon. But mistakes happen, and he would have been satisfied if his Outback had simply been fixed. While the unit was "in" warranty for parts, it was unfortunately "out" of warranty for labor; and nobody at Sony Corporation of America would budge: no pay, no play.

SONY: If we fixed it for you, we would have to do it for everyone.

CUSTOMER: That sounds like a good idea.

SONY: Our warranty is industry-standard; Panasonic and everyone else have the same policy.

CUSTOMER: But I don't buy from Panasonic, I only buy from Sony.

SONY: Read your warranty—it says you have to pay for labor after ninety days.

CUSTOMER: But I don't read the warranty when I buy a Sony product.

There were more phone calls, and letters, and the tape player went back and forth twice to Sony. The logjam was broken only when a letter was sent directly to Akio Morita, head of Sony in Japan. Soon after, the machine was replaced for free. The people in the front lines at Sony, while always polite and certainly patient, clearly had no authority to make an exception to the rules. Just as clearly, Akio Morita, many thousands of miles away, did. But not before a lifelong customer was lost.

You can live with a portable tape player that does not work. What about your company's communications or computer system? If the software developers that keep this equipment up and running—and the people who approve what they do—are twelve time zones away and don't speak your language, you have problems. When your job is on the line, you want decision-makers there *today*. This is the problem many Japanese companies face despite billions of dollars in investment overseas.

No amount of public relations spending will mask this central control, although most of the large Japanese multinationals are in the process of image-building, touting their concern for Americans. Honda, for example, ran a series of ads boasting of its exports from the United States. Toyota ran a campaign with the theme of "investing in the individual" that publicized its philanthropy in America.

Such PR might be greeted cynically in the United States; in Europe, carpetbagging is met with action. In 1991, the European Community reached a comprehensive agreement with Japan limiting imports and local production of automobiles until 1999. Imports will be frozen at 1989 levels (equal to an estimated 9 percent of sales at the end of the decade), and all growth must come from "transplants," cars made in Europe.[20] Ironically, the cars Honda exports from the United States to Europe posed a dilemma for the European Community, forcing the U.S. government to go to bat for Japan, at the same time as the U.S. manipulates its own "voluntary" restraints.

In electronics, the EC is forging a combination of restrictive trade practices and government subsidies to turn back the Japanese threat. Another decade of mercantilism will almost certainly kill what's left of the European electronics industry, but will make life for Japanese suppliers miserable in the meantime.

While the Europeans do what they can to keep out Japanese products, be they imported or locally made, Japanese companies have nevertheless rushed to build their plants before the 1992 deadline for European customs integration.[21] It's the same strategy as the Japanese used in the United States, with poorer chances of success perhaps, but still the right move for the wrong reason. These plants are controlled directly from Tokyo (or by Japanese expatriates in daily contact with headquarters); they do not get Japanese suppliers closer to customers. Unimpressed by such actions, Europeans are erecting real barriers: one thing the Europeans are good at is state control.

Local investment is not just in factories but R&D laboratories as well. The rush to build plants in Europe and America has been accompanied by many new research centers. But like the plants, these are usually controlled directly from Japan, reducing the benefit of exposure to customers that would be derived from local management, especially in combination with local sales and manufacturing. Stand-alone operations work on specific projects fed to them from Japan, and serve as listening posts for new breakthroughs.[22] In locating these labs, Japanese companies often "buy brand name," choosing high-profile university sites like Princeton, New Jersey, and Cambridge, Massachusetts, in the United States and Oxford and Cambridge in England.[23] On the public relations front, local R&D often does not stand up to close scrutiny: there's lots of final development to local tastes, but little basic research.[24] The sexy stuff—dreaming up the new products and turning them into reality in close collaboration with manufacturing and customers—is kept close to the vest in Japan. Fujitsu ran into this problem in the United States with its big communications systems—conceived, designed, and produced in Japan. Fujitsu still wonders why they don't appeal to Americans.[25] Toshiba manufactures its portable PCs in California, but designs them in Japan, an unwieldy process that has lost it business to more nimble competitors.[26]

Local R&D and local manufacturing do not mean local control. NEC produces in America over 40 percent of what it sells there;[27] Fujitsu supplies more than half of North American telecommunications product sales from local production.[28] Laboratories have been established by many companies to do local research. Yet factories and labs are generally controlled directly from Japan or by Japanese stationed in the United States, and have little or no customer exposure. While competition has taken its toll on NEC in personal computers, NEC gave its offshore PC business a big boost when it shifted both production and design to the United States.[29]

As long as Japanese companies pull the strings from Japan, they will respond to their customers more slowly than competitors with decision-makers on the spot. Government pressure to increase investment and reduce discrimination will eventually force the Japanese to come around. But for now, this handicap can be exploited to great advantage by companies willing to trust their managers.

Danger Sign No. 5

An earthquake that destroyed any of your overseas locations would have no "material" impact on corporate operations.

Trusting the Locals

When Tokyo calls the shots, the company comes first. Customer relations deteriorate, along with employee morale. Locals in touch with customers every day know what customers want. But if these employees can't act without permission from halfway around the world, competitors will respond first. And as often as not, these same powerless employees end up getting the blame for failure. This is not to say that strategy cannot, or should not, be directed centrally. But corporate strategies must be developed in close consultation with customers and the people who see them every day, and executed without constant interference from headquarters.

Customer service is improved by fast decision-making, which is perforce based on fragmentary information. When customers are on the line, they will not wait for you to develop a consensus about your future plans; they want action now. Customer frustration increases exponentially as the number of people required to resolve problems increases. If questions must be relayed back to Japan for careful consideration, dissatisfaction will be endemic, ultimate failure certain. To stop the German invasion of France in 1940, Field Marshal Gamelin tried to direct French forces from his GHQ in Vincennes near Paris, many hours from the front. Orders were methodically issued every morning to Gamelin's commanders in the field. By the time Gamelin's orders arrived they had been overtaken by events in the field. Your Japanese competitors rely on this approach, and they will share

France's fate if you are prepared to empower your frontline people to act quickly, with the information at hand, and without fear of reprisals.

Decisions in Japan are made laboriously, by small groups and networks of groups, close together, communicating informally. The process works well in Japan, a small country in which most customers are a subway or train ride away. But this management system does not travel well. Informal networking simply cannot reach halfway around the world.[30]

Perhaps Japan Inc.'s greatest strength is that employees are trusted—but only in Japan. Sharp distinctions are made between Japanese and American managers. All important decisions are made in Japan; local decisions, generally low-level ones of limited value to customers, are made by the Japanese collegially, excluding Americans. Locals made titular company presidents are often given responsibility for administrative functions, like personnel, legal, and public relations. Japanese managers control line functions like manufacturing and R&D.[31]

Purchasing seems like a relatively low-level decision, but many Japanese companies in the United States buy from their Japanese suppliers—the sale is clearly made in Japan. In 1990, NTT, the Japanese phone company, announced plans to set up a data communications operation in Jersey City, New Jersey, to provide services for its big Japanese customers.[32] Chances are, NTT's new company won't be selling to Americans, but to the real decision-makers in Japan. Those stateside managers will simply get their marching orders from Tokyo.

While career opportunities for non-Japanese overseas may seem limited, promotions to headquarters in Japan are simply out of the question. Many companies do send engineers and even plant workers to Japan for training or special projects. But managers and executives are virtually never transferred to Japan; there is no place for them in the group, which has been bound together since college days. When you sign on at a Japanese company, you'd better do it for the money you are getting now, because you have no shot at the top jobs. With no real options for advancement, locals must move on to realize their career goals. A fast-track sales executive for Hitachi in America will never be president of the parent company in Japan. If he wants new challenges, he must look elsewhere. With little future to of-fer their local employees, recruiting is tougher for Japanese com-panies than for their better-managed European and American competitors. What they get stuck with is deadwood. So do their customers.

Sometimes these employment problems turn legal: a string of suits has hit some big Japanese companies. Two NEC Elec-tronics executives charged that their former employer had an anti-American bias and denied them the authority they had been promised to do their jobs. A Canon USA employee charged the company was biased in favor of Japanese men for management positions.[33] Fujitsu was sued by three former American employ-ees who said they were fired because they were not Japanese.[34] A federal judge ruled that Quasar, a subsidiary of Matsushita based in Illinois, violated civil rights laws when it fired most of its American managers but kept on the Japanese. Fifty-seven of eighty American managers were laid off when business soured, while all nine Japanese kept their jobs.[35] On appeal, the federal court ruled that because of treaties between the United States and Japan, Matsushita had the right to treat Japanese nationals differ-ently, just as American companies can—and do—treat Ameri-cans posted overseas preferentially.[36] There is no doubt Americans like to sue their employers, Japanese or otherwise, but the impression nevertheless remains that Japanese employees have jobs for life, while American employees are expendable as business conditions change.

Most of the lawsuits against the Japanese seem to involve disgruntled white-collar workers. In a few cases, blue-collar workers may be better off with Japanese employers; certainly it is tough to beat American business when it comes to shortsighted employment practices. Honda and some other Japanese car com-

panies, for example, did not lay off production-line employees
when sales took a dive in 1991.[37] In a rare show of cultural adaptation, however, Japan Inc. on the whole seems to have embraced the American "slash and burn" attitude toward workers.
When recession set in during 1991, Fujitsu, Subaru, and Toshiba
axed hundreds of workers in response to poor sales.[38]
Bridgestone hired people aggressively in the late 1980s, only to
lay them off again when business soured in 1991.[39] At least
Bridgestone decimated the ranks of management before starting
in on its production workers,[40] a major deviation from Detroit's
tried-and-true methods.

While Americans and other foreigners hired by Japanese
companies face dead-end jobs, Japanese managers are expected
to do time abroad on their way up the corporate ladder. But even
for the Japanese, time spent abroad can be risky if they lose
touch with the intricacies of corporate politics at home. Many
managers prefer to spend huge amounts of time traveling from
Japan rather than lose their place in the decision-making process.
Never try to impress a Japanese manager with the number of fre-
quent flier miles you have under your belt; their stories of dozens
of trans-Pacific flights in a year are not uncommon. ("So many
free first-class round-trip flights to Hawaii, so little time . . .")
One executive we know made thirty-six such trips in twenty-four
months, all to avoid moving his family to the United States. Another spent fifteen years abroad without his family to ensure that
they remained in the Japanese mainstream. Furthermore, a manager's "foreignness" can make reentry into Japan difficult. In
other words, the more successful he is in learning from his overseas experience, the worse his reception at home will be. We
know one outspoken manager who is known by his colleagues as
"the American," a none-too-flattering sobriquet. Perhaps most
difficult of all, if his children are educated abroad, his foreignness can limit their chances for success in Japanese society: the
sins of the fathers are visited on the sons. *Kikokushijo,* or return-
ing children, have great difficulty getting back on track in Japa-

nese schools, and apparently are ridiculed by other kids for their speech and "foreignness." In the United States and Europe, foreign exposure for children and adults alike is generally considered a benefit. Some observers, like Roger Goodman in his book *Japan's International Youth: The Emergence of a New Class of Schoolchildren,*[41] argue that the *kikokushijo* presage a new generation of outward-looking Japanese. Perhaps—but it will be a generation or two before these children are in decision-making positions.

Sometimes products are so good and competitors are so bad that it doesn't matter how you treat your frontline employees. Sony and Toyota for many years had products you couldn't buy from American companies; what's more, their competitors were probably even more centralized than they were. But Japan has already picked off most of the pigeons, and good products are no longer enough.

In service markets, people are everything. In advertising and publishing, for example, success depends solely on full understanding of local tastes. Dentsu, which became the biggest advertising firm in the world on the strength of its top spot in Japan, gets only a small fraction of its revenues from overseas, and does little more than follow its domestic customers around the world.[42] Kodansha, a large Japanese publisher, set up shop in New York, but for the most part translates selected Japanese texts, despite ambitions to publish original works in English.[43]

As long as Japanese companies do not trust their local employees, especially the ones who see customers every day, they will be handicapped outside Japan. Competitors with aggressive hiring and promotion practices can fill the breach.

Danger Sign No. 6

Locals are not running every one of your overseas operations; less than two of your corporate officers are foreign nationals.

Stranger in a Strange Land

Perhaps more than any other Japanese company, Sony represents the success that is the reward of quality and technical leadership. Sony has invested heavily in America, in local production for its consumer electronics, but also in movie and music entertainment. Indeed, Sony may have gone farther than any other major Japanese company in decentralizing authority overseas. Many promise to give their foreign employees real power, but don't deliver. Sony is trying to deliver, especially in its entertainment operations, where autonomy for local management has translated into significant market share gains.

Unlike any other big Japanese company, Sony has not one but two foreigners—both American—on its corporate board. Peter G. Peterson, an investment banker, chairman of the Council on Foreign Relations, former federal Secretary of Commerce, and no patsy on Japanese trade issues, was appointed in 1991.[44] Michael Schulhof, a lifelong Sony employee, was appointed in 1989.

Schulhof, a Ph.D. in physics who joined Sony in the early 1970s, had by 1991 become not only a board member, but also vice chairman of Sony USA (the American holding company) and president of Sony Software (the movie and record company). Ron Sommer, a German and star performer for Sony in Europe, became president of Sony Corp. of America, the marketing arm for Sony's hardware business. While Sony has turned much authority for its American business over to non-Japanese employees, letting go of control is not easy.

While Schulhof is vice chairman of Sony USA, Norio Ohga, president of the parent, is chairman of Sony USA and, until recently, Akio Morita's kid brother Masaaki was executive vice chairman. At Sony Software, Schulhof also has Ohga looking over his shoulder in the chairman's spot. Schulhof in fact told *Business Week* that he talks to Ohga, based in Tokyo, every day. Furthermore, while a German runs U.S. marketing, Masaaki

Morita, as chairman of Sony Corp. of America, had local manufacturing firmly under his grip. He will be replaced by Sony insider Ken Iwaki. Are these real decision-makers at Sony America?[45]

When Sony shifted control to the front line, the payoff was clear. Sony Pictures became the box-office leader in 1991, taking an unprecedented 20 percent of the market with a string of hits, including *Hook, My Girl,* and *Prince of Tides.*[46] Sony deserves a lot of credit; handling Hollywood is not easy for anyone. Coca-Cola couldn't control Columbia, which is why it was sold to Sony in the first place.[47]

Sony promised to give Columbia Pictures and CBS Records complete artistic authority, but that promise was not easy to keep once the honeymoon was over. In response to lavish spending and mixed results, Sony started, in 1990, to rein in Peter Guber and Jon Peters, two hot producers originally hired to run the show. Then in 1991, Guber helped squeeze out his longtime partner Peters (whose freewheeling management style did not sit well with Tokyo) and then he canned Columbia president Frank Price.[48] For a while it seemed like the quickest way to get rich in Hollywood was to get fired from Sony: Peters left with $15–25 million, Price with $10–20 million, and Walter Yetnikoff, former head of CBS Records, with $20 million.[49] Sony gave Yetnikoff, the head of CBS Records, free reign artistically, but he nevertheless left in 1990. Ohga then took control, virtually commuting from Tokyo to the U.S.[50]

Market share gains came at a high cost financially. To cover the acquisition expense and ongoing cash-flow drain of the movie business, Sony in 1991 began raising money (ultimately the company may require several billion dollars) on the equity markets (the first Sony issue in Tokyo in November 1991 was about as well received as *Hudson Hawk,* one of Columbia's early duds).[51] It's not clear Sony will make money in movies, but if market share is what it wanted, it succeeded. Trying to build this

business from Tokyo would have been a disaster, but Sony cut
Guber enough slack to do his job.

Movies were new to Sony, and as American as you can get.
Perhaps the company realized it had no choice if it wished to
avoid disaster. On the hardware side of the business, Sony has a
choice, and it's keeping control in Japan. In the early 1960s,
Sony president Ohga centralized all product design into one center near Tokyo, where it remains.[52] New products, the lifeblood
of a company like Sony, are the exclusive domain of Japan. Centralized control may have worked at one time in TVs, radios, and
tape players. But the next generation of consumer electronics will
require closer cooperation with customers. And if it continues to
mastermind its computer strategy from Tokyo, Sony will have no
better success in the future in this market than it has in the past.

Sony has signaled its desire to decentralize operations, os-
tensibly to bring decision-making closer to its customers. Ron
Sommer, the German head of Sony's U.S. sales, told the *Wall
Street Journal* that he thinks the time will come when Sony's
center of gravity will be in America, and that a non-Japanese
might head the parent company.[53] One of Sommer's European
counterparts does not sound so sure. Dr. Rainer Kurr, the general
manager of Sony's European television operation, told the *Financial Times* that he doubted Sony's plans to decentralize authority,
particularly when it comes to manufacturing. Tokyo keeps its eye
closely on Sony's eight European plants.[54] If Sony's Japanese
managers can't give up control even of its overseas TV plants,
they are unlikely to let go of the hot new projects on which
Sony's future depends.

Centralized control has already cost Sony business in computers. A small company which does optical disk storage applications work on subcontract offered Sony America an
opportunity to sell relatively inexpensive image storage systems
using CD-ROMs in a jukebox-like configuration. Image management would have given Sony an entrée into the high-end office
market that it prized. Sony, however, wanted to use this as a

"platform" for selling a complete line of Sony business products only. Large corporate customers were willing to spend several hundred thousand dollars, much more than the price of a Sony "platform," if only Sony would customize this new system for their individual needs. In other words, these customers would pay Sony big dollars to provide a complete service, to use this image management system to integrate all images generated by the competing PCs and other computer equipment they already had. However, American executives at Sony could not sell Tokyo on the idea of using Sony expertise to make competitors' computers work better together. All they were worried about was keeping the factories running in Japan. If customers were not prepared to junk their existing investments for completely new end-to-end Sony systems, supported by a third party, Sony wasn't interested.[55] Neither were its customers interested in Sony.

While Sony has a tough time letting go, at least it is trying. Eventually it will succeed, to the detriment of its competitors. Most Japanese companies have not even started trying in any serious way, although all talk a good game when hiring, as many disgruntled ex-employees will tell. According to its president, Yataka Kume, Nissan "views localization as a five-step process. First, we increase local production and create new jobs; second, we raise the local content through expanded use of locally sourced parts and components; third, we strengthen our local R&D capabilities; fourth, we localize management functions; and last, we localize the decision-making process."[56] Clearly decentralization is a pretty low priority for Nissan. (No wonder U.S. market share fell in the 1980s.) Others go to great lengths to circumvent the problem altogether.

What works well in some cases is to send a Japanese executive overseas essentially for life. Minolta's U.S. company, a leader in cameras and copiers, was run for twenty-two years (until 1992) by Sam Kusumoto, a Japanese. In a sense, Kusomoto had brought Tokyo with him: more than half his vice presidents were Japanese and he traveled back to Japan four or five times a year.[57] He could thus stay "plugged in" to decision-making at home, while himself "going native" in America. While this approach to decentralization can perhaps work for well-focused manufacturers like Minolta, it requires a kamikaze pilot like Kusumoto who is willing to abandon his life in Japan for the good of the company. In today's Japan there are few shouts of *"Banzai!"* anymore when the call for volunteers is sounded.

Another less successful technique to avoid decentralization is to make financial investments without assuming a management role. To gain a piece of the mergers and acquisitions mania of the 1980s, Nomura paid out $100 million for 20 percent of Wasserstein Perella.[58] Tobu Department Stores backed a 1990 management buyout bid for Saks Fifth Avenue to obtain this prestigious name in retailing.[59] Kumagai Gumi, the construction company, bankrolled a partnership with an American developer to buy into the high-stakes New York real estate game.[60] A number of Japanese investors financed movies in the late 1980s, presumably to bask in the California sunshine.[61] When the M&As dry up, retail sales fall flat, real estate tanks, and the movies flop, these risk-minimizing investments look like a poor substitute for getting involved.

Striking the right balance between effective control and decentralization is not easy for anybody. British retailer Marks & Spencer prospered in the 1980s through a no-frills combination of food and clothing sales ("pies and panties," according to one wag) under one roof. Marks & Spencer has eliminated suffocating layers of management by empowering all employees to get things done. Its success in the U.K. may be repeated on the Continent; one of us recently visited an M&S store in Paris and was astonished to see French shoppers grabbing off the shelves English pork pies, white bread, shrimp-flavored potato chips, and irradiated vegetables faster than they could be restocked. Despite its strong performance close to home, Marks & Spencer's expansion into North America, using Canada as a beachhead, was a disaster. Assuming that all Canadians are Anglophiles, M&S ran its business there like an extension of its English retail network. In 1991, the company began localizing decision-making to turn the venture around, but a turnaround will be tough.[62]

Such hubris ("If it works here, it'll work there") can be especially damaging and is common among American and European companies. Surprisingly, it is rare among Japanese managers we have met. On the contrary, they believe that Japan is so alien from its overseas markets that communications and trust are next to impossible. Perceiving themselves as strangers in a strange land, they struggle with decentralizing their organizations and giving real power to their overseas employees. At several companies we have encountered, they know they must come to terms with decentralization if they are to get beyond the export stage and achieve the ambitious goals they have set for themselves. A few, like Sony, are making real progress. But the vast majority of Japanese companies you come up against are likely to be completely adrift.

Danger Sign No. 7

Your overseas executives are contacting headquarters more than once a week.

Fat and Happy

The old Soviet Union's central planning organization, Gosplan, could have taught Japan Inc. a few things about streamlined bureaucracy. From headquarters in Tokyo, layer after layer of management masterminds Japan Inc.'s every step. Somehow, the process works in Japan. Personal networking can overcome organizational complexity to serve Japanese customers. Said Guy de Jonquières in the *Financial Times,* "To the western eye, the system may appear inefficient because it occupies so many people. It works because it encourages highly efficient diffusion of information. Not only do face-to-face communications at every stage of product development forge close links between different corporate functions, regular rotation of staff ensures that all concerned understand each other's jobs."[63] That's great in Japan. Unfortunately, overseas managers and their customers are simply excluded from the process. Companies exclude customers at their peril.

We have seen Japanese companies with as many as ten layers between frontline employees and the CEO. Sometimes these layers are triplicated, once in the U.S. holding company, again in the Japanese line division, and finally in the Japanese regional marketing organization. In such a case, for example, a computer disk drive salesman in Atlanta who has a request from a customer that requires a change in the product would send a memo to the disk drive division in suburban Tokyo. At the same time, the sales rep would copy his memo to the North American marketing group at headquarters in downtown Tokyo. The disk drive engineering and manufacturing managers then study the feasibility of the request, since they would have to make any changes in the product that are ultimately required. Within this line organization, an endless number of meetings between managers, market planners, development engineers, and product engineers takes place, each generating further meetings and studies. The headquarters marketing people, with a disk drive sales quota for North America to meet, analyze the market potential of a product change and keep tabs on the disk drive line people to make sure the request doesn't get swept under the carpet. Meanwhile, the U.S. holding company management could get dragged in if the change has an effect on another division or raises legal or regulatory questions. Confused? Imagine how the poor salesman feels six months after making his request. Customers, however, are not confused by all this—they have long since moved on to another supplier.

Examples like this are not only real but common in Japanese companies. Ironically, if the customer were in Japan, the organization would work well, expanding and contracting organically to meet the needs of customers, who are close at hand (particularly big government customers and other buyers from the *keiretsu*). To control overseas operations while meeting the number one goal of leaving cozy relations at home intact, complex matrix structures are required. When confronted with elaborate, multilayered, three-dimensional organization charts, Japanese executives will retort that these charts don't reflect the real links that connect real decision-makers. They are right: often as not, you can circle the University of Tokyo graduates and draw lines between them to see where the real power flows. Unfortunately, none of their overseas employees or customers are likely to be Todai grads, and so are off the power grid. Competitors willing to flatten their own organizations and decentralize decision-making can run circles around such Byzantine bureaucracies.

Of course, the Japanese do not have a monopoly on bureaucracy. AT&T's notorious failure in computers can be traced to the extraordinary number of layers of management between customers and decision-makers. AT&T tried to solve its problem in computers by acquiring NCR, avoiding the root cause of its woes. For too long, General Motors refused to deal with the layers of management that make the company inward-looking and all but oblivious to the needs of its customers, preferring to hack away at the factories and blue-collar workers who got left holding the bag. The main purpose of the bureaucratic ramparts at GM was to protect top management from the assaults of customers and shareholders. And IBM continued to push all important decisions up to its celebrated management committee at the top of the huge Big Blue bureaucracy long after it was clear that IBM's agenda and not that of its customers was being served. One expensive example: IBM thought that it could rejuvenate its mainframe business by making PCs into perfect mainframe access points; the result was OS/2, a new generation of PC software perfectly designed to solve IBM's problem. Selling OS/2 to other customers has proved a big challenge.

To deal with its own inefficiencies, the bureaucratic morass in Japan grows and grows. Teams of managers study information about overseas markets, without ever actually talking to overseas customers. As one Japanese executive said to us, "the biggest problem in our company is that we have too many general managers." Meanwhile, salesmen in the field methodically gather from customers information which is carefully transmitted in detailed memos back to headquarters, where it disappears, as light into a black hole at the center of some distant galaxy, never to be seen again. In one company we looked at, the salesmen on the ground in the States were patching together account plans from out-of-date press releases, newspaper clippings, and handwritten notes. Meanwhile, the market planners in Tokyo had detail on customers in the United States that would make the NSA blush. But this bureaucracy was not supporting sales; quite the reverse.

Most American businesses once worked this way, but competitive pressures during the 1980s—largely from Japan—forced American industry to thin or eliminate layers of middle management. By the early 1990s, even the biggest and most successful companies in America, like AT&T and GM, finally had to face fully the horrors of these irresistible pressures. Throughout America, the process continues, as layoff after layoff decimates the ranks of white-collar workers. Japan's middle managers have been spared such restructuring. Flush with cash from the appreciation of the yen in the mid-eighties, Japan spent its way to growth. As with carpet bombing, however, occasionally you hit something strategic. Successes are in spite of decisions laboriously made in Tokyo, not because of them.

While in the United States "fat and happy" now means "dead and gone," in Europe government-sponsored industrial policies encourage mergers and consolidations to keep the bureaucratic dinosaurs alive. Europe will probably take longer to face the music than even Japan. With a degree of wishful thinking that can only be called inspirational, former Prime Minister Edith Cresson of France decided in 1991 to combine state-owned nuclear power, biotechnology, and information technology into one high-tech powerhouse.[64] Colbert would be proud. By contrast, Japan's Asian competitors are not living in a dream world. Change may be coming to the companies from which Japan has the most to fear. Daewoo, a diversified Korean conglomerate with its sights set on information technology, fired a third of its middle managers in 1991 to speed up decision-making.[65] Japan cannot resist this tide of change.

Honda, for one, has tried to come to terms with its own bureaucracy. Honda was a superstar of the 1980s, but its growth slowed dramatically in the early 1990s, forcing the company to admit that it could not act fast enough. Consensus decision-making was resulting in designed-by-committee cars that were boring. Honda will now make managers individually, not collectively, responsible for their operations. Layers of management will be reduced.[66] Honda is on the right track, but there is little indication it is transferring real power to the United States, where most of its sales are. Nevertheless, this change is bad news for American competitors.

During the 1990s, the swollen ranks of Japanese corporate management will break under the pressure. As Japan invests and manufactures overseas, the inadequacies in its current management structure, designed for export, will become ever more apparent. At the same time, the postwar era of the great Japanese industrialists—like Shoichiro Honda of Honda Motor Co., Konosuke Matsushita of Matsushita Electrical Industrial Co., Koji Kobayashi of NEC Corp., and Akio Morita of Sony Corp.—is rapidly coming to an end. Once these single-minded visionaries are gone from the scene, the faceless, soulless bureaucracies must take over.

The transition will not be easy; the sheer willpower of these men, which drove their companies forward, will disappear. Such change is ongoing in the United States (as everywhere else).

DEC, for example, faces the retirement of Ken Olsen, a real leader who has driven product development at DEC since day one. But the United States made the big transition from the rule of the great entrepreneur-industrialists—when the likes of Alfred Sloan at GM, Thomas Watson at IBM, and J. P. Morgan reigned supreme—to one of professional management during the immediate postwar period, a time when its place in the world was unchallenged. Japan will enjoy no such luxury.

Bureaucracies—Japanese or otherwise—insulate decision-makers from customers. In the bad old days, suppliers could get away with such inefficiencies because they held all the cards. Governments could be counted on to stack the deck in favor of business, especially national champions. Today, especially in America, the customers hold all the cards, and they are aces.

Danger Sign No. 8

Your company has more than four layers of management between shop floor and boardroom.

Emptorphobia

Outside Japan, few Japanese companies sell direct. Rather they rely on dealers, manufacturers reps, wholesalers, retailers, and job-lotters to reach their ultimate customers. As a result, product managers in Japan are out of touch with their customers, who are an ocean and several layers of distribution away. Over the years, we have hosted many Japanese road shows: groups of designers and planners touring the United States. Invariably they had made the trip to see competitors and market researchers, but not customers. Designing and selling products that people want without talking to them is pretty tough—unless, of course, your competitors have even less interest in customers.

Nowhere is Japan suffering more from the lack of customer contact than in information technology. With computers, the degree of human interaction required increases directly with the sophistication of the product. The need for ongoing support has reached the point where networks of computers, for example, have become services, not products. Without the benefit of direct customer contact, Japanese companies can't sell the networks and all the computers attached to them. That's why more than three quarters of Japan's computer exports remain low-end parts (like memory chips) and peripherals (like printers), which can only be sold on price.[3]

Competitive pressures are forcing change: NEC began selling its communications systems directly because its distribution system fell apart. Hitachi and Fujitsu sell mainframes through companies in which they were part owners. Fujitsu decided to sell its business products direct in Canada in 1991, as a kind of dress rehearsal for the U.S. market.[4] Not all change comes easily, however: NEC turned over direct sales of its supercomputers to Control Data in 1992 after trying direct sales on its own.[5] Nevertheless, direct sales abroad could eventually force these companies to change. If change is resisted, the results will be predictable: market failure (and in the case of Japan's information technology industry, an enormous crisis). If change is embraced, watch out!

Competitors that reach their customer directly are dangerous—witness the Japanese car companies. Now that Detroit has closed much of the gap in product quality, competition in cars, particularly in luxury cars, has shifted to service. For their Infiniti and Lexus luxury lines, Nissan and Toyota sell through dealers, but they exert strong control over the "buying experience." Through training and contract requirements, they ensure that service-level standards are met. As they see the payoff from better customer relations, these two pioneers are trying to improve the experience of buyers of all their cars, no matter what the price. More customer contact eventually forces decentralization, but places enormous stress on the fabric of the Japanese management and promotion system, a problem with which the car companies are now grappling. They are likely to succeed, and when the benefits of customer contact become apparent to other Japanese companies, real change will be afoot. Meanwhile the big three (at least when they are not beating the drums in Washington) continue to fight the last war: product quality.

Danger Sign No. 9

Intermediaries account for more than 25 percent of your sales.

Customers Define Quality and Service

Quality is not an abstraction, it is defined by customers. "Six sigma," the statistical term for 99.9997% defect-free production, is the quality goal of Motorola.[6] No defects is a worthwhile goal for any company, be it Motorola, General Motors, or UPS. But customers do not judge you by the number of defect-free solder connections or spot welds. They judge you by—well, whatever they want to judge you by. The point is, if you focus on your own measure of quality and not customer satisfaction, you will end up with warehouses full of cellular phones and parking lots full of station wagons. The same holds true for services: the post office may meet its own "quality" goal of clearing all its pick-up boxes on time, but when the mail arrives two days late, who cares?[7]

Customers define quality. Their satisfaction with your product or services is in large measure shaped by expectations: if you buy a Honda Civic, you expect less from your car and dealer than if you bought an Acura. So too, if you send something by Express Mail, you have a reason to hope that it will get there the next day; if you drop a letter in a mailbox with a first-class stamp on it, you know you have only yourself to blame if it gets there late. What your customer expects from you and your product cannot be left to chance: you must *control* customer experience—or at least manage it closely. You are kidding yourself if you think you can leave this to someone else, no matter how high the "quality" of your product.

In the high-powered computer markets Japan has targeted, customers want their suppliers to be partners—to help them help their customers do better. Decisions are long-term and made at the highest levels. Benefits are measured in increased sales and improved customer relations. Japanese companies do not reach these decision-makers and cannot provide the benefits they are looking for. As long as they sell commodity hardware through third parties, their problems will persist. You can exploit this.

Benefits from such simple products as photocopiers and fax machines are immediately evident to customers: reliability, low cost, and ease of use. Decisions are typically made by an office manager or even by a consumer. The benefits of big systems accrue indirectly: a supercomputer allows an aircraft manufacturer to design more fuel-efficient planes; a local area network allows a department to be decentralized; a communications system improves customer response time, raises service levels, and increases cash flow. These complex products solve complex problems, requiring highly sophisticated interaction; getting them to work requires close and ongoing consultation with customers. They are not bought on price: the revenues they bring in or expenses they reduce far overshadow the initial investment (likewise, if they fail, the cost is measured in lost revenues, not mere inconvenience). Purchase decisions are made by top executives, not by office managers or purchasing agents. Sales require contact at high levels between buyer and seller—the proverbial golf-game sale. Buyers need to feel comfortable with the seller, to know where the seller's business is going, and whether the buyer will get prompt action when problems arise, as they inevitably do. A third party cannot provide this kind of contact; neither can a lone salesman.

Once a Japanese firm asked us to explain its sales failures in California. We explained that in California, by itself the sixth-largest economy in the world and one of its most complex markets, this firm had one salesman working from an answering machine at home. California has thirty million inhabitants, we pointed out, roughly as many as the Kanto area around Tokyo. How many salesmen covered the Kanto? One? Indeed, there were hundreds working from beautifully appointed offices with support that the poor soul in California with a country-sized territory to cover could only dream of.

Ironically, some of America's top companies are imitating Japan's mistake, looking for "new channels" for their products. Kodak, disappointed with the performance of its office equipment business, announced in 1991 that it would stop selling complete systems directly to customers in favor of pushing its hardware components through third parties.[8] Rather than focus on its real strength, customer relations, IBM wants to boost its market share and keep its factories running by selling its systems through others. Ricoh and Hitachi sell IBM's notebook PCs in Japan. Mitsubishi sells IBM's flagship mainframes and minicomputers in Japan under its own label, [9] and Wang distributes IBM's minicomputers.[10] Who will customers blame if these products don't work as expected? What will IBM learn about its customer's needs? If IBM wants to be more like its Japanese competitors, it had better be careful that it does not get its wish: Big Blue will become Medium Blue, an also-ran in the computer hardware game.

Danger Sign No. 10

You are spending more time with fellow employees than with customers.

Ship and Forget

Exports built Japan. And exports remain the number one priority of Japan Inc. But the "ship and forget" approach that worked for cars and TVs in the past will not work in the future. Consumers expect more: they want first-rate products and first-rate service to go with them. Japan just wants to keep the factories at home humming. This is not a meeting of like minds.

Managed by engineers, the big Japanese electrical companies would rather dream up new technologies than solve customer problems. Convinced by its loss in World War II that America's power derives from its technology, Japan has been determined to catch up—and maybe surpass—its old enemy. Technology is crucial to military and business success. Japan is right. Well, half right. When you buy a computer mainframe, a commercial airliner, or a truck engine, technology is critical, of course. But—even more critically—you need to depend on your supplier, day in and day out. When you buy a car or TV, an answering machine or fax, the less you see of your supplier, the better. At least that's the way it used to be.

The need for close contact with customers is creeping

downmarket. Personal computers were traditionally sold through third parties. But the level of support that customers expect is increasing. Compaq relies on third parties to deliver computers with the power of minicomputers and mainframes. Customer satisfaction problems are the result: Compaq finished poorly in a 1990 *PC Magazine* reader survey. Two of the strongest performers, Dell and Northgate, sell direct.[11] It may make great hardware, but if Compaq can't control its customer's experience with the product, it loses.

Apple Computers has been slam-dunked by this shift: its products are now too sophisticated for its distributors to support. To fix this problem, the company tried selling direct to big buyers, making its distributors nervous. So Apple then tried recruiting systems integrators. Later the company began selling to discounters, further alienating its distributors. Apple is now dangerously removed from customers, who doubt that dealers can deliver sophisticated applications, and its dealers, who control customer relationships but may feel confused or even angry.[12]

Not surprisingly, Japanese PC vendors, none of which sell direct, are generally rated poorly by customers, except on price. In a 1991 J. D. Powers survey of personal computer customer satisfaction, none of the top spots were held by Japanese companies.[13] In a survey of PC users done by Dataquest in 1990, Japanese suppliers received low marks for customer satisfaction and customer commitment. At one company that did well on these questions, Dell Computer, customer calls are answered, on occasion, by the CEO.[14] Try getting hold of the CEO of Toshiba if your computer doesn't work. Or Apple: the company refuses to answer telephone calls for technical support, referring all problems to its dealers.

Japan Inc. may have hoped that computers would become "consumerized," playing to its strength, but expectations have changed. You might buy a $100 VCR that fell off the back of a truck, but not a $2,000 computer. In 1991, Sony began manufacturing one of Apple's laptops,[15] perhaps hoping to learn from its new partner something about the PC business, where it has failed repeatedly. So Sony will get its customer contact thirdhand: somebody complains to the dealer who complains to Apple who complains to Sony . . . it's like a game of telephone. Who knows what ultimate message will reach Sony's engineers in Tokyo. As for disputes between Apple and its dealers, the fallout can only hurt Sony.

Japanese companies are not the only ones to suffer from the "ship and forget" problem. In the early 1980s, Mitel, a Canadian company, revolutionized the market for small and medium-sized communications systems with a new design, cheap but loaded with features. Selling through distributors, the company became the top supplier in its segment. In the mid-eighties, Mitel came up with a new and simple upgrade for its old system. The problem was, Mitel did not know who its customers were, because somebody else had sold to them. Without direct contact, Mitel could not keep customers who may have been thrilled by its new technology. It paid the price in lost sales and market share.

In cars, the Japanese are way ahead of their competitors in taking control of customer contact by dealers. In consumer electronics, they are getting sloppy and are probably vulnerable. Recently one of us bought a Panasonic minicomponent stereo from a discounter in New York. When the system arrived, it was apparent that it had been used as a demonstrator in the discounter's showroom; all the boxes had been opened and carelessly retaped, and there was even a tape in the cassette deck with the handwritten notation "Charlie's songs—oldies. Do not tape over." A month later, he bought a Panasonic answering machine from another discounter in New York. This one seemed new, but he couldn't get one of the features to work. Call the dealer? Forget it; service was not the dealer's strong point. So he looked in the manual. No toll-free number, but a listing in New Jersey. He called at about 4:30 P.M.; they were closed for the day. Called again the next day; was put on hold for ten minutes. Finally somebody answered: sorry, that feature doesn't work on your machine. Philips, are you listening?

Danger Sign No. 11
You cannot name your top ten customers.

Limited Direct Sales

Look at where Japan has made a splash overseas: cars, cameras, copiers, computer chips, faxes, machine tools, stereos. All these products are bought by somebody else for resale; none are sold directly by Japanese manufacturers to their overseas customers. Look where Japan had trouble overseas: advertising, construction, investment banking, retail sales, and, worst of all, information technology. In these areas, direct, daily contact with customers is necessary. Admiral Yamamoto warned his compatriots that there was no point in attacking Pearl Harbor unless Japan was committed to attacking, and conquering, the entire continental United States, "to march into Washington and dictate the terms of peace."[16] Either they resist selling directly, as in information technology, or they won't trust their foreign employees when they do sell directly, as in investment banking. As long as your Japanese competitors stay in Tokyo, refusing to empower their local employees and avoiding direct dealings with customers, they are vulnerable.

If they want to become major players in information technology away from their home base, the Japanese must reach their customers directly, as the leaders in that market now do. However, replacing your dealers with your own salesmen can be a nightmare. Fujitsu and NEC now sell their communications systems directly in the United States, but continue to use distributors as well. Customer confusion is often the result, with two or even three different distributors selling the same product to the same companies. By contrast, two of the top three suppliers in this business sell direct. The third sells indirect but has an elaborate premier accounts program.

In Europe, Japanese mainframe computer sales relations are Byzantine. In Italy, Hitachi distributes its mainframes through Olivetti, and in Germany through a joint venture with Siemens and BASF. Fujitsu sells through Siemens in Germany, and Amdahl elsewhere in Europe; on top of this, Fujitsu bought ICL to sell throughout Europe.[17] With these competing channels of distribution, the opportunities promised by the European customs union in the 1990s will be difficult to realize. Consolidation will take years, and woe betide customers who need pan-European or global support for their computer networks. NEC, Japan's other big mainframe supplier, limits distribution to the French computer company Machines Bull. What do NEC computer users in Europe think of Bull's service? What do they think of NEC's products? Does NEC know or care?

Many organizations are turning over their computer and communications operations to somebody else, lock, stock, and barrel. That somebody else won't be somebody they never see. Since they are out of touch with their customers, Japanese suppliers are not cashing in on this business.

Such "outsourcing" comes in several flavors. With facilities management, the supplier, for a monthly fee, runs (and perhaps even owns) your entire data processing or communications operation. With network management, the supplier ensures that your voice and data communications stay up and running. With systems integration, the supplier acts as the general contractor for major information technology purchases, bringing all the manufacturers together. The common denominator here is responsibility: the supplier makes sure everything works and "holds the bag" when problems occur. Outsourcing means knowing the customer and acting fast. It is not an activity that can be exported or managed from halfway around the world.

In establishing its partnership in 1989 with EDS, an outsourcing giant, Hitachi opened the possibility of participating in large facilities management and systems integration projects. And this new organization did the right things, like opening new service centers in New York and California.[18] But Hitachi remains the hewer of hardware and drawer of MIPS, selling IBM-compatible mainframes at knock-down prices,[19] while EDS gets all the gravy from its big contracts.

NEC plays no significant role in systems integration, even where it sells direct. Sold by CDC, its supercomputers are targeted at scientific organizations which require little or no applications support.[20] Mainframes are sold through Bull. In other words: ship and forget.

Once computer manufacturers could bind customers to themselves with proprietary hardware and software. But software standards have made hardware a commodity, lowering prices and bringing once unimaginable power to desktop computers available anywhere. This diffusion of computing power has given anyone with a PC and a telephone jack the power to set up worldwide networks. Customers are looking for partners that can help them use this new power to solve real business problems. You can't be somebody's partner secondhand; you must deal directly.

Even if you want to switch to direct sales, sometimes the distributors do not want to let go. Nissan found itself in court when it tried to cut off its sales agent in the U.K.; its bid to take over French distribution in 1991 needed government approval at a time when the French, the original *dirigistes,* were trying to exclude the Japanese altogether from Europe.[21]

Making direct sales work takes a change in attitude that may be alien to Japanese managers far removed from the grim realities of sales outside Japan. Anyone worried about Matsushita's selling direct should go to the Panasonic "Office Automation" store on Park Avenue in New York. Lavishly appointed, in a prime location, and well advertised in the local press, this site is meant to be a showplace for Panasonic products. But don't ask to buy, because in this showroom they don't sell anything. We first visited the store to find that none of the Panasonic PCs we were shown were correctly installed, many of the products were no longer in production, and the Panasonic employee who reluctantly helped us appeared to be nursing a hangover—or worse. On a second visit, a much better informed Panasonic spokeswoman explained to us at some length why the PCs prominently displayed near the front had been withdrawn from the market. She also apologized for the poor setup of the products that were still for sale (no Microsoft Windows, no mouse). All in all, she seemed rather sad and lonely: we were the only "customers" there. We were left with a nagging question. If on a swing through New York a Matsushita executive toured this showplace (something they presumably do) and concluded that everything there was just fine (something they must have done), how much do Matsushita executives know? The only possible conclusion is that the people who run Matsushita don't know too much about their products or their customers. A very sorry state of affairs.

Bridgestone has not exploited an unusual opportunity to reach its customers directly in the United States. With its purchase of Firestone in 1988, Bridgestone also acquired 1,550 Firestone car service centers. Millions of customers are coming to Bridgestone directly every year with their car problems, many of which must involve their tires. But Bridgestone has its heart in manufacturing, not marketing. As soon as business turned sour, Bridgestone started to question the value of these outlets. To turn around its floundering U.S. operations, Bridgestone needs to make many changes—surely listening to customers must be one of them. In the end, Bridgestone wisely held on to its tire stores. If fully exploited, this direct link to customers could become the cornerstone of Bridgestone's success in America.[22]

Selling direct does not automatically confer new powers on companies unwilling to listen to customers. When we bought our first IBM PCs in 1983, we went to an IBM computer store in

New York for them. We were met by a young woman who said that she couldn't really negotiate with us because she was just a trainee. Then she called in a floor manager, who in turn called in the store manager—three layers in one store. All prices were fixed at full retail; there was no discounting and no price flexibility unless we bought twenty or more PCs, and that was handled by a different sales organization. The trainee volunteered that none of them were on commission, so that if our business went somewhere else that was fine because it would have no impact on their compensation or job security. We went back several times, and finally decided to buy eleven PCs. Unfortunately, IBM would not accept our purchase order, because it didn't meet IBM's internal accounting requirements. We had to produce a PO that looked like an IBM PO in order to buy from them. Eventually, we wended our way through this maze. When at last our IBM PCs arrived, the first one we turned on caught fire! Needless to say, we never bought from IBM again. And advised all who asked us about buying PCs to give IBM a wide berth. IBM eventually got out of the retail business. Small wonder.

One-Way Information Flow

"Ship and forget"—even if successful for a time—leaves decision-makers in the dark. They get orders from their distributors, but no feedback from customers, no "feel" for the market. Competitors with constant contact enjoy a great advantage. With nothing else to go on, Japanese companies focus on technical improvements and price alone, often with poor results.

Japanese companies have a great feel for their home market, where they have continual customer contact. Japan's physical compactness makes staying in touch easier than in the United States, for example. Nearly a quarter of the country's population live in the Kanto plain surrounding Tokyo, a short train ride from one end to the other. Short distances make it easier, but Japan's successful exporters work hard at customer relations at home. Sony has its own stores, and its designers wander around the streets of Tokyo to see what trendsetters there are buying.[23] Matsushita operates its own chain of retail stores, so it can see for itself what Panasonic TV buyers want or don't want. The big Japanese car companies employ their own door-to-door salesmen, so they find out what people are thinking in a hurry. In consumer electronics and cars, Japanese customers have generally been successful proxies for overseas customers. But whether it's station wagons or stereos, the strategy is not listening to customers (beyond basic questions of quality and value) so much as churning out an endless stream of new products in Japan just to see what will happen. If it sells, great; if not, move on to something else.[24] What people like in Sendai they are supposed to like in Brussels, Chicago, and Jakarta. Sometimes this works, but Japan Inc. has made the mistake of thinking that Japanese consumers can act as proxies for all types of products.

In some areas, like information technology, customers outside Japan have very different requirements from the Japanese. No amount of cruising Akihabara can bridge this gap. Sometimes computer hardware can be successfully adapted for overseas. Software rarely can; the Japanese use computers in radically different ways, if only because their language is so different from English and other European tongues. Just ask Apple, which met with abysmal failure in Japan until its personal computer operating system was rewritten in *kana* and *kanji*. For their Japanese customers, computer manufacturers often go to extraordinary lengths. The big three mainframe manufacturers toppled IBM in Japan once they started pushing their engineers out into the field to develop software for customers.[25] But what they learned about customer requirements in Japan has little or no value elsewhere.

New product ideas cooked up in a vacuum can be shockingly poor. In 1990, Hitachi, Sharp, and Toshiba all introduced laptop computers with color displays. However, these "laptops" weighed more than fifteen pounds, did not run on batteries—and they had to be plugged into an electrical outlet![26] Japanese companies are not the only ones to dream up such gravity-defying products. In 1991, IBM introduced a "portable" computer that weighed twenty-two pounds and cost $16,000. The machine had a fast Intel 486 processor, but how IBM planned to sell such an overpriced clunker was not clear.[27]

With no feedback from their customers, Japanese engineers direct their energies to topping competitive technologies. Look, for example, at the "war of the gigaflops" in supercomputers. One Japanese supplier after another has announced a faster machine in what seems to be some kind of competition between these Japanese rivals with little regard for what customers may think. When asked about this obsession with speed, one NEC manager told *Business Tokyo,* "Many of our users are research institutes, so they devise their own programs."[28] Computer speed is of the essence when selling supercomputers, of course. But the idea that manufacturers can tinker with hardware and let their customers worry about making these silicon juggernauts actually do something useful is the very essence of the "ship and forget" mentality. Outside Japan, customers, especially businesses with no interest in such feature wars, will find their solutions elsewhere. Or, at best, extract huge price concessions from the warring competitors. The problems this lack of contact causes cannot be offset by sending a team of engineers to California for a week to observe how women get in and out of their cars (as one Japanese automaker did) or studying American TV-watching habits to find out if they want another TV set (as another Japanese company did).[29] You need the day-in, day-out exposure, just like your Japanese competitors get in Japan.

Some American observers fear that Boeing is sowing the seeds of its own destruction by subcontracting production of key aircraft components to Japanese giants like Mitsubishi Heavy Industries and Kawasaki Heavy Industries. Boeing is taking a calculated risk, sharing its know-how in exchange for Japanese airline contracts. But co-opting these potential rivals while keeping them well removed from airline customers outside Japan is probably the best way to keep them at bay. If Mitsubishi and Kawasaki think that airlines worry about whether their planes are made out of aluminum or plastic composites, that's fine. Boeing knows that what's really on the mind of airline executives is nuts-and-bolts questions that affect cash flow. (For example, can the galleys and lavatories be moved quickly to increase business-class capacity?)[30] The biggest risk to Boeing is simple complacency, not Japanese subcontractors.

Danger Sign No. 12

You have no programs to bring customers into your labs, plants, and offices every single working day.

"What Features Must We Add?"

Suffering from the one-way flow of information, our Japanese customers invariably ask us, "What features must we add?" Looking around at competitive products outperforming their own, they want to know how to catch up. Higher capacity, lower power consumption, faster bit rate, brighter screen—what will it take? They are looking for technological shortcomings to explain their poor performance. What we tell them is *"Don't ask us, ask your customers."* Americans will tell you if a product stinks—but you have to ask. You cannot substitute any amount of market research or technical navel-gazing for a couple of hours talking to a customer. *Why did you buy this product? Who budgets for it? What do you spend your time doing? How is your performance evaluated? What are the pressing issues you face this month?* You will quickly find that what is on your customer's mind is not technology.

In the late 1980s, Canadian telecom supplier Northern Telecom became one of the top players in small communications systems, climbing right over the backs of Fujitsu, NEC, and Panasonic, among others. Northern's U.S. strategy was based on next-day drop shipment right to the customer's doorstep. Northern eliminated inventory (a big concern in low-ticket items) for its distributors and speeded up service for their customers. The formula was a winner. Technology played no role. While the Japanese are in retreat in this market, Northern Telecom has expanded internationally. Since the product was first introduced in 1988, it has been installed in more than forty countries, including ten European markets. Even overseas, rapid delivery is the key. Supplied from its North American plants and made virtually to order, the Norstar, as this product is called, can be installed by British Telecom in ten days.[31] During a series of presentations made in 1989 to Japanese suppliers, we were grilled about the features of the Norstar. We found it difficult to get the message across: the Norstar's features are unremarkable; the complete service, not the product, created Northern's success.

Nowhere have "features" gotten more out of hand than in consumer electronics. Whether it's a TV, VCR, CD player, camera, telephone answering machine, or instant breadmaker, each successive generation is laden with a geometrically increasing number of features. Naturally, the manuals for these electronic wonders are getting fatter still: one of us recently bought a new stereo for which the manual was as fat as the local phone book! Japan got where it is now in consumer electronics by giving its American customers what they want, no question about it. But now that they have buried General Electric, Motorola, RCA, and Zenith, are they still listening? In Japan they love gadgets, the more complicated the better, so that's what Sony and Panasonic crank out. Americans are different, but we still get VCRs that require a Ph.D. in computer programming to operate.

Until now, that is. Two California scientists introduced in 1990 a new product called VCR Plus, a hand-held remote-control device you use to program your VCR by punching in a single number (between five and twelve digits, depending on the show) printed in the local newspaper TV listings.[32] Another California start-up called Frox is developing a TV-VCR entertainment system that is controlled with Apple Macintosh–like symbols (some Frox engineers worked on the original Mac design).[33] These are great ideas, and a long time coming. Why didn't they come from Sony or Panasonic?

To keep the consumer electronics boom going, now that everybody has a TV and a VCR, manufacturers are experimenting with "home theater," an expensive combination of high-definition TV, laser disks, digital music recordings, next-generation video cassettes, and home computers (to name just a few of the possibilities). Sounds complicated, but the idea is simple: get everyone to replace everything he or she has now with something new and more expensive.

Predicting the fate of such an idea is virtually impossible; electronic toys do not exactly solve consumer "needs." But if Walkmen, why not home theaters? If the idea catches on, there will be a unique opportunity for Western companies to wrest back from the Japanese control over consumer electronics.

Many of the home theater concepts being batted around now will make today's VCR programming look like a piece of cake. What is needed is somebody to do for consumer electronics what Apple did for computers: make them easy to use. In fact, Apple hopes to do it all over again; in 1992 it launched its foray into "multimedia" systems (a variation on the home theater theme). We believe, however, that Apple's diversification into consumer electronics is more likely to drag its computer business down the tubes. What's needed is not another Apple, but another Steve Jobs, Apple's founder. Somebody who knows what customers want: fewer features, not more; a home theater that doesn't need an operator's manual. Keep up the good work, Frox.

Pumping Iron

Fatal Flaw No. 4: Japan's Technostrategy

When Takuma Yamamoto, chairman of Fujitsu, announced his company's acquisition of British computer leader ICL in 1990 he could look back on what appeared (to most American and European observers at least) to be an unbroken record of success. From a mere $6 million in sales in 1961,[1] Fujitsu had rocketed to $16 billion in 1990 and built a major presence in computer, telecommunications, and semiconductor markets in Japan, the United States, and elsewhere. With the addition of ICL to his portfolio, Yamamoto could look forward to his next conquest: Europe.

Perhaps more important, ICL would enable Yamamoto to reach his customers directly instead of through distributors, recouping the spread now lost by Fujitsu to others. While at home Fujitsu was a full-line supplier, internationally the company was having a hard time getting beyond job lot hardware sales. In Japan, of course, Fujitsu was top dog in many coveted electronics markets. Internationally, it was another story: Fujitsu was an also-ran in PCs, workstations, computers, and communications systems. Fujitsu could barely muster a quarter of its sales in 1990

from foreign operations, compared to 61 percent for archrival
IBM. What was worse, Fujitsu could not break out of commodity
hardware sales. Fujitsu was selling look-alike printers, PCs,
faxes, computer chips, and disk drives, under relentless price
pressure from the Koreans, Taiwanese, and upstart American en-
terprises. Leadership (outside Japan) in mainframe computer systems, a cherished goal of Fujitsu's, remained elusive. All Fujitsu
could manage was selling IBM knockoffs at knocked-down
prices. Other companies in Europe and the United States pack-
aged, sold, and serviced Fujitsu's hardware, keeping all the gravy
for themselves. In their 1990 letter to shareholders, Yamamoto
and his president Tadashi Sekizawa said, ". . . companies need
creative information systems that help them gain the edge on the
competition. Fujitsu's major objective in the 1990s is to
strengthen its system integration business to meet these customer
demands."[2] Tired of being the turkey, Fujitsu wanted the gravy
for itself.

Yamamoto decided to marry ICL's strength in software and
services with Fujitsu's hardware. With ICL's expertise, Fujitsu
could develop the customer smarts needed to get top dollar for its
equipment. Once these skills were mastered, Fujitsu hoped to sell
its computer products directly in the United States and Europe,
rather than getting hammered on price by selling peripherals to
its distributors.

The strategy seemed sound, the fit good. ICL would help
raise Fujitsu to the next level in its development. But winning
will not come easy. Computer acquisition success stories are
rarer than foreign nationals on Fujitsu's board. Worse, ICL's
strengths in sales, service, and software depend on people, not
technology. Unfortunately, Fujitsu is a "technology" company,
not a "people" company. And this technology is made in Japan.
To make a splash in Europe (and America), Fujitsu must sell
peace of mind, not technology. To do so, Fujitsu must transfer
corporate management, R&D, and big-ticket production to its
overseas operations.

Will Fujitsu succeed? History says no. In the United States, Fujitsu has already tried to make the big move upmarket in telecommunications, with poor results. In 1989, Fujitsu introduced its new, large communications system (the 9600) to the United States. Developed for the Japanese market, the 9600 was later adapted to American needs by a local software team. A sophisticated product requiring complex installation and after-sales service, the 9600 was poorly received. Two years later, R&D was pulled back to Japan.[3]

At the same time, Fujitsu tried to crack the U.S. telephone company market for large systems with a product designed and manufactured in Japan. Fujitsu says software development and production will move to the United States eventually. Pulling the strings from Japan, Fujitsu is trying to develop a new business that requires trusted, professional employees on the ground, in daily contact with customers. Without sufficient authority in the front lines, Fujitsu's efforts are doomed to failure. While boasting of his own autonomy and the flexibility of his employers, one sales executive at Fujitsu told us, "We work until nine o'clock every night so there is time transparency with Japan." He went on to say that he was in constant, daily contact with his boss in Japan. Fujitsu Network Switching's biggest competitor in the United States, Canadian Northern Telecom, is run by an American.[4]

Within months of its acquisition of ICL, Fujitsu threatened to pull R&D back to Japan in response to European protectionism.[5] Nevertheless, Fujitsu has won many kudos for the autonomy it has granted ICL and its other overseas acquisitions.[6] But Fujitsu will not become a major player outside Japan with a ragtag collection of acquisitions. It is not enough for Fujitsu to leave these subsidiaries alone while the parent company remains in splendid isolation at home. Will ICL turn Fujitsu into a hands-on, "service with a smile" business partner for its foreign customers, or will Fujitsu turn ICL into a factory outlet for its domestic technology? Experience says the dog wags the tail.

In a two-page Fujitsu advertisement in the *Economist,* the headline boasted, "This year we'll spend more on R&D than most of the Fortune 500 will make in sales." So what? A special advertising supplement announced, "Heart and soul, Fujitsu is a technology company."[7] Who cares? Its annual report proclaimed, "For over 50 years, Fujitsu has used advanced technology to help people achieve their dreams." Fujitsu's dreams, maybe. Until Fujitsu stops selling technology, Yamamoto's vision of the global, upscale Fujitsu will remain a dream. In Japan, Fujitsu built itself into one of the top information technology power-houses on the strength of close relations with customers. Outside Japan, the company will remain the hewer of disk drives and drawer of memory chips until it exports something more than technology.

The Technical Fix

Most Japanese companies sell what they like best about themselves: technology. Customers, on the other hand, think about themselves, their own problems, needs, and desires. Japanese decision-makers are heavily drawn from the ranks of engineers—those most fixated with technology and farthest removed from customers—who like to dream up new products, then try to find a home for them.

Companies that are technology-driven believe their mission is to lead their customers; they think that customers are waiting to be "told" what to do. Such visions of the future can be costly when customers have ideas of their own. In Japan, centralized control and lack of customer contact reinforce a technology-driven management culture by insulating decision-makers from the real world.

With nothing else to go on, feature and product proliferation is the first line of attack of Japan's cloistered engineers; when that fails, prices get slashed. Occasionally these shots in the dark hit their mark, but it's an expensive way to do business. In the past, Japan has been lucky to choose markets in which competitors have underinvested in technology, allowing Japan Inc. to maintain and even widen its technological edge. Innovative and aggressive Japanese companies struck sleeping American giants hard, knocking aside the likes of GM, Ford, Zenith, and GE.

Indeed, when a new technology is unique and desirable, product development is easy: the technology sells itself. How could Sony sell a portable CD player in 1983 that used so much power that the batteries went dead in less time than it took to listen to one CD? Because in gadget-mad Japan, it was the only such device on the market.[8] As competitors catch up, the rules of the game change; Sony soon had Matsushita breathing down its neck in portable CD players. Ultimately, technology is reduced to a commodity, and suppliers can compete only on service or price. Today, look-alike portable CD players get cheaper and cheaper. Japan's technology-driven companies invariably choose price to differentiate themselves, leaving the way open for competitors prepared to seize the high ground.

Postwar Japan is transfixed by technology, believing its security and progress depend on technological know-how. The Atomic Bomb convinced Japan that technology is power. But Hiroshi Kashiwagi, director-general of the MITI Electrotechnical Laboratory Technology, told *Business Week* in 1990 that Japan was closing in on the United States because America "has allowed its stock of technology to disintegrate."[9]

Like the engineers who run Japan Inc., the Tokyo University Law School graduates who call the shots in the bureaucracy have bought into the big technical fix (who could possibly know less than a Tokyo bureaucrat about the needs of a shopper in Peoria?). Japan may be right about the pivotal role of technology in modern warfare, but where customers fit in this equation is not at all clear. Competition can be likened to war, and military metaphors are often well applied to marketing. But business is not war and customers are not the enemy.

Selling technology is about looking into the mirror and seeing what you want to see. Your customers, however, see something different when they look at you: different qualities and different faults—that is, if they look at you at all. We have sat through innumerable Japanese sales presentations which invariably reveal glossy photos of new products, intricate close-ups of integrated circuits, aerial shots of brand-new plants complete with local employment numbers, and vague corporate statements of "commitment to advancing the needs of society." These presentations are about "us and our technology." Not a word about customer problems and possible solutions. In one sales call to a large American utility, a Japanese electronics giant presented over a hundred mind-numbing overheads that said *not a single word* about its customer. Incredibly, the countless schematic diagrams, tables, pages of dense text, and development schedules for existing and yet-to-be-developed products repeatedly drew the prospect's attention to the supplier's faults. As if anticipating objections, the supplier raised them in relentless succession. While this was an extreme case, let's-talk-about-me sales presentations are the rule, not the exception, among your Japanese competitors (but before you start snickering, listen again to your own sales pitch).

Japan has earned a premier reputation for R&D excellence. By some measures, Japan does the best research in the world. In a "world competitiveness" survey (conducted by Swiss business school IMD) in 1990, Japan ranked highest in R&D (the U.S. was highest in "market orientation").[10] Japanese corporate R&D expenditures as a percent of sales rose steadily during the 1970s and 1980s,[11] producing a growing share of the world's patents.[12] U.S. performance by these measures has declined, particularly when government R&D outlays are factored out. Many take this as another sign of U.S. decline: Japan invests for the future, while Americans eat their seed corn.

Certainly, scrimping on R&D is not a virtue. But neither is throwing money at research. Japan's enormous investment in semiconductor technology bought it a top billing on the world stage. But there have been failures, as well. Japanese expenditures—both public and private—on high-definition television (HDTV) and aerospace have run into the billions of dollars. Japan's HDTV standards were out of date before they were commercialized in 1991, and this next-generation TV technology is considered a disaster even by Japanese executives: "One of the miscalculations is high-definition TV," commented Ken Iwaki, deputy president of Sony, to the *Wall Street Journal* in 1992, regarding his company's stock market problems.[13] Thirty years of investment in aerospace have produced two commercial airliners which were complete flops (the YS11 in the 1960s and the Asuka in the 1980s) and some blueprints for a successor to the Franco-British Concorde, a misguided enterprise if there ever was one.[14] In short, Japan hasn't had a successful airplane since the Mitsubishi Zero. The point is not that R&D is a bad investment—Sony will make TV sets no matter who sets the standards for HDTV; and Mitsubishi, Kawasaki, and Fuji Heavy Industries will remain major subcontractors for Boeing and McDonnell-Douglas even if they can't design an aircraft anybody wants to buy. Rather the point is that spending more than your competition on R&D is not the key to success. Only your customers have that key, and they will give it to you for free if you just ask.

Politicians should be concerned about their country's industrial problems. In Europe, development policies encourage large-scale mergers in search of critical mass, that bloated state, always one combination away, in which competition with Japan seems possible. Meanwhile, heavily funded research programs keep Europe's industrial predators off the one scent they need to follow: their customer's. Across the Atlantic, the United States lavishes tens of billions of R&D dollars a year on defense research and megaprojects like supercolliders and space labs that do virtually nothing for America's competitiveness. Caving in to narrow protectionist interests hurts those left to fend for themselves. Favoring debt over equity in the tax code leads to chronic underinvestment. These kinds of government policies reduce America's export potential. Perhaps more to the point, poor product quality hurts America's competitiveness. General Motors cannot be faulted for its R&D spending and investment in plant and equipment. Unfortunately for GM, better quality, not better technology, put Japanese cars in every third garage in America. Better service will keep them there.

The Ivory Tower

Engineers at labs in Tokyo or Osaka have no idea what Western customers want. Their ivory towers, far removed from the day-to-day problems of real customers, are a prescription for disaster. Moving the ivory towers closer to customers is not a solution, if the product designers remain cloistered. All the minilabs sprinkled around the United States and Europe by Japan's electronics giants will do nothing for market share if they report directly to Japan. From these cloisters, the ideas can sometimes be bizarre. Hitachi and Nissan are working on a mobile office of the future, a car equipped with fax, telephone, TV, VCR, and on-board navigation system.[15] Will anyone buy such a car? Maybe, but it won't be because these companies tried to solve customer problems. They are applying leading-edge technology to solving a sales problem of their own. Their solution will intersect with the needs of their customers by chance alone. And it will be up to their customers to fix their mistakes. These companies are developing a 1990s version of GM's visionary, if wide-of-the-mark, world-of-the-future exhibit at the 1939 New York World's Fair.

Product development in isolation from customers leads to solutions in search of a problem. The Canon "Navigator" all-in-one office introduced in 1990, with PC, fax, answering machine, and printer combined, is just such a solution. "High-tech merger gives home offices a big advantage," said the ad.[16] Customers setting up home offices no doubt have many problems, but desk space is probably not at the top of the list.

Japan has no monopoly on ivory towers, of course. Battered minicomputer suppliers in the United States prospered while they could cook up new ideas and sell them through third parties to customers willing to work their own solutions. Said Data General founder Edson de Castro to the *Wall Street Journal* when he was finally squeezed out of the company, "My biggest mistake was failing to get Data General into the PC business."[17] Spoken like a man who never talked to customers! Xerox is another company in search of the technical "fix." In 1990, the copier giant introduced a $200,000 all-in-one copier, scanner, fax, and computer.[18] No doubt when there is a market for such a machine, a Japanese company will introduce one at a price that will make it practical. While in the 1970s its Palo Alto Research Center dreamed up many of the ideas embodied in today's personal computers, Xerox was unable to commercialize them. In the 1990s, this famous lab has cooked up what it calls "ubiquitous computing," a twenty-first-century vision without keyboards or monitors. Such work may help the United States in the patents and scientific-paper sweepstakes, but it will not help Xerox's sales anytime soon. Xerox would be smarter to have these engineers talking to copier customers about their business problems.[19]

AT&T has routinely developed new products that were revolutionary, but then dropped the ball on delivery. Perhaps the most egregious example was the transistor, which Bell Labs invented but did not commercialize. We have personal experience of two examples. Early in the 1980s, AT&T asked us to try out a personal computer called the 3B1 that was powerful, well priced, and had capabilities that were quite visionary. But it never quite worked, and AT&T did not follow through with the software or support to make the 3B1 a really useful product. The company ended up with warehouses full of 3B1s that could be used as boat anchors and little else. Then, in the late 1980s,

AT&T developed an electronic mail service that enabled Apple Macintosh computers located anywhere in the world to operate as if they were on the next desk. This product could have quadrupled AT&T's e-mail business (not to mention what it would have done for Apple) if it had been sold and supported properly. It quietly slipped into obscurity.

How could AT&T drop the ball like this? One former AT&T manager with a half-dozen employees told us how his job was to develop new applications for AT&T's computers. "Did you talk to customers?" we asked. No, he explained, he hired a market research company to find consultants with expertise in the areas they thought needed new applications. Their job was to develop ideas that AT&T could translate into new software. He admitted that he had not seen a customer in ten years. No wonder AT&T Computers was an abject failure.[20] You may be surprised to know that this is also how your Japanese competitors find out what customers want—we know because they came to us.

Companies succeed with well-differentiated products that meet real customer needs, which may or may not have anything to do with the level of spending on R&D. Technology seldom differentiates a product, and then only for a short time. Companies—even small ones—that spend far less on R&D but listen to their customers can do better than competitors that have well-financed labs but are out of touch with reality.[21] In the early 1990s, a host of small American companies like Thinking Machines and nCube developed parallel computers. These replaced supercomputers at a fraction of the cost by using hundreds or even thousands of standard personal computer chips all running at once. Their Japanese competitors, meanwhile, were introducing faster and faster supercomputers that nobody outside of Japan wanted to buy. The Japanese have run headlong into a market with no future.

Of course, where underinvestment by competitors is egregious, Japan has zeroed in. In the 1970s, Westinghouse's Unimation unit dominated robotics in the United States, but stuck with its antiquated hydraulic technology. Japanese competitors pushed ahead with electrically geared systems that soon knocked Westinghouse out of the running. Technology was crucial, but the Japanese suppliers were also willing to work closely with their customers to integrate robots into their manufacturing procedures. American suppliers were trying to move iron—and rusty iron at that.[22]

Danger Sign No. 13

Your engineers do not spend at least 50 percent of their time with customers.

Hit and Miss

Feature and product proliferation is the competitive response of the weak, and, as we have seen, it is often the first line of attack of Japan's cloistered engineers. In an effort to avoid price competition, Japanese suppliers bring out an endless stream of new products with ever more features nobody uses. When was the last time you programmed your VCR to record *General Hospital* while you were at work, left a "memo" on your own answering machine, used the "camp on hold" feature (see page 274 of the owner's manual) on your telephone, or timed your fax to send after midnight? Such clutter confuses customers.

Experimentation is good, but Japanese companies go too far. In gadget-mad Japan, companies release new experimental products to find out what consumers want. Matsushita, Sony, and their innumerable competitors introduce new camcorders, radios, stereos, TVs, and VCRs in relentless succession as prices go down, down, down. We call this the "spaghetti testing" method: throw it at the wall and see if it sticks. The process works well in consumer electronics (and in cars, in Japan at least), but in most markets, hit-and-miss produces too many misses and poor returns.

As a senior Sony official told the *Wall Street Journal,* his company's computer strategy was "not really based on any grand design; it's a kind of trial and error."[23] Lots of trials; lots of errors. Other Japanese electronics giants also use this product strategy in computers. Toshiba had no less than a dozen models in its laptop PC line up in 1991, a tough year for the company.[24] Toshiba used the right approach to launch its original laptops, which were highly successful. A group of designers was sent to the United States to find out what Toshiba's distributors wanted.[25] To maintain its position of leadership, these designers must be located in America, and they must talk to customers, not just distributors, every day.

If spaghetti testing doesn't work well in personal computers, it's a disaster with more complex systems. Customers with big investments in older systems and software will not tolerate new products that make their old ones obsolete. IBM learned this lesson the hard way. When it tried to foist a new operating system on its mainframe customers in order to boost software sales, IBM spent the 1980s recovering from its mistake. Complex systems must evolve, requiring ongoing and close customer relations. And not just in computers: MITI would like to leapfrog Boeing technologically with a supersonic airplane. Boeing understands the ongoing needs of its customers, particularly their training, spare parts, and service requirements.

Breakthrough technologies must often be developed without a commitment from the ultimate customer, but their application requires close cooperation with those who use them. Thinking Machines may have the fastest parallel processors dreamed up in splendid isolation, but no one will sell many of these computers without a clear idea of how they will affect organizations using them. Thinking Machines wisely decided in 1991 to cooperate with IBM to adapt for its computers existing mainframe software in which potential buyers have invested billions.[26]

Despite its much-vaunted R&D strength, Japan does not do well in some markets in which breakthrough technologies do differentiate products. One of Japan's most conspicuous failures is in pharmaceuticals, in which success is based on blockbuster new drugs. In Japan, pharmaceutical companies make fast, incremental improvements to their products; outside Japan, major new qualities are what sell. As a result, there are no credible Japanese threats to the Mercks and Glaxos of the world. And despite a generation of heavy investment in biotechnology, Japan's prospects are no better there.[27]

Japan has perfected fast product development that delivers incremental improvements in rapid succession. With an eye to competitors, engineers in close cooperation with their production and marketing counterparts turn out one generation of product after another. But the value of these skills outside the markets already conquered by Japan may be limited. Most critically, the hit-and-miss strategy is simply too expensive—it's no wonder Japan's electronics giants have to spend so much on R&D. Even owning the bank, Japan Inc. cannot for long squander precious R&D resources on such trial-and-error methods. Particularly when the alternative is so cheap: just ask customers what they want!

Danger Sign No. 14

One of your senior people is compensated for the number of new products introduced.

Markets Evolve Over Time

Emerging technologies give suppliers great power because they can deliver large, previously unenjoyed benefits. Customers will take what they can get and make it work themselves. They might even pay a premium for what may be a flawed product.

But as competitors catch up, delivery, price, and quality take precedence. What was once acceptable becomes second-rate, since alternatives are available. Finally, as the market and the technology driving it mature, customer relations and after-sales service are paramount.

The car industry has followed this pattern closely over the past twenty years, and the Japanese have exploited each shift most effectively. Stage one began with the oil crisis of the early 1970s, which gave the Japanese their first real shot at the big time. Fuel-efficient Toyotas and Datsuns (now Nissans) were a sharp break technologically with the land yachts then available from Detroit. While those early Japanese cars were not especially well made—many were underpowered, rust-prone death traps—they were cheap to buy and cheap to run. More to the point, there were few alternatives: Volkswagen had decided to move upmarket by this time, forsaking the beloved Beetle. As for Detroit, remember the Gremlin, Pinto, and Vega? In stage two, in the early 1980s, the big three started to get with the program, introducing a wider selection of small cars. Competition then shifted to quality, and moved upmarket. Those Toyotas got bigger and better. In the late 1980s, when the big three improved the quality of their cars dramatically, stage three began. The Japanese, while maintaining a clear quality edge, shifted competition to service. Better-made cars need less service, but Honda, Nissan, and Toyota nevertheless pushed their dealers to improve service, starting with their luxury models. The idea was to make the entire experience of owning and maintaining a car more enjoyable—or at least less of an ordeal. Service will remain key until another major shift in technology occurs.

This next shift may be "green" cars. While Detroit does its level best to resist emissions and fuel-economy legislation, Japan's auto giants are looking to the future. They are investing in electric cars, better fuel economy, and lower engine emissions, of course. But green means more. In 1992, we talked to the manager of one Japanese plant in the United States who said his company's goal was zero emissions from its factories. No smoke out the chimney, no solvents in fifty-five-gallon drums, no cardboard boxes to take to the dump. To reach its objective—and the plant manager said it was almost there—this manufacturer is completely rethinking its business from end to end. Why? Because zero emissions means no waste, and no waste means low cost. If Detroit ever catches up on service, this will be its next fright. The real challenge for the big three will be to get the U.S. government to force Japan to be less green.

In other areas, the Japanese have never gotten ahead of the market evolution curve. Most information technology markets are in the final, service-intensive stage where the Japanese are weak (outside of Japan, at least) because of centralized management and distributor sales. In the late 1970s, when computerized communications systems were introduced, simply having digital technology was enough to capture sales. In 1983, when AT&T introduced its own digital system, the rules changed. Manufacturing skills, cost, and quality determined success. Finally, in the late 1980s, when differences between suppliers' technology and production capabilities were minimal, service became the key to effective sales. Customers now want solutions to business problems, not technology.

Some high-tech markets, including advanced materials, biotechnology, and superconductors, are still in early stages of development—and Japan is investing heavily in these areas. But as they commercialize their products, your Japanese competitors will be vulnerable if you work closely with your customers. NEC and Fujitsu got the jump on many of their foreign competitors in fiber optics, a focus of strategic investment by Japan Inc. But when this technology matures, these companies will see their market shares slip if they do not provide a high level of support for their customers. While technology can differentiate at key times, no one can use the technology card indiscriminately, without regard to market evolution. Touting technology in personal computers, for instance, makes no sense when everyone has the same microprocessors, memory chips, hard drives, keyboards, and displays.

If you compete with Japan in process control, machine tools, and robotics, the time may have come to turn the tide back. Advances in technology cracked this market wide open for the Japanese—American suppliers were sitting ducks for anybody willing to invest in better products. But now that most of the survivors in the market have improved product quality, competition will shift to service. Manufacturers in America or Europe know that they must automate their production techniques, but they need help putting these new tools to work. We know of one company that bought its process control computers solely on the basis of the vendor's manufacturing know-how—the computers themselves were the same as everybody else's.

Selling service gives customers what they want, of course, but there are other benefits for suppliers. Demand for service long outlives the demand for new hardware, and often exceeds it in dollar volume. Service revenues can pay for new product development. But best of all, when you service a product you find out what customers really like and dislike about you—and your competitors. To sell products successfully, you must sell service first.

Putting Technology to Work

To "get closer" to consumers, those selling to them have to decentralize. When consumers demand better service from whoever sells to them, the pressure works its way from supplier to supplier. Every supplier in turn must decentralize to understand its own customers. Those who don't improve their service so that their customers can improve their service in turn simply get squeezed out. What holds this all together and enables companies to decentralize effectively is the modern computer network.

Corporate America invested heavily—literally hundreds of billions of dollars—in information technology in the last decade,[28] and now wants a return on that investment. Whether they are CEOs or office managers, the people who buy computers and communications systems don't want to hear about technology, they want solutions to business problems. If they can't use their information systems to offer better service, they may soon be out of business. The electronics companies that will prosper in the coming decade will be the ones who can put this technology to work.

Networking is what makes computers pay.[29] Networks can turn computers into problem solvers, by allowing companies to decentralize, to integrate closely with suppliers, to track customer buying patterns and improve customer service. But the level of service customers need when they buy a network is much different from what they need when they buy a photocopier. Nobody ever went out of business because the copier broke, but you can be sure American Airlines will take a big hit if its reservation network goes down. Japan's computer giants talk a big game about being "total system suppliers," but are conspicuously absent from networking. While they sell some bits and pieces here and there, they offer little in the way of software and virtually nothing in network services and support. Japan is leaving money on the table—big money. Customers are looking for solutions to operational problems, and are willing to pay for them. Japanese manufacturers want to sell hardware—now a commodity—at ever declining prices.

Networking, like other services, cannot be exported. You have to be on the ground and with your customers. Service cannot be engineered out of networking—networking is pure service. Suppliers that want to "pump iron" are cut out of the action.[30] To make matters worse, they do not benefit from the close customer contact service sales require. In the 1990s, information technology is a "contact" sport. You cannot substitute R&D spending for customer experience. Each customer is unique; the "perfect" customer solution cannot be developed in the lab. While technology is clearly the enabler for better networks, successful networking is not about technology, but about putting technology to work. Japanese companies looking for something better in their labs will not find it.

Most worrying perhaps for Japan Inc. are the sales missed because of poor or unavailable service, the result of relying almost exclusively on indirect sales channels. This does not mean Japan gets to keep the hardware sales while others attend to service. In 1983, we purchased a small Minolta photocopier for convenience copying in the office. We were delighted with the machine, but all copiers need service sooner or later. Minolta's distributor, we soon found out, was more interested in new sales than after-sales service. We simply could not get the distributor to take care of our copier properly, and we ended up threatening each other with lawsuits because we would not pay for service work that had been done poorly. Tired of being treated like criminals, we trashed the Minolta and got a Xerox machine with a full service contract. Minolta lost our business—hardware, software, or otherwise—forever.

Danger Sign No. 15

Service for your three best-selling products is provided by third parties.

Customer Power or Supplier Power?

The question is simple: who calls the shots? Customer or supplier? In many markets, technology has been reduced to a commodity; suppliers can compete only on service or price. This gives customers extraordinary power. Regardless of what new technologies emerge from the labs, customer power will not be reduced anytime during the next generation.

Deregulation in transportation, broadcasting, financial services, and telecommunications has further increased customer power. When Trabant's monopoly over the East German car market ended with German reunification, sales skidded to a halt. Trabant had power over its market, until customers had a choice. Telephone companies around the world have lost their monopolists' lock on markets and technology. Today anyone with a PC and a modem can create his own network.

On another level, the widespread distribution of computing resources has caused a secular shift in market power from producers to consumers. Like the printing press, the microprocessor has created social change unanticipated by its creator. The printing press permitted multiple versions of the Bible, shattering church control. The microprocessor permits every individual to have a unique edition of the Bible, and a custom-made network to deliver it to the faithful. In short, consumers are appropriating power in our society, and information technology is making it happen. The diffusion of computing power to individuals in Japan occurred later than in the United States and Europe, but with the boom in notebook computers that started in the early 1990s, Japan will catch up. Then it will be more difficult for Japan to be run for the benefit of its producers and not its consumers.

If Japan Inc. cannot adapt to the needs of its overseas customers, we have reached the end of an era. If people want cheap manufactured goods, they'll go to Korea, Taiwan, or Mexico. No one will buy me-too hardware with poor or mediocre service levels even if the price is right. Reluctant to face the need for radical change in rethinking, organization, and strategy, Japanese companies are frantically looking for technical points of differentiation that do not exist. Japan risks becoming the job lotter of high technology.

Danger Sign No. 16

You pay commissions for sales regardless of customer satisfaction.

Four Fatal System Errors

There can be only one reason for Japan's failures: Japanese companies are not giving customers what they want.

Four fatal "system errors" described in chapters 3 through 6 keep Japan from meeting customer needs. Like a system error that makes a computer freeze up, these flaws are big enough to crash Japan's strategy for the future. They have locked Japanese managers out of step with their customers. Japan's technology is not in question; rather, the application of its technology is simply wide of the mark.

All four flaws are "internal." They are not problems over which Japanese companies have no control, like the high costs of capital, poor roads, or badly educated workers in the United States. On the contrary, these are problems that could be corrected by the companies that suffer from them. But Japanese managers are making decisions every day that keep customers at a distance.

That's not to say the Japanese are oblivious to their shortcomings. Working with Japanese customers, we've encountered many managers who are all too aware of some or all of these system errors. Some were looking to us, as outsiders, to deliver the bad news. All seemed overwhelmed by the inertia that keeps their companies on their present course.

Japan's many strengths mask these weaknesses now undermining the drive for leadership in new areas, particularly high tech. Extraordinary manufacturing skills and unwavering commitment to R&D, combined with a dogged perseverance in markets they have chosen for growth, give Japan's competitors nightmares. But without the right customer relations to capitalize on these strengths, they count for little.

Our four rules of counterattack follow in chapters 7 through 10. Where your Japanese competitors are vertically and horizontally integrated, you must be focused; where they are bureaucratic and centrally managed, you must be agile and decentralized; where they avoid customer contact, you must relish it; and finally, where they sell technology, you must sell peace of mind.

—7—

Disintegrate Yourself

Counterstrategy No. 1: Do What You Do Best

*There are three steps to implementing successfully the first rule
of counterstrategy against your Japanese competitors: focus, focus, focus. You must disintegrate your business by eliminating
vertical and horizontal integration. You must zero in on what
your customers value most about you, then do it the best. While
your Japanese competitors are building hardware and building
empires, you must focus on one activity where all your energies
can be brought to bear. If you try to compete on many fronts,
they will crush you. If you attack at a single, vulnerable point in
their broad and deep formation, you will break through. Your
customers will greet you with open arms.*

When Ed Fitzgerald took over Northern Telecom in September
1984, his company was like a Japanese Zero ready to crash into
the deck of an American carrier somewhere near Okinawa. In
this case, the carrier was the American Telephone and Telegraph
Company, at the time the largest telephone company in the
world. How much damage the carrier would suffer was not clear;
about the kamikaze pilot's fate, there was little doubt.

Outwardly, Northern Telecom looked like an unquestioned success late in 1984, a Cinderella story come to life. When it had entered the U.S. market in 1971, this Canadian manufacturer of telecommunications gear had just $500 million in sales (almost all to its parent Bell Canada), about 1 percent of AT&T's revenues. Like AT&T, Northern made virtually everything a phone company could want, from telephone poles to exchanges. Northern's technology came secondhand from AT&T, which had set its poor Canadian cousin up in business a century earlier, and which maintained residual technology transfer arrangements with Bell Canada. Gradually, however, AT&T was cutting off Northern's access to its labs, and by the early 1970s it was apparent that Northern could not pay for its own R&D just by selling to Bell Canada.

The company looked south of the border for growth. Starting with the first new product it designed on its own, Northern began selling to small U.S. telephone companies outside the Bell System, then the exclusive domain of AT&T's own manufacturing arm. Sales grew modestly, but were not the breakthrough the company was going to need for survival. At that point, Northern decided to stake its future on a new computerized communications technology that AT&T thought was premature. The DMS, as it was called, was introduced in 1977 and was an immediate hit.

Soon Bell System companies began to look enviously at this new technology not yet available from AT&T. In 1982, New York Telephone decided to buy the DMS, against the wishes of its parent AT&T. When the U.S. government broke up the Bell System in 1984 and the telephone companies were free to buy from anyone they wanted, Northern's sales took off like a rocket. By 1985, Northern had grown to $4 billion in revenues, eight times what they were when the company first entered the United States. But beneath this outward appearance of success was a house of cards ready to collapse.

By 1985, AT&T was shipping its own advanced products in volume. Northern's one simple advantage—it had the only product on the market—was gone. Also, during the late 1970s,

Northern had spent hundreds of millions of dollars to buy two computer companies with products it wanted to combine with Northern's own to produce an all-electronic pipe dream: the "office of the future." Northern's heavy hand had transformed these two winners into losers; the investment in computers had turned sour and had drained off financial and managerial resources the company could ill afford to waste.

Rapid sales growth also bankrolled vertical integration. The company believed that only by producing its own leading-edge computer chips could it remain competitive in the markets it had staked out for itself. At the same time, engineers were hired by the suburban-office-park-full: Northern Telecom processor chips needed Northern Telecom programs to make them work. Northern was spread paper-thin over too many markets.

Then, in 1985, the telephone companies, with plenty of encouragement from Northern, started to install the DMS in heavily trafficked urban environments to serve their biggest and most demanding customers. Exchanges that had performed well in rural America began to crash. The Cinderella tape began to play backward. New orders began to dry up.

This is the mess Ed Fitzgerald found himself in not long after he became Northern's CEO. His solution: a forced march to simplicity and focus. Computer operations were wound down. A new DMS system was designed to use off-the-shelf Motorola processors running standard Unix software. Hewlett-Packard was brought in to revamp manufacturing. In short, Northern redirected its energy away from vertical and horizontal integration to what its customers were looking for: advanced features running on standard hardware and software.

The "disintegration" of Northern Telecom paid off. Sales have doubled since 1985. Today the company is the largest telephone exchange manufacturer in the world, well ahead of American, European, and Japanese suppliers many times its size. Indeed, quality is so good that Northern is now a major supplier in Japan.[1]

Focus, Focus, Focus

To maximize leverage with your customers, you must focus on what you do best. The *Queen Elizabeth 2* can't turn on a dime, and neither can you if your company is busy making everything from toasters to jet engines. Vertical and horizontal integration build in costs and risks, and build out flexibility. Companies without clear focus are driven by the internal political needs of their organization, not by the all-important needs of customers. Focused companies are often smaller than their less flexible competitors. Observing that the most profitable computer companies are ones in the $3–$4 billion range (compared with Fujitsu at $20 billion and IBM at $60 billion), Vittorio Cassoni, managing director of Olivetti's computer group, said to the *Financial Times,* "Size is no longer the issue. Focus is the issue."[2]

With conditions changing quickly, you can't work to two (or more) agendas. If your company and your customers have different requirements, you're competing with an arm and a leg tied behind your back. You have a simple choice. You can focus, and share your customer's goals. Or you can work to your internal agenda, and watch your business vanish.

Companies succeed today by serving their customers well, not by securing their own sources of raw materials and components, not by making rolled steel, minicomputers, and fax machines. Mitsukoshi is trying to make its department store in New York different by buying from its own factories in China, and must perforce respond more slowly than competitors without such constraints.[3]

At our company, we realized that we were overextended. We were tracking high-tech markets from aerospace to computer chips. Since our customers valued our telecom research above all, we dropped our other products, which were second-rate anyway. When we realized that accounting was commanding too much management time, we subcontracted the whole process to ADP, the payroll people. Although our business was publishing, we kept only a convenience copier in the office: all printing was done out-of-house. Our customers didn't care who printed our reports.

Be lean and mean: make only what you make best, and buy the rest! But remember, you can't apply this rule and not our others. AT&T has reduced its vertical integration dramatically, but the firm remains obsessed with being a "full-line supplier." The benefits of disintegration have not been fully achieved, and for a while write-downs followed each other in a seemingly endless stream.

American manufacturers have much to learn from their Japanese competitors. Vertical and horizontal integration is not one of these lessons. In Japan, the *keiretsu* system seems to work as a substitute for disintegration. Outside Japan, *keiretsu* bonds reduce flexibility to near zero. Most of your big Japanese competitors cannot release these bonds without abandoning their home market, a step none will take. Giants Fujitsu, Hitachi, and NEC generate more than half their sales in Japan; *keiretsu* sales and purchases keep their business safe. You have the freedom to maneuver; they do not.

Flexible Outsourcing

Flexibility is speed; speed is customer service. When the customer says jump, you have to respond—fast. Upstream activities, like component design, have to respond too. If you're locked into too many of these activities, you won't be able to change as fast as your customers. And you will lose their business.

All operations not directly related to customer requirements are nothing but excess baggage. You must focus on what your customers really want from you and subcontract—or outsource—everything else. You will get better quality, better prices, and a better night's sleep. Outsourcing shifts risk to your suppliers, allowing you to focus scarce resources on customer service.

For your Japanese competitor, tied to the complex system of obligations and relations inherent in the *keiretsu* system, there are few such options. Regardless of their market share, Japanese managers remain firmly committed to vertical integration, which they believe gives them lower costs, higher quality, and greater control. We have been lectured by Japanese managers who repeat these supposed benefits like a tired mantra. One communications systems manufacturer with sales in a decade-long slide told us most emphatically that it could not use outside components because it was too risky, even though its two biggest competitors use nothing but parts from the open market.

Selling computers is a tough enough business. Do you really want to compete in semiconductors and machine tools at the same time? That's what you're doing if you make your own components. If you're trying to do two or three things at once, chances are you're doing a poor job of both. You certainly move more slowly than someone who is focused. And your components are probably higher-cost and lower-quality than those you could buy from others. As for protecting your proprietary technology, if nobody buys it, it's not worth protecting. Unisys wisely decided in 1992 to turn all chip production over to Motorola.[4] We think this greatly increases Unisys's chances for survival.

Perhaps most important, your customers don't care who makes the parts in your products. Or who cleans your offices and who does your payroll, for that matter. They want their problems solved. If you can solve them, you get their business. If not, *sayonara.* Your people must have the flexibility to find the best sources of supply for all their purchases. Why should they saddle their customers with second-rate products just because you have factories to run?

IBM and AT&T are outsourcing to a degree that would have been unthinkable a decade ago. Repeating the success of its original PC, IBM introduced a well-received laptop computer in 1990 in record time, cutting the development cycle from its usual two or three years to fourteen months. The key was letting designers specify virtually all parts off-the-shelf from other suppliers. Only a few chips are made by IBM. The theory: worry about what customers want, and not what IBM's own technology can do.[5] At one time AT&T made its communications systems out of sand and iron ore (well, almost). Today it outsources all but the most critical parts.

Many companies are wisely subcontracting entire staff functions, entire departments that serve internal, not customer needs. Kodak transferred its data processing operations to IBM in 1989 and communications to DEC in 1990. Said Kodak's head of information systems Katherine Hudson, "We are not in the business of supporting computers. We decided that outside vendors could supply systems and support services better and more cost-effectively than we could."[6] Diesel Technology Corp. turned over its entire information system to EDS. Looking to grow its business rapidly, Diesel thought about expanding its own computer resources, but then, CEO Derek Kaufman said to *Computerworld,* "We asked, what do we do best around here? . . . The answer that kept coming back to us was 'We're very good at making fuel system componentry. We ought to maximize the focus of every single person here on that.' "[7] With fewer internal headaches, these companies can turn their energies to where they will best serve their customers.

You can go too far, however. Conner Peripherals, the hot supplier of PC disk drives, even subcontracts manufacturing, doing only design work in-house. But component shortages have hurt some new-product introductions.[8] You can't outsource your core business. If you sell minicomputers, you should make them. But you don't have to make the chips, the metal cabinets, and the machines that press the cabinets. Honda likes to keep in-house production of components that the customer sees, like bumpers, fenders, and dashboards. The quality of these parts clearly affects Honda's relationship to its customers.[9] Conner may have gone too far, but this upstart is nevertheless closing in on industry leader Seagate, which makes many of the components that go into its products.[10]

Action Item No. 1

Reduce internal sourcing by 25 percent per year until less than 5 percent of purchasing is made internally.

The idea is simple: if an activity doesn't add value directly for your customers, don't do it. List all operations by degree of customer interaction required; outsource everything your customers don't see.

Trusting Your Suppliers

Outsourcing does not mean endless shopping for the lowest price. It means building long-term relationships with companies that are the best at what they do. Your initial costs may be higher, but life-cycle costs will be far lower. While GM outsources far fewer parts than Toyota, it has more suppliers. These suppliers are forced to compete aggressively to keep their business. By contrast, Toyota incorporates its suppliers into the design process and guarantees a supplier business over the life of a new model.[11]

Quality control is often cited as the greatest advantage of vertical integration. But the price is usually higher inventories and overhead (read: higher costs). If quality is a problem, the first step is to get rid of the quality control department. In one of its plants, Northern Telecom gave responsibility for quality to all workers; as a result, quality improved by 50 percent while the number of "quality inspectors" fell by 40 percent.[12] Problems have to be identified when they occur, not after production is complete. The second and most important step to better quality is to shift the responsibility to your suppliers. But you must do more than subcontract, you must trust your suppliers. That means you cannot check everything they do. Besides, if your suppliers know that you are not testing their products when they arrive, it will put the fear of God in them. The best Japanese companies know these lessons—and they learned them from the best American companies.

Companies with a high level of vertical integration don't trust outside suppliers. We have been told by vertically integrated European and Japanese suppliers, "We test everything to maintain our high quality standards." Quality levels can be kept up, but at enormous cost. At every point testing occurs, inventory (parts, work in progress, or finished product) accumulates. Inventory carrying costs can spell the difference between cost leader and cost loser. If you do it right the first time, you don't need to test for quality, and you save time and money. Your customers get better products sooner, and you grow faster.

The top Japanese car companies have applied these "lean manufacturing" principles. Many other Japanese companies have not. You can be sure that when your Japanese competitors buy American chips because the government is twisting arms, they are reluctant to work closely on designs with these suppliers, and they test everything they buy from them. Japanese buyers maintain that American chips have greater failure rates than Japanese ones. Maybe they do—but such lack of trust and the testing that goes with it eat up time. You can use this time to advantage in fast-changing, high-tech markets.

Efficiency and simplicity seem to go together. We have toured plants in America, Japan, and Europe and have found the best ones appear the most simple: clear layout and no clutter. In fact, we have found a high correlation between plant cleanliness and market share. If the plant is a mess, the company is a mess, and performance reflects it. Some of the messiest plants we've been in are Japanese. Japan wrote the book on manufacturing and quality. But you should imitate the winners, not the losers. How do you get quality better than the Japanese? By being smarter. Rely on your suppliers, and rely on your own operations. In short, you can drive quality up and costs down by letting other people—inside and outside the company—do what they do best.

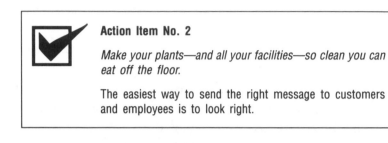

Action Item No. 2

Make your plants—and all your facilities—so clean you can eat off the floor.

The easiest way to send the right message to customers and employees is to look right.

The "Vision" Thing

Forget your vision of the future. Your customers are not interested.

A visionary agenda makes sense on paper, but leads to horizontal integration. The thinking goes like this: "If we put together this great plan to make all the computers in the world work together, then supply all the pieces, we've got it made!" The temptation to fill in all the missing pieces in your product line is irresistible. But as they say at the track, "The horses don't read the *Racing Form.*" What you consider a great plan and what customers consider a great plan are, in all likelihood, two very different things. Particularly when you and the guys at headquarters cooked up the plan without talking to any customers.

Xerox spent fifteen years trying to turn its copiers into an "office automation" business. Xerox's vision of where it wanted to go had nothing to do with real customer needs, and was a complete fiasco. More dangerous for the company, while it tried to live out its own fantasies, it nearly lost the entire copier market to the Japanese. In the late 1980s, Xerox abandoned this dream and set to fixing its copier business. Now the company has set more modest goals for the "document" business that are probably in line with customer expectations.

The reality is that customers want to mix and match their

purchases from different suppliers, picking the best from each. Few Americans settle on one company for all their purchases. Customers intuitively know that different companies have different strengths; chances are slim to nil that one supplier can meet all their needs. When American Express wanted to replace its human resource and payroll systems in 1991, the company did not look to a single source because, human resource executive Richard O'Gara told *Computerworld,* the best packages "come from different vendors."[13] In Europe, there is probably more brand loyalty than in America, but greater competition during the past decade has greatly reduced its value to suppliers. In Japan, by contrast, relations with a single company are highly prized. Transferring such loyalty overseas is a nonstarter, but the Japanese haven't figured out why.

Sister companies in diversified organizations rarely dance to one tune. They have their own ideas, and they must vie for the attention of headquarters to secure the resources they need for growth. Ever-expanding bureaucracies are needed to manage these battles, and the inevitable result of political infighting is deteriorating sales. AT&T needs computers to make its communications network operate. So it figures it is an expert in computers and ought to sell them. Unfortunately, customers don't see it that way. They like AT&T telephones but find little use for its computers. When AT&T tried to combine sales forces for these two product lines it experienced complete failure. In big companies, communications and computers aren't even bought by the same people. The vision thing simply has nothing to do with the people who buy your products.

Action Item No. 3

Eliminate all staff planning functions.

Your customers can tell you where you should be in the year 2000. Strategies dreamed up by MBAs at headquarters will almost certainly lead you down the garden path.

Focus on Customer Value

"What do we do best?" is not always an easy question to answer. And your customers will invariably have a different answer from your own. So why do your customers buy from you? Sounds silly, but most companies don't have the faintest idea. Companies without any customer contact are particularly clueless. Knowing what customers value about your firm is the flip side of knowing what your customers want. To sell your products, you must know what customers need. But if you don't know what customers value about you, you will find yourself constantly missing the mark in advertising, new product development, and strategic direction.

Philips, the Dutch electronics combine, cannot decide exactly what it does, so the company flounders, while withdrawing from huge markets like semiconductors, computers, and telecommunications. If the company were to focus on consumer electronics, it could probably give its Japanese rivals a run for their money. At the other extreme, Zenith has shed all its mediocre attempts at diversification and is back to basics: TVs. The time is right for Zenith to take back the TV market from Sony and Matsushita, two companies that now have diversified well beyond plain old television sets. If Zenith simply gives its customers what they want while these two competitors slug it out in high-definition TV and Hollywood, its success is assured.

Many observers think Boeing faces a threat from the Japanese. But virtually all of the resources of this aerospace powerhouse are focused on one industry. Its designs focus on the mundane needs of its customers, like fuel economy, seat arrangements, and load factors. This is where Boeing shines, and the company is smart to subcontract production to its potential Japanese rivals to keep them off the scent. Airlines are not interested in technology, or white elephants like the second-generation Concorde that MITI wants to develop. But load factors? Now we're talking cash flow!

We were once asked by a computer company client why it was consistently losing business from a valued customer to lower-priced competitors. The competition was much less service-oriented—our client had a large number of salesmen posted right on its customer's premises—but always bagged the biggest deals.

The customer, it turned out, was only tangentially interested in our client's computers. Computers are a commodity: you can always find somebody who will bid a lower price for hardware. What really attracted the customer was the computer company's manufacturing expertise, which had helped establish the customer as the low-cost producer in its own market. This expertise was given away, while hardware orders dwindled, because our client did not know what its customer valued most. What our client valued most about itself was its computer hardware.

If you don't know what your customers value about you, you won't know where to focus your energy. Your customers can tell you which of your organization's unnecessary activities can be pruned. You will discover that what you do best is also where you make the highest return. The bean counters may be skeptical at first, but they will like the results.

Action Item No. 4

Knock the bottom 5 percent of your products off the catalog. Once a quarter.

The simplest way to figure out what your customers value is to look at what they buy. Nothing slows down effective management like products that don't pull their own weight.

Decentralize Yourself

Counterstrategy No. 2:
Abandon Headquarters!

Start with this simple rule: the only people who should make executive decisions are the ones who talk to your customers every day. This will force you to decentralize and shift power closer to your customers. Your Japanese competitors are trying to mastermind their every move from office buildings in suburban Tokyo; they don't talk to their overseas customers and they don't listen to their own foreign employees who do. But don't kid yourself: if you think you can achieve daily customer contact from your office in Atlanta any better than the Japanese can from Osaka, you are wrong. Move out into the field, flatten your organization, and empower your front-line employees. Your Japanese competitors won't know what hit them.

When in four short years Hampton Inn became the top economy hotel chain in the United States, CEO Ray Schultz was worried. While he felt his company had earned its place in the industry, he knew that Hampton could not keep expanding in the face of growing competition and rapid personnel turnover and still make sure that, as he wrote in the *Wall Street Journal*, "every air conditioner was working, every carpet was clean, and every bed was freshly made in each of our 23,000 rooms."[1]

The next step that Schultz took was not unusual. In October 1989, Hampton introduced a 100 percent satisfaction guarantee: any guests who had problems that were not resolved to their satisfaction by the time they left would get one night's stay free. But everybody—even the post office—offers some kind of "satisfaction guarantee." If this had been all Schultz planned to do to keep his customers happy, he would have been in trouble. Like the mint on your pillow, such an offer would probably be greeted with a yawn, even if it was a first in the hotel industry.

Schultz made more than an empty offer. Every hotel employee—bellhop, chambermaid, front desk clerk, or manager—was authorized "to take whatever action is necessary to keep the customer satisfied." More to the point, they could do so without asking for permission. Problems were not kicked upstairs or put on hold: frontline employees, on the ground, had to respond to customer complaints as they occurred. They were told that "their job is not just to make the beds or to mow the lawns, it's to keep our guests happy." And they were convinced that management would not second-guess decisions made under fire—in fact, that they would be rewarded for their actions.[2]

By treating his employees with respect, Schultz reduced turnover, the bane of hotels and other service operations. More important, he put a quality control manager into every room, in every one of his over two hundred hotels. As a result, Hampton is able to maintain an extraordinary level of service, perhaps unparalleled in the economy hotel field. We talked with one customer who had stayed there more than one hundred times, virtually without a hitch. He added, "Once in a while I'll stay at the Hyatt if I get a 50 percent off coupon, but frankly it's still not worth it. Hampton is better. I even stay there when I go on vacation." That's quite a testimonial.

Conventional wisdom would have led Hampton to increasingly detailed manuals, procedures, and reporting requirements to keep track of all the thousands of details necessary to make a hotel work. The alternative was much simpler and effective: Schultz decentralized power into the hands of his frontline employees. As he puts it, ". . . the front desk clerk, the housekeepers, and the maintenance crew—not our senior executives—face our hotel guests every day."[3]

Talk to Your Customers—Every Day!

To maximize leverage with your customers, you must restructure to determine and exploit customer needs. Most companies are organized for historical and internal reasons; their organization charts look like one of the great pyramids, with the pharaoh (a.k.a. the CEO) himself at the top, of course. The customer is like some poor Egyptian slave at the bottom, crushed under the weight of this entire edifice. Cries for help must wend their way to the top, through endless memos and meetings, defying the push and pull of internal politics. The only problem with this pyramid analogy is that the Egyptian slave had to take his lumps. Your customer can walk.

There is no mystery to getting in front of your Japanese competitors. Focusing on what you do best means focusing on your customer. If you want to keep your customers, get in their face, as they say in New York. The only way to consistently develop, make, and deliver products that people want is to see them every day, and to make sure that the employees who do see customers every day are the only ones making decisions. Authority must be pushed out from the center—better yet, get rid of the center. Headquarters staff groups should be disbanded, to prevent bureaucracy from frustrating those in the front lines. If your company operates like a poor caricature of the U.S. Army, it's time for change. If you can turn the pyramid on its head, so your entire organization supports sales and service—and hence sup-

ports your customers—you can effectively neutralize the highly
centralized management style of the Japanese.

Even in a small company like ours, we had consolidated
decision-making to the detriment of customer relations. One
summer we both took a month-long vacation at the same time,
and were concerned about how the business would run without
us. Despite serious misgivings, however, we didn't call in while
we were gone. What the hell, we thought, it's only money. When
we got back we were surprised to find that the place was running
like a top. Without us to bother them, our employees were making good decisions fast. Our customers never missed us. In fact,
we had had a record month.

Remember, decentralizing isn't enough. Overcoming great
inertia, Sony is trying to localize management of its overseas operations. At the same time, however, the company is diversifying
at a rapid pace. As long as it applies our rules selectively, Sony
will remain removed from its customers. In a similar fashion,
German electrical giant Siemens eliminated many layers of management at its headquarters in Munich, but clings to vertical and
horizontal integration. In many of the high-tech markets Siemens
has selected for growth, performance remains lackluster.

In Japan, every worker has a say in how his business is run,
and virtually all managers are in routine contact with customers.
The results show: Japan is a tough market to crack. Away from
home, Japan Inc. is not employing these enlightened practices—
not yet, anyway. The pressure to change is becoming irresistible.
You'd better get to the customer first.

Get the Boss Into the Field

Give them the word: *Hit the road, Jack.* Everybody must
get out of the inner sanctum and into direct contact with customers. Senior management has to set the example by moving to the
front—taking headquarters with it. Well-publicized tours of the

sales offices by the CEO are not enough: the CEO must move to one of your sales offices, and live with your customers. The rest of the brass must do the same. If executives working daily with your customers call the shots, you will make the right decisions and make them fast.

During the 1980s, hardening of the decision-making arteries set in with a vengeance at IBM. Having almost single-handedly colonized the entire northern half of Westchester County in suburban New York, IBMers faced themselves at every turn. In this environment, IBM—once the consummate sales-driven company—became the paradigm of bureau-sclerosis. In endless meetings in which anybody could kill an idea, managers filtered information up to the management committee, a tribunal of five top executives, which ultimately made all decisions. Customers were not getting heard in this process, as IBM's sales slump showed quite dramatically.

Eventually CEO John Akers and his number two man Jack Kuehler got the message. They decided to bust up the IBM bureaucracy and get their executives out into the field. Between 1988 and 1991, Akers and Kuehler cut seven thousand out of eight thousand staff positions at headquarters, decentralizing to the divisions those functions that were scrapped in Westchester.[4] We saw these changes firsthand, visiting several IBM sites in Westchester in 1989 that were eerie, empty monuments to the glory days. One of the executives who managed these cuts was Ed Lucente, nicknamed "Neutron Eddy" because, like a neutron bomb, it was said that he got rid of the people but left the buildings standing. While IBM, to its detriment, did not go so far as to decentralize right out to the sales offices, many of its redundant managers were offered sales jobs in a valiant effort to maintain the company's no-layoff policy.

Unfortunately, these cuts were not enough: IBM tightened the girdle, but only rearranged the fat. Stronger medicine was required. Early in 1991, IBM moved the headquarters of its communications group from Somers, New York, to London; Europe is IBM's biggest communications market. Ellen Hancock, the head of this line of business, made the move along with her entire staff of 120.[5] Then at the end of 1991, IBM announced that it would break itself up into five companies, presumably to get decisions and decision-makers closer to customers.[6] We expect some of the new companies to be headquartered away from New York, and at least one more to be moved overseas, most likely to Tokyo.

Too little too late for IBM? Will IBM follow the New York Central Railroad, U.S. Steel, and General Motors down the ignominious path from superstar to has-been? Unlike these predecessors, IBM is making radical changes while there is still time. However timidly, IBM's leaders are facing up to customers, who clearly believe they are getting the short end of the IBM stick. And to a greater extent than most companies, IBM does listen to its salesmen—they tell the market planners, who tell the marketing VPs, who tell the engineering VPs, who tell the engineers, who tell the programmers. In most Japanese companies, it's the other way around (i.e., the engineers make the decisions and the word filters down to the salesmen—sometimes). But good intentions are not enough; it's not clear that IBM has again found its way; the company has not figured out what it does best. Like the Roman Empire, IBM will take a long time to decline, but not centuries. The Vandals—in this case Fujitsu, Hitachi, and NEC— will not wait.

To help turn around Ford in the early 1980s, then-CEO Donald Peterson went out to focus groups and listened directly to customers himself.[7] Focus groups are a controlled environment, compared with a Ford repair shop waiting room, for example. Nevertheless, a CEO getting within punching distance of a customer is probably without precedence in modern Detroit history. Given Peterson's success with Ford at that time, the value of customer exposure cannot be underestimated.

If getting the boss out of the office is a good idea, moving the office is even better. In 1990, Hewlett-Packard transferred the headquarters of its personal computer division to Grenoble, France; more than half of H-P's PC sales are generated internationally, primarily in Europe.[8] Du Pont manages its entire Lycra fabric business from its European headquarters in Geneva.[9] Faced with market exit, the Siemens telephone exchange group boldly transferred to the United States decision-making authority in such vital areas as product engineering, development, procurement (i.e., the make or buy choice for components), and manufacturing. For the Germans, releasing control of their core technology to Americans was difficult, but the results show that it was the right move: after many frustrating years, in 1991 Siemens received an order from Ameritech (one of the biggest U.S. phone companies) large enough to keep it in the game. Perhaps the best example of a decentralized company is Swiss-based Asea Brown Boveri, a $28 billion engineering and heavy equipment manufacturer, which has a mere 140 headquarters staff managing 4,500 independent business units. That's what we call traveling light.[10]

By keeping top management so far away from customers— that is, in Tokyo—Japanese companies are offering you a critical advantage, if you will just take it. You can move your entire management team into the field and expect little, if any, response, anytime soon. The Japanese government came down on Nintendo like a ton of bricks when the company suggested that it might move its headquarters to Seattle to be closer to the vast majority of its customers.[11] Besides, tight-knit relations within Japan are central to Japan's decision-making process, which cannot be changed without unraveling the country's social fabric—a difficult, if not impossible, process. In short, outside Japan, Japanese suppliers are easy pickings for any firm prepared to pay more than lip service to customers.

Incredibly, most managers will tell you that they would like to see customers more but are too busy. As one executive at a large New York publishing company put it to us: "The word came down from senior management that we had to spend more time with customers, and we did for a little while, but then, you know, other things came up."[12] Fundamentally, executives don't like dealing with customers; it's certainly easier to command respect (which you richly deserve, no doubt) from your subordinates than from your customers—especially unhappy ones. If you are one of the big boys, you probably expect someone else to do this dirty work for you, and type up the results in a well-sanitized report (imagine the language Don Peterson would have heard from his disgruntled Pinto customers in 1981). But you cannot escape *direct* responsibility for serving customers if you want to outperform your Japanese competitors. You can be certain that, cultural problems or not, Japan Inc. will eventually get to your customers if you don't.

Three Japanese car companies with problems responded, in part, by moving some design responsibility out of Japan, with significant results in all cases. Nissan was a sales laggard in the United States throughout the 1980s, but by the end of 1992, half its cars sold in the United States were fashioned by American designers. To reach this point, twelve long years had passed since Nissan's first design studio opened in California. While second-guessing and resistance from Japan continued, proximity to customers produced exciting new cars, which stemmed Nissan's American market share slide.[13] Mazda, a marginal performer throughout the 1980s, conceived its hot-selling Miata MX-5 sportscar at its design center in California.[14] And Honda, running out of steam in the early 1990s, decided to shift some product development overseas, although the "real work," like engine development, remains in Japan.[15] Testing the waters, these car companies will eventually move more decisions overseas. Other Japanese companies will follow their example.

Changes in attitude have to start at the top, with the CEO. If he is out in the field, everyone else will get the message. If it's "Do as I say, not as I do," everyone will know it's business as usual. For you, as an employee, it's like a canary in the mine shaft: if the CEO doesn't talk to customers, it's time to get out.

If you're too busy to see customers, spending your time fighting internal battles, your firm has problems.

To one of our customers, a Japanese CEO who was concerned about customer service, we recommended that he carry a cellular phone twenty-four hours a day, and that his customers be given a toll-free number they could call with any problems they had. This executive laughed and said he'd never be able to sleep. We responded that he had nothing to worry about: there were tens of thousands of people working for him who would make very sure that phone did not ring.

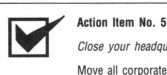

Action Item No. 5

Close your headquarters.

Move all corporate activities to your regional sales offices.

Going Native

While Japanese competitors remain Japanese first, many American and European companies long ago realized the benefits of going native. Ford and General Motors turned in their best performances worldwide in the 1980s in Europe, where both companies have long acted like local suppliers. GM Europe is overseen by a mere two hundred staffers in Zurich; the real power resides in the local companies.[16] Through long and patient investment in Japan, Texas Instruments, headed by a Japanese since the early seventies, has come pretty close to achieving "local" status in semiconductors, striking at the very heart of the Japanese industrial giant.[17] Apple enjoyed a sudden boost in sales in Japan in the early 1990s after it localized management (and introduced a Japanese-language version of its software, certainly a long-overdue step).[18] Successful as these companies are internationally, they all employ foreigners at their corporate headquarters in the United States.

Perhaps no company has done a better job of "going native" in Japan than IBM. IBM knows it cannot solve its customers' problems from halfway around the globe, so IBM Japan is run by Japanese in Tokyo. IBM remains a leader in Japan despite four decades of government effort to build a domestic industry at its expense.

Of course, the head of IBM Japan is Japanese. And of course, IBM develops and makes locally what it sells in Japan. But IBM Japan is also a unique combination of IBM and Japanese cultures. For example, IBM Japan employs a compensation system based more on merit than a typical Japanese firm. Base pay and benefits are geared to Japanese, not American, standards.[19] IBM is influential in government circles and attracts the best university graduates to its ranks.

While IBM Japan was established in the 1930s as a sales and maintenance operation, Big Blue has had local production and R&D for over two decades. Investment is not based just on what IBM thinks it will take to keep the market open. Rather IBM takes advantage of local skills—Japan is the source of laptop computer, liquid crystal display, optics and semiconductor technologies for IBM worldwide—to service its customers best. Basic research is done in image recognition, multiprocessor and other systems applications.[20] IBM employs Japanese outside of Japan as well. Four of the directors of the IBM World Trade Asia Pacific board, to which IBM Japan reports, are Japanese nationals. And one of IBM's corporate officers is Japanese.[21] By the end of the century, we expect IBM's CEO to be foreign, perhaps Japanese.

For thirty years, IBM dominated computers not because IBM did everything right, but because everyone else did so many things wrong. Unfortunately for IBM, hubris is the first sin, and IBM became just as unresponsive to its customers as everyone else in the 1980s, and is paying the price in the 1990s. In Japan,

IBM's mainframe competitors sent armies of programmers out to work with customers developing the software applications they needed, an activity IBM ignored. Suddenly, IBM found that Fujitsu and NEC knew more about IBM's customers than IBM itself, and Big Blue's market share in Japan has taken a beating as a result.[22]

For all its shortcomings, IBM dominates the Japanese computer industry in a way that no Japanese company does anywhere outside Japan. To renew itself now, IBM is decentralizing with a vengeance. How long will it take for IBM's Japanese competitors to respond to *perestroika* at Big Blue?

Flatten Those Organizations!

When you move the boss into the field, you must slash the size of your staff groups, or eliminate them entirely. Layers of management will disappear, and ideally, no single employee will be more than a phone call away from customers. Every function will have formal ties to them. The sales organization must be in control, but customers will be exposed to every link in your company from product conception to after-sales service. While your Japanese competitors remain overstaffed and rigid, you can build a flat, customer-driven organization that is responsive and less costly to run.

Don't expect everything to go smoothly. Flat organizations work, but when the shift takes place, management must be prepared for a different style of decision-making. Once forced to face outward, everyone becomes an expert on what customers want. Disagreements can be heated, but at least everyone is focused on customers and aimed in the same direction. You'll know you have made real change when the fights start about what customers really want, when one-upmanship is based on the number of customer calls you have made, when your people are bragging about the lengths they went to to meet a customer's requirements.

Flat organizations can be messy. In one company we know with a mere four layers between shop floor and CEO, each manager has twelve or more direct reports. Dotted-line, informal relationships abound. Memos are banned and meetings are limited to brief, infrequent, and impromptu sessions. Gone are the freshly minted "org" charts that show precisely everyone's spot in the hierarchy. Unnecessary are those well-choreographed announcements of dramatic reorganizations so beloved by Wall Street.

The key to managing the flat organization is information technology. Close communications (via PC, electronic mail, and voice mail) can allow loose and evolving teams to function effectively—in short, to make anarchy work. Computer networking can bind your company to its suppliers and customers at once. On the "buy" side, maximum outsourcing depends on close communications with vendors. On the "sell" side, technology can give frontline personnel the tools needed to respond quickly to customers. Citibank customers can get mortgage loan approval in fifteen minutes, instead of the month or more required at many banks. PCs in particular offer an affordable means to provide the information needed to facilitate decision-making at the local level.

Your Japanese competitors have been especially slow to exploit computer power. In Japan, computers are used extensively in product design and manufacturing, but not in management decision-making. Japanese offices are remarkably devoid of computers, even telephones. It is said that the telegraph killed the British Empire; before the widespread introduction of this technology, decisions had to be made in the field, and so were made quickly and in full awareness of local conditions; after its introduction, all decisions could be kicked upstairs to London. With cheap PCs, you can transfer power back to the front, reversing the negative effects of one hundred years of telecommunications.

If Japan Inc. keeps control centered in Tokyo, this will spell the end of the Japanese empire.

With technology facilitating communications within your company, you are liberated from the need to have all your decision-makers in one building. Managers can be relocated to your sales offices, to see customers face to face, and stay in touch with coworkers electronically. This is the shift that is required to unleash the power of the enormous investment made in information technology by American business in the 1980s. The flat, customer-integrated organization is within reach. But remember: no amount of electronic networking will obviate the need to flatten your organization.

A popular method for bypassing internal bureaucracies is the "skunk works," a group set up on its own to develop a new product outside normal corporate channels by bringing together a small number of design, production, and sales people under one roof. IBM launched its original personal computer this way, and tried to repeat this success in PC software in 1991 by setting up an independent team in Boca Raton, Florida.[23] With quick results, Motorola let loose in 1989 a twenty-two-man team to start up a new business to produce electronic components for fluorescent lights.[24] And in 1991, a small team of engineers introduced Chrysler's well-received Viper sports car in record time with a tiny budget.[25] If it's such a great idea, why not institutionalize the "skunk works"? All products should be developed by small, closely knit groups unrestrained by corporate bureaucracy. Don't bypass the problem, eliminate it.

For some, the flat, decentralized organization is a way of life. The British conglomerate Hanson has defied gravity by restricting corporate interference of its operating companies to financial matters. As long as they meet the numbers, subsidiaries—which span a wide range of consumer and industrial markets—run themselves.[26] While Hanson does demonstrate the power of decentralization, the strain of serving too many markets will undoubtedly catch up with this latterday ITT. IDG, a large publisher serving the computer industry, has prospered through decentralization: each publication is independent; each publisher has responsibility for only one publication. T. J. Rogers is trying to keep growth organic at Cypress Semiconductor by spinning off each new product into a separate new company that must sink or swim on its own.[27] Decentralization is not the same as spinning out of control: when Whirlpool took over Philips's European appliance business in 1989, it found out that there were no parts in common between washing machines manufactured in Germany and in Italy.[28] This is where technology comes in: all those washing machines should have been designed on the same computer network.

In the pursuit of clean organization charts, many companies split into sales and product organizations, a formula for disaster. Some Japanese companies go even further, with separate manufacturing, development, and sales companies. This structure denies product designers the benefits of everyday contact with customers. Perhaps worse, power-hungry headquarters staffers are required to broker disputes between the groups. Chances are that headquarters will frustrate the plans of everybody else, to make sure its power is not bypassed.

Flat organizations are essential to managing customer-responsive companies, especially in the high-tech areas Japan has targeted for growth.[29] Decision-makers have to be close to customers and to their technology at the same time. In other words, sales and product development must be bound together. You have to know what customers want, but also what you can really deliver.

Action Item No. 6

Promote everyone on the same track: you make customers happy, you move up. Otherwise, move on.

Make sure all employees, particularly foreign ones, play by the same rules and have the same opportunities. Send the brass on the road for at least one week per month to see customers.

Customer Co-location

When you decentralize, go one step further. Locate across the street from your customers for maximal contact. For big-ticket items, you can literally let your customers determine where you locate your offices, plants, and labs. If you want to sell supercomputers, determine where your top five prospects are and put your operations as close to them as possible. If you run a bank, move into the same building as your biggest account. Northern Telecom, the U.S. market leader in telephone switching systems, has its regional offices located within view of its big telephone company customers. This way customers can count on you to help run their business—you become as essential to them as their paychecks. And you can see who pays the bills by gazing out the window.

For mass-market products, you may have to pick out your biggest distributor, not the final consumer. If you make hammers, and your biggest customer is Sears, locate your head office in Chicago, or near the Sears store that sells the most hammers. In some cases, a more creative approach to customer co-location may be in order. Finding motorcycle riders to co-locate with might seem like a bizarre idea, but Harley-Davidson formed clubs throughout the United States for its customers, aptly called the Harley Owner Group, or HOG. By mixing with them where they want to be, Harley can stay in touch with these inherently mobile consumers. During the 1980s, Harley recaptured the U.S. market for big bikes; government protection got it back on top, but responsiveness has kept Harley there. GE sells its appliances through dealers, but heavily advertises its "GE Answer Center," a twenty-four-hour toll-free number you can call to get help with minor repairs or to arrange service for an appliance. This gives GE a direct line on customer concerns and prevents small complaints from escalating into anti-GE hysteria.

Just as effectively, Dell Computers established what might be called "virtual co-location" with its personal computer customers, taking mail-order sales to new heights. Employing well-trained sales operators, five-day shipment of custom-ordered systems, toll-free technical support, and fast on-site repairs, Dell can give its customers the kind of service they would expect from someone located across the street, except that the service they get from Dell is probably far better than any nearby PC dealer could offer.[30]

Dell's Japanese competitors are playing catch-up ball, but catching up they may be. NEC, the leading Japanese contender in PCs, shifted to the United States responsibility for design and production of its products that are sold to national accounts by NEC's own sales force.[31] And Toshiba, the leader in laptops, beefed up toll-free telephone service for its personal computer customers in response to a decline in market share. With a little persistence, you can get past the recorded message labyrinth and the busy signals to a live technician who will try to solve your problem over the telephone, but refer you to a local dealer for anything complicated, or any repair out of warranty. Nevertheless, the direct link to customers is there, and Toshiba will benefit if management listens. Watch out, Dell!

For small companies, a half-dozen locations are not feasible. But you can "live" with your customers nonetheless. DOD Electronics makes signal processors for electronic musical instruments. Its 285 employees are in twenty music bands, including the company band, in which the CEO performs. DOD is giving

Japanese competitors like Yamaha a run for their money, even in Japan.[32]

Spreading production of commodity products around is not co-location, as many Japanese manufacturers have discovered. Japan Inc. has built many factories in the United States and Europe, but they do not serve as communications channels to reach customers.[33] In 1990, the *Financial Times* reported that Hitachi had established two R&D labs in Europe and one in the United States; these three "research centers" between them had twenty-seven technical employees, while Hitachi's nine labs in Japan had some four thousand scientists on staff.[34] To localize operations, you must hire natives to run your business, doing real research and real production in your overseas markets. Most important, customers must know they can talk to real decision-makers, in their own language and in their own time zone.

Action Item No. 7

Locate all activities near your customers.

Corporate headquarters, factories, laboratories, and sales offices should be across the street from key customers.

Get Your Lights Punched Out Every Day

Our rule of thumb is simple: if you are not close enough to your customers to get your lights punched out every day, you are not close enough to understand what keeps them awake at night. And that means that you don't know enough about their business to sell to them. It's not easy to find experienced managers who are comfortable dealing directly with customers. When recruiting college graduates for our business, we looked for people who had had summer jobs as waiters and waitresses. Nobody has had that job without getting their lights punched out quite a few times. As you change your organization, chances are you will have to change the habits of the people who work for you now.

In touch at home, out of touch overseas is a common problem. Japanese product developers work the music districts of Tokyo to find out what is hot. But walking the back alleys of Shinjuku won't tell you much about customers in America and Europe. At one Japanese customer of ours, every single manager all the way up the hierarchy to the CEO's office dealt with the company's Japanese customers on a regular, if not daily, basis. Few had anything to do with American customers, yet this company was looking to the U.S. market for growth. Typically in the big Japanese electronics combines, a half-dozen layers of management in a foreign country are added to the bureaucracy in Tokyo, leaving a dozen or more layers between CEO and customer.

Where Japanese companies have done best, they are indeed flatter: as recently as 1990, Ford Motor Co. had fifteen levels of management compared to Toyota's seven. Too many American companies are sitting ducks; today, for example, only 53 percent of those working for U.S. manufacturers (down from 77 percent in the 1950s, America's golden years) are actually in hands-on positions, making things. The rest are doing—well, what exactly are they doing?[35] In 1991, GM still had nearly 100,000 white-collar employees;[36] that's one for every few dozen customers, if anyone was talking to customers, that is. There is no reason why your company should not be able to run circles around its unwieldy Japanese competitors—unless you simply don't want to change.

Microsoft, the virtually unchallenged leader in personal computer software, may have learned the lesson that some of its rusting industrial predecessors did not. When we first purchased personal computers in 1983, the owner's manual for the operating system software (MS-DOS, the product that built Microsoft) did not even list a telephone number for Microsoft. If you couldn't get it to work, you could join a computer support group and hope for the best. By 1988, when we went to Apple Macintosh computers, the manuals for the Microsoft products we had did indeed list the number of Microsoft's headquarters in Redmond, Washington, but it was not a toll-free number. Our calls were answered by operators who knew nothing about software, and who redirected us aimlessly from one department to another (each attempt requiring another toll call). Then in 1990–91, Microsoft began to change. We received newsletters giving us the direct telephone number (regrettably still not a toll-free number) of Microsoft's product development teams, who, when called, were well informed and anxious to please. What's more, we found the Microsoft booths at computer trade shows manned by product engineers who knew what was going on and wanted to hear what we thought. This company has made a genuine effort to reach out to its customers. Now, if they would just pay for the call . . .

Many American businesses have tried to streamline their organizations through mass layoffs, without pushing decision-making authority down the line and out into the field. One Unisys manager told the *Wall Street Journal* in 1990 that his department was cut in half and two layers of management were eliminated. But decisions took longer than before, because authority was raised, not lowered.[37] Likewise, forced early retirements eliminate the most seasoned managers without regard to ability. Worst of all, perhaps, are layoffs that decimate the ranks but leave the number of layers intact. This approach was a favorite at AT&T at one time.

Letting your customers manage you entails risk. When managers get their lights punched out enough, they start suffering from the "Stockholm syndrome," which occurs when kidnapping victims identify with their captors. We have seen companies that have flattened and decentralized suddenly lose control of their own destiny, spinning off in too many directions as they try to please each customer, in every way, indiscriminately. In short, their customers take them for a ride. Unless you are well prepared to sell at a premium what the customer values most about your company, you will end up giving the shop away. Decision-makers close to customers find it hard to say no when calls for price cuts and freebies come up. You can't say no unless you know what the customer really wants—and will pay for.

Market Share and Customer Integration

There is no easy way to find out what keeps your customer awake at night, but if all your operations are well integrated with those of your customers, you will find out. Very quickly. When engineering, production, and sales decisions are made with the customer, the customer buys. The best measure of customer integration is the number of levels of management between CEO and customer. In fact, in information technology, our research shows that market share is inversely proportional to this metric.

Responding fast to customers' needs leads to success. You must base most decisions on fragmentary information. But when you're close to your customers, decisions can be made with partial facts. When you're removed from them, you need reams of statistics, reports, market research, and other details that are out of date when printed.[38] No number of focus groups will substitute for just getting out there and pressing the flesh.

While AT&T is grossly overmanaged in many parts of its business, its Network Systems organization, which sells communications products to telephone companies, runs lean. There are just four levels of management from salesmen to CEO: salesman to regional VP, to Network Systems group executive, to AT&T CEO. In fact, one of CEO Bob Allen's key functions is working these customers. The results show: AT&T remains a leader in this market.

Sometimes these changes are forced on you. In the mid-eighties, Storage Technology, a manufacturer of IBM-compatible mainframe disk drives, sank into bankruptcy as it strayed away from its core business and got crushed under the weight of its own bureaucracy. Ruthless layoffs ensued, and without their go-fers to go for them, managers and researchers alike were forced out into the field to see customers. They came up with the idea of an automated tape library based on customer feedback, and within two weeks they had twenty orders for this multimillion-dollar system. Japanese competitors, which sell through distribu-tors, were simply left in the dust. And Storage Tech was no longer simply copying IBM, but leading the market.[39]

The benefits of streamlining are real, but will not be real-ized unless the boss comes out of his hole, and unless authority to make decisions is decentralized. Perhaps toughest of all, man-agement must stand behind tactical decisions made in the field. For your VPs to overrule line sales people, who best know what customers really want and will pay for, is very bad for morale. And even worse for sales.

Action Item No. 8

Reduce layers of management from CEO to salesman to a maximum of four.

Those closest to customers—the salesmen—must be in daily contact with those who determine corporate policy. Any extra layers can only obstruct your objective: serving the customer.

Maximize Customer Contact

Counterstrategy No. 3:
Make Everyone Sell

To maximize leverage with customers, make everyone sell. There isn't a single person in your entire organization who should not be directly responsible in some way for sales and service. Make all decisions based on what you hear from customers, not what you want to believe about yourself. Your Japanese competitors still think that (outside Japan, at least) they can either subcontract or delegate to underlings responsibility for customer satisfaction. They can't—and neither can you if you want to turn back the threat to your livelihood from Japan. Nobody can come between you and your customers.

If building market share is your goal, look no further than Roger Penske. When Penske took control of the Detroit Diesel subsidiary of General Motors in 1988, it was a shambles. One problem after another—botched new products, poor service, fractious union relations—had sent this manufacturer of heavy-duty diesel engines into a tailspin, from nearly a third of the market in the late 1970s down to a rock-bottom 3 percent in 1987.[1] Detroit Diesel had the technology—its electronically fuel-injected Series

60 engine introduced in 1987 was a rare leap forward that reduced emissions and boosted fuel efficiency—but had lost the confidence of its customers.

Penske had more than customers to win over. Diesel's factory in Detroit had become a caricature of the American rust belt, a beat-up old place with even worse labor relations. As the company's fortunes declined in the 1980s, layoffs ensued and management became pitted against labor. The number of union grievances soared. Penske decided to solve his two problems at once. One of his first steps at Detroit Diesel was to round up the union leaders and take them for a tour of the country on his private airplane—to see customers. They got an earful about what was wrong with Detroit Diesel, its products, and its service. Penske gave his dealers the attention they needed—we spoke to one of his biggest dealers, who praised him in almost messianic terms. When a customer balked at buying Detroit's new engines, Penske gave him one to try. When cutbacks were needed, it was not labor that took the heat: Penske reduced the number of white-collar workers by a quarter, eliminating the marketing department entirely.[2] The message was clear: everybody sells, and the boss is the chief salesman.

There's nothing like leadership for success. Penske convinced his customers: by the end of 1991, market share rose to 25 percent, and as high as 33 percent in some months. From the back of the pack, Detroit Diesel improved customer perceptions of quality and service to the point that it had pulled up with Caterpillar, the service leader in the heavy-duty truck engine business. What's more, Penske convinced the people who make customer service a reality: his workers. Labor cooperation improved efficiency and quality at the same time. The union even joined with management to build a multimillion-dollar training and recreation center for the plant in Detroit.[3]

Before he acquired Detroit Diesel, Penske ran Hertz's truck leasing operation, so he knew trucks. He was also a Detroit Diesel dealer, so he understood the concerns of those selling his engines. And he was smart enough to adapt Japanese lean manufacturing practices to increase efficiency and production speeds. But mostly what Penske did for Detroit Diesel was simple common sense: serve customers, and support the people who serve customers. Penske likes to tell the story of his first car dealership, where he had his retired father (who was looking for something to do) come in every day. He gave his father a stack of completed repair work orders and had him call every customer to make sure everything was fixed properly. Seems pretty simple—no Harvard MBA required—but decades later, few of his competitors have adopted this practice.[4]

Cut Out the Middle Man

Selling direct is the simplest way to counter the preference of your Japanese competitors for distributors outside Japan. If you control customer contact, you can maximize your sales and follow-on sales opportunities. Just look at the phenomenal success of mail-order sales during the last fifteen years. With mail order, you find out every day what your customers want. You will not reap the potential benefits of focusing on your best products and decentralizing your organization if you turn over customer relations to somebody else.

It's much easier to rely on distributors to sell your products, but the cost is high. A distributor controls a customer's experiences with your product. One of us bought a Dodge Caravan from Potamkin, a Chrysler dealer in New York. The car has worked virtually without flaw for four years, but every car needs service occasionally, if only to be tuned up or to have its oil changed. During the first year, when it was still under full warranty, he took the car several times to Potamkin for service, and waited as long as an hour and a half just to drop it off for an appointment that had been scheduled in advance. A very minor repair to the power steering had to be repeated three times before it was done right. One surly employee told him, "We don't care about service, we just want to sell new cars." Buying another Chrysler product—no matter how well made—becomes a difficult decision under such circumstances (particularly when you hear about Japanese companies offering pickup and delivery for service appointments).

When you sell through third parties, not only do you lose control of the customers' experience, but you don't have the benefit of their feedback. Distributors have their own agenda, and what you hear indirectly from customers about problems, ideas for improvements, and future buying intentions will be heavily biased by that agenda. Certainly nobody at Potamkin was interested in what anybody thought about Chrysler's cars or their service.

In our own business, we experienced a great awakening when we went from direct mail to direct sales, replacing junk mail with salesmen. We thought our customers bought our publications because they were accurate and detailed. This was only half true; they bought our information to reduce the risks of their decisions. They wanted not facts and figures, but authoritative advice. We changed our whole approach to sales, exposing our methods of doing research so our customers would be comfortable with them. Previously we had kept our methods secret, so we didn't "give away the recipe with the cake." Before long we were selling our methodology more than our information. Once we had salesmen talking to our customers, we could no longer treat customer inquiries as an annoying intrusion; if we did, the salesmen, who measured customer service levels every Friday in their paychecks, went ballistic. Soon we were providing free, unlimited telephone support with each of our publications. Our business changed completely—and for the better.

You can't sell direct to everybody, and you shouldn't sell to some people at all. After you see the whites of their eyes, you'll know whose expectations you can meet, and whose you can't.[5] There's some business you just have to walk away from, because your customer will be unhappy no matter what you do. After we started selling direct, we found out that our primary U.S. customers were corporate librarians, not executives as we had thought (and flattered ourselves). We soon realized that we should avoid selling directly to executives, who would only call us at 5:00 P.M. on Friday when they needed information in a panic for a board presentation at 9:00 A.M. Monday morning. While we prided ourselves on our quick turnarounds, these customers, in their hysteria, were inevitably dissatisfied.

Some companies do well when they focus on a single type of customer. In the early 1990s, NCR was one of the few computer companies selling products using industry-standard UNIX software and making money at it. While its competitors were selling commodity hardware at a loss, NCR sold its retailing expertise to its customers in the form of software, hardware, and service.[6] Just as its cash registers automated the retailing industry earlier in this century, so do its computers today. The only way NCR can know one industry so well is by selling direct. If it tried to wholesale its computer hardware through third parties, no one would be interested.

Selective application of the "sell direct" rule does not work well. Local production won't do anything for your position without local control over decision-making; the benefits are lost. Without disintegration and decentralization, direct sales simply remain a burden for the manufacturer. In the early 1980s, IBM's attempt to sell personal computers directly through its own retail stores failed: saddled with Big Blue's lumbering bureaucracy, these outlets could not compete with more nimble competitors. IBM got rid of the stores; it should have gotten rid of the bureaucracy.

At home, your Japanese competitors sell directly everything they can, even the simplest products, like TVs. Customer service is a matter of personal honor. Outside Japan, they use distributors to sell and service even the most complex products, like communications systems and large computers. Customer service is nothing but a nuisance for somebody. No wonder Japan's share of these markets is low. If you want to get between your Japanese competitors and their customers, sell direct. If you can't sell everything directly, at least reach the 20 percent of your customers who generate 80 percent of your sales. If you can't sell anything directly, do what the Japanese do at the high end of the car market: set tight standards for your dealers.

Everybody Sells

Selling direct means turning the entire company into a sales force. With everybody, including R&D and manufacturing people, involved in sales, decision-making is faster and more focused. There will be arguments, but at least they will be about what customers want, not internal politics. Involving everybody works best when you shed unnecessary upstream activities. In other words, if you manufacture the headlights that go into your cars, you should not bring headlight designers along to meet customers, but rather subcontract headlight production. Furthermore, everybody who is making decisions should be in the same time zone; there's no point in debating customer requirements if every decision you make will be second-guessed by your head office halfway around the world. In short, "everybody sells" works best when decentralization and disintegration have been implemented.

IBM is trying to turn the "everybody sells" rule into reality. During the late 1980s, IBM decided to thin its ranks, but wanted to maintain its (somewhat tarnished) no-layoff policy. Forced retirements were one approach. But the company has also turned thousands of middle managers into salesmen. In Europe, the goal was to have some 65 percent of white-collar employees in direct contact with customers by 1993 or 1994, up from 58 percent in 1989. In Japan, IBM in 1991 decided to transfer three quarters of its seventeen hundred headquarters staffers to three new sales organizations.[7] Not enough, perhaps, but how does this number compare to your company?[8] Worldwide, IBM has scratched thousands of staff positions. By the end of 1990, some 65,000 employees worldwide had been retrained for frontline jobs.[9]

IBM has the right idea here. But because it is so vertically and horizontally integrated, as well as centrally managed, IBM has a hard time *acting* on the information it gets from customers. One IBM salesman told *Business Week* in 1991 that it was "politically incorrect" to raise doubts about new products; consequently, R&D does not hear about what customers want.[10] In 1991, IBM set up an autonomous group to develop and sell a new graphic supercomputer. Covering the development, a *New York Times* reporter thought it was noteworthy that the head of the group went on sales calls personally; the marketing director of the group told the *Times* that she could take customer feedback directly to product engineers, adding, "That's something that is frequently not possible elsewhere in the company."[11] Clearly, IBM has a long way to go.

Everyone who works at Lexus in the U.S. is expected to talk to a new car customer at least once per week, a requirement that would have a revolutionary effect at Toyota's American rivals.[12] GM is worried about high costs and declining market share. It should be worried about customer relations—and not in the public relations sense. If GM understood its customers' needs, and met them, market share and costs would take care of themselves.

Japanese electronics giants dominate information technology in Japan in large part because of the close ties with customers at all levels and in all functions (and thanks to a healthy dose of government protection). Everybody sells in Japan; elsewhere, it's patchy at best. In Europe, Japan's big electronics companies are eager to participate in government-sponsored research projects designed to bail out the European electronics industry.[13] It is hard to imagine anything that has less to do with customer needs than a European Community–sponsored research program.

If you are selling to business, the purpose of putting everyone in the front lines is to identify real customer operational problems. Customers want to maximize cash flow and profits; what's slowing them down? How can your products help them attain their goals? If they can't, how can your products be improved? If you are selling to consumers, making everyone sell gives you a direct line on changing tastes, concerns, and buying patterns, long before they show up in conventional market research. Your Japanese competitors have thousands of bureaucrats in Tokyo studying your customers; each project they do is transported thousands of miles, translated at least twice, and analyzed to death. If you can't do better, faster, you're just not trying.

Action Item No. 9

Shift two thirds of your people to sales and service.

Any activity (except manufacturing) that does not need daily customer interaction should be outsourced. At least once every six months, each plant worker should be assigned to track a customer delivery, from initial shipment to follow-up calls at intervals of thirty, sixty, and ninety days.

Let Your Customers Manage You

Once you have decentralized your company and flattened your management hierarchy, everyone will be exposed to the real world: the people who pay money for your products and services. Turned inside out, your organization can be managed on a daily basis by your customers. When your VP of new product development is located in the field, there's no waiting for marketing staff groups to "approve" a customer request passed up by the sales office. He can take prospects right into the labs and make decisions on the spot. With customers in the driver's seat, the risk of new product failure is minimized; new ideas can be commercialized in the certain knowledge that buyers not only need them, *but have already budgeted for them.*

With direct lines of communication to all your people, customers can quickly tell you what they value most about your company. You can build on those qualities, eliminating activities customers do not need, reducing your costs dramatically in the process. In response to intense pressure from customers, your employees can quickly recognize unnecessary costs, and eliminate them. Your customers will, in effect, run your business for you.

Product developers in particular need customer contact. But moving the labs away from headquarters and into the hinterland isn't enough, as the experience of the Japanese has shown. If the labs can only communicate with headquarters and not with customers directly, the benefits are lost. Typically, when your Japanese competitors set up labs in prestigious college towns like Princeton or Stanford, the labs work under the direction of Tokyo. There a market research team works in isolation from the U.S. lab and the U.S. customers to identify hot new technologies for the U.S. market. Indeed, we have even seen U.S. labs being told by Tokyo-based market research groups what products to develop for third markets, like Europe and Asia. This is ridiculous. There is little or no contact between researchers, salesmen, and customers. Market research is no substitute for such contact. Without direct customer input, the labs can only develop something somebody wants to buy on a hit-or-miss basis.

While Japanese companies lavish huge amounts of money on research, there is no direct correlation between R&D expenditures and success. If you develop a small number of products in close cooperation with customers, chances are they will sell.[14] Conner, the disk drive supplier that excels at subcontracting, has taken the lead in hard drives for laptop PCs using a philosophy called "sell, design, build." Engineers work closely with customers before a product is designed.[15] Conner has its challenges, but introducing products customers don't want is not one of them.

Manufacturing also benefits from some outside exposure; customers should be encouraged to poke around your plants. Workers on the line feel better if they can see the people that use their products. When everyone knows that customers are around, the plant will be cleaner and better organized. And engineers on site might just get some useful suggestions. Best of all, customers have more confidence in your product when they can see where the "real work" is done. Whether you make chocolate in Hershey, Pennsylvania, minivans in Windsor, Ontario, or mainframes in Montpellier, France, your customers would like to tour your factory. You will both benefit from the experience.

Japanese companies are "globalizing," slowly moving plants and labs out of Japan and into foreign markets. But they are not decentralizing, since decisions continue to be made in Tokyo. Globalization is driven by politics (to get around protectionism in the United States and economic unification in Europe), not by customer needs.[16] At home, Japanese companies let their customers talk to the labs, see the factory—in short, "kick the tires." Abroad, your Japanese competitors are not letting their customers have a hand in managing them. You must.

Action Item No. 10

Let customers set your priorities.

Eliminate or delegate all items on your "to-do" list that have nothing *directly* to do with customers. Give key customers *formal* sign-off authority on all new product development. Don't let internal procedures kill good customer ideas.

Set Your Sales Force Free

You have to trust the people who talk to your customers every day, your salesmen. Listen to them, let them tell you what customers want, and involve them in product design. Most managers don't trust their salesmen, a real irony, since salesmen spend more time with customers than anyone else. Your Japanese competitors are not taking advantage of the knowledge and experience their overseas salesmen can offer. They may even be contemptuous of them. Speaking of the need for innovation in electronics, Sony CEO Akio Morita says in his autobiography, "It may sound curious, but I learned that an enemy of this innovation could be your own sales organization, if it has too much power."[17] If you meet Sony head-to-head in any market, ignore your salesmen at your own peril.

You must compensate your sales staff for what the customer wants to buy, not for what you want to sell. Base quotas on accounts, not products, so your salesman can figure out what's best for each customer. No company can shoehorn its production schedule into its sales plan and long survive. Most compensation plans are designed to fail. They reward inertia, not initiative. They serve accounting and production needs, not customers. They are designed to keep factories running, not to satisfy customers. If your salesmen are paid to sell boxes, customers can always find cheaper boxes someplace else.

Let your salesmen design your compensation plan, and it will be designed to succeed. This may sound like heresy, but trusting your salesmen will work if you have good people and take them into your confidence. Let salesmen design a system for tracking customer satisfaction. And involve them in building your business plan, don't just hand them quotas on January 1 (or worse, tell them to keep up the good work in January and give them their quotas in April). For some companies, this kind of change requires a radical rethink of accounting and human resource policies. On many occasions, we have heard salesmen complain about their employers because they were not getting paid on time. Shortchanging your salesmen is not a formula for better customer relations.

Salesmen need to be well armed with detailed account plans. We're amazed how often salesmen are completely ignorant of customer objectives, of basic facts in customer annual reports. Sales presentations we see invariably emphasize the seller's business goals, expansion plans, technological breakthroughs, and other facts of no import to a customer. Each account requires a detailed battle plan keyed to that company's goals and needs, but salesmen cannot do this kind of groundwork without help. Your Japanese competitors may have armies of functionaries building business plans in Tokyo, but they are not supporting their salesmen in the field outside of Japan. Don't make the same mistake.

Successful motivation begins with better relations with your staff. Sit down with your people. Figure out what keeps customers from being fully satisfied with your products. List the changes required to improve customer satisfaction and pay people to make those changes. Remember (p.148) Hampton Inn, where all employees, right down to the bellhops and housekeepers, have the authority to do whatever it takes to keep their hotel guests coming back.[18] At L.L. Bean, the first person you reach when you call has the authority to accept returns and make other adjustments required to keep you happy. You won't easily find a Japanese company that offers this kind of service outside Japan, unless it's Honda, Nissan, or Toyota. But your Japanese competitors will inevitably learn the value of direct customer contact and good account control. You'd better get there first.

Action Item No. 11

Free your sales team.

Put sales and service personnel on product development committees. Turn sales into the management fast track. Let your salesmen design your compensation plan. Knock a point off your market share every time you overrule the sales department.

Manage Your Customer Relationships

In Japan, relations with customers are a lifelong concern for most companies. Outside Japan, it's ship and forget. Close account management is necessary to ensure customer satisfaction throughout the life of your product. The real benefits of close contact accrue over the long haul, but the payoff is enormous. With better account management, you can make sure that your product works properly for your customers throughout its life. With the ship-and-forget approach, you have no idea what happens after your product leaves the loading dock. Unless a product fails and is returned, you have little opportunity to redress problems. If the customer is simply unhappy or is not fully exploiting your product's capabilities, you may have lost the next sale without even knowing it. Services perforce require direct contact with customers, but the benefits of that contact do not accrue automatically. You must *work* to understand your customer's needs, and to benefit from what you learn.

Account control is essential with large and complex products, which often incorporate products and services from many vendors. Problems can arise with your product that may be caused by one of your competitors. When your customers come to you, they don't want to hear about the other guy. If good account control is in place, you can handle such volatile situations properly. If not, you have lost a customer forever. You can run into this problem even if you're not selling supercomputers. A friend recounted to us the sad tale of her Jeep Cherokee that kept stalling, despite repeated trips to the shop. The dealer insisted she was buying cheap gas, that the problem was not with the Jeep. Maybe she was buying cheap gas, but her next car was a Volvo, and Chrysler lost one more customer.

Close account management allows you to bring customers into the development process for the next generation of product, ensuring that they buy into the design. Applied Materials, a leader in semiconductor manufacturing equipment, broke with its American rivals when it decided to sell its products directly in Japan in 1979. By shifting some product development offshore and building close relations with its Japanese customers, Applied survived the shakeout in the early eighties among its American competitors, survived the collapse in semiconductors in the mid-eighties, and now prospers as a leading supplier in Japan.[19]

Close contact is essential in electronics, if only to ensure "backward compatibility," i.e., that new products will work with the old ones the customer already has. There was a time when suppliers could make everything they had previously sold obsolete at the time of their choosing. IBM and AT&T did this for years, until competition ended the scam. The forced march to product upgrades doesn't work anymore. Customers control life cycles, and if you don't spend time with your customers, those cycles will pass you by. Most Japanese electronics companies have no experience outside Japan replacing their own equipment. They often abandon hardware markets when they mature, which is just when the best opportunities arise for service and add-on sales. Consequently they are relinquishing to others the ongoing revenue and new-idea stream from devoted customers just waiting to buy from them. Winning new customers to replace these is much harder than keeping old ones.

Sony made this mistake with DAT, its failed digital recording process. We are putting our money on Sony competitor Philips and its digital compact cassette recorder (dubbed DCC),[20] which has CD quality but is compatible with existing analog tapes as well.[21]

No Pain, No Gain

There's no shortcut to customer integration. Acquisitions, joint ventures, joint marketing agreements, and other "global" strategies may seem like painless ways to avoid selling direct, but they are not. Downstream activities, like sales and service, must be kept in-house. No one can come between you and your customers! You can safely unload upstream activities; nobody will notice if you stop making the fenders that go into your cars, knobs that go on your computers, or the accounting software that runs your back office. These do little for your competitiveness and nothing for your customers. In short, all activities that involve customers directly you must do yourself. Everything else should be outsourced.

Can you use acquisitions for instant customer access? Fujitsu is certainly trying in computers. This company made itself the second-largest computer manufacturer in the world by acquiring the fifth- and sixth-biggest computer suppliers in Europe, ICL of the U.K. (bought in 1990) and Nokia Data of Finland (1991).[22] Fujitsu has invested in a number of American computer ventures over the past twenty years, most notably a 46 percent interest in mainframe maker Amdahl, started in the 1970s. More recently, Fujitsu invested in Hal Computer Systems (1991) and disk and tape drive maker Intellistor (1987).[23] History has produced few successful computer acquisitions, but Fujitsu's brood has done reasonably well, largely because Fujitsu has kept its hands off. In particular, Amdahl, now a $2 billion company, has been a good investment, and has served as a useful sales channel for Fujitsu hardware. If Fujitsu's goal is to run a profitable venture capital fund, it may have the right formula. If it wants to build a global computer company that solves customer problems in a unique fashion, Fujitsu has a long way to go. Fujitsu's best investment may have been the thirty-man direct sales force the company established in Toronto in 1991, which will give the company some real frontline exposure.[24]

Avoid joint marketing ventures, for which most partners have unrealistic expectations. Few of these arrangements are well conceived and almost none are well executed. IBM pulled the rug from under Fujitsu in factory automation by buying one of its key software suppliers; Fujitsu responded in 1991 by forming an alliance with McDonnell-Douglas, which will sell Fujitsu's products in Europe and Asia (outside Japan).[25] Fujitsu's mishmash of overseas distributors could be the undoing of its computer acquisitions in Europe, where three or four Fujitsu distributors, each competing for customers, can easily cause confusion.

Apple Computers decided in 1991 to use third parties (not its regular dealers, but systems integrators such as EDS, Peat Marwick, and Arthur Anderson)[26] to reach its sophisticated customers, but this approach could prove disappointing for all involved, particularly Apple. Some of Apple's most demanding users already feel they are getting second-rate support from Apple, yet the company seems to feel it can subcontract this problem. Later in 1991, Apple embraced its longtime rival IBM to share hardware and software developments in order to meet the perceived needs of customers it does not deal with directly.[27] This is no way to protect yourself from sudden shifts in customer needs in a fast-changing business.

In a limited number of special circumstances, creative approaches can be used for "virtual" direct sales. Close cooperation with retailers improves the flow of information from customers. Many cosmetics manufacturers have set up their own counters in department stores, staffed with their own sales clerks. Food processors maintain the racks in supermarkets that display their products. Another option is to replace retailers with franchisees, which you can make march to the same tune, called by you, the franchiser.[28] All these steps give the supplier better control over relations with customers, but they do not eliminate the need to see customers directly, and they require close management.

Not everything can be sold direct. Procter & Gamble is not going to open diaper stores. But by listing toll-free numbers on its products, P&G maintains direct links to customers. And P&G sells directly to retailers, not through middle men, and works as closely with them as possible. P&G maintains computerized links to its biggest retailers, like K Mart and Wal-Mart, to shorten delivery intervals and reduce inventories.[29] The idea is simple: keep K Mart and Wal-Mart happy, and they will move the diapers.

During the boom years of the 1980s, most personal computers were sold through dealers of some kind. Then up-and-comers CompuAdd, Dell, and Gateway revolutionized the business by selling PCs through the mail with better prices and better service. While they all began in the United States, Dell, for one, has duplicated its success in Europe.[30] In response, market leader Compaq was forced to abandon its sole reliance on dealers and to offer toll-free technical support and on-site service, even inviting customers to its headquarters to keep them up to date on its plans.[31] When it decided to take another crack at the PC market in 1992, DEC took to mail order to reach its customers directly. Even IBM is looking at mail-order sales of PCs.[32] Toshiba, by contrast, still wholesales its laptops through a distributor, which sells to retailers, which sell to customers.[33] Who knows where these machines end up?

The bicycle company Performance pulled the same trick as the PC direct mailers, selling bicycles and accessories through catalogs to build a $50 million business in ten years—the largest bike shop in the United States.[34] Doing an end run around local retailers, who traditionally sold all bicycles, Performance offered better service and better prices—we know, because we are both customers. Direct sales may be the best way for Detroit to do an end run around its Japanese competitors. They might begin by targeting women, who may be intimidated by a dealer system dominated by men and designed for a time when men bought all the cars. If some such radical move to direct customer contact is not taken, the great strides in customer service that the Japanese car companies are now making will be the death knell for the American car industry.

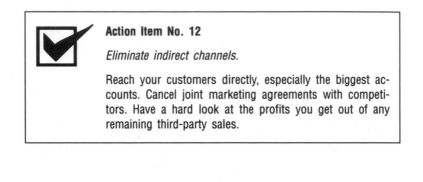

Action Item No. 12

Eliminate indirect channels.

Reach your customers directly, especially the biggest accounts. Cancel joint marketing agreements with competitors. Have a hard look at the profits you get out of any remaining third-party sales.

—10—

Sell Peace of Mind

Counterstrategy No. 4:
Let Customers Set Your Goals

To maximize leverage with your customers, sell relationships, not products. What your customers value is peace of mind—what the Japanese call anshinkan. *And if you've followed our first three rules, this fourth will take care of itself; if you are focused, decentralized, and in daily contact with customers, you will know what to do. Forget about your goals and your problems. Forget especially about your technology. Figure out what your customer's needs are and how to meet them.*

It's not easy to sell books for $18,000 a copy, but Gideon Gartner does, to the tune of $75 million per year. Not surprisingly, these aren't ordinary books: Gartner is selling paper, but his customers are buying peace of mind. In 1989, while planning a new product for our own publishing company, one of us spent six months talking to Gartner's customers. During that time, we did not hear one significant complaint about Gideon Gartner, his company, his products, or his service. Try that on your own business.

A Wall Street research analyst with an IBM background, Gartner set up his company, the Gartner Group, in 1979 to track the computer market. At that time, IBM still set the pace for the entire industry. When Big Blue brought out a new product, competitors scrambled for cover. Gartner found a receptive if somewhat modest-sized audience among those suppliers looking over their shoulders at IBM. But it wasn't just competitors that were getting whipsawed by IBM; so were customers. Companies that owned old IBM machines when the new ones came out found a big hole in their balance sheets where their old, undepreciated equipment used to be. For those with lots of big IBM mainframe computers, unanticipated swings in the value of the hardware could run into the hundreds of millions of dollars. Once Gartner began tapping into his mother lode of uneasiness, he was off to the races. Between 1983 and 1988, revenues jumped tenfold from $4 million to $40 million. Later that year, Gartner sold out to the big English advertising conglomerate Saatchi & Saatchi for $86 million, an astounding thirty-eight times net income.[1]

For $18,000 per year, a Gartner customer receives about 250 sheets of paper, called "Research Notes," prepared by the company's in-house team of analysts. These notes analyze the technology, price performance, new product plans, and service capabilities of all the big players in computers and communications (Gartner's net is cast far beyond IBM today). They read much like articles you can find in *Business Week,* the *Wall Street Journal,* or computer industry trade journals, which are available at a tiny fraction of the cost. The first time you read one of these notes you have to ask how it is possible to charge so much for them. The key is in service: Gartner's research staff spends its time supporting customers, not writing research notes. Gartner customers can call for telephone support as often as they like. Customers contemplating major equipment purchases can visit Gartner to air their ideas and concerns, obtaining the Gartner Group *nihil obstat* before they make their final decision. In short, Gartner customers spending millions of dollars every year on computers can feel comfortable that they are making the right choice. In a $50 million computer budget, $18,000 for peace-of-mind insurance is money well spent.

Anshinkan

To make your customers happy, you must understand them well enough to give them *anshinkan,* or peace of mind. Then you can figure out how to meet their needs with what you have to sell. American Airlines wants to keep its planes full and on schedule; it uses its reservation system to reach these goals. Federal Express wants its packages to arrive on time, and to answer with precision customers' questions about their deliveries; its tracking system enables it to do so. American Express wants to produce accurate statements efficiently, as well as to answer customer inquiries promptly; its billing system permits it to do both. The common denominator here is computers, but the different applications of technology are what makes these computers valuable to those buying them. If you are selling computers, or any other high-tech product, you ignore this at your peril.

Our rule applies to low-tech products as well. When it makes TVs, Sony must consider the wishes of consumers buying its products: good value, reliability, power requirements, cable and VCR compatibility. But Sony must also consider the needs of its distributors, which, in a tough market, might be obsessed with inventory. How can Sony keep dealer inventories to a minimum? In a recession, solving this problem will do more for Sony TV sales than any new feature it can dream up.

Ericsson's performance in high-end communications systems illustrates the benefits of relationship selling. This Swedish company rang up new sales in the United States in the 1980s, while its Japanese competitors bumped along. Ericsson realized that U.S. telephone companies wanted to expand internationally to escape domestic regulation after the Bell System was broken up in 1984. Capitalizing on its strong presence in Europe and many third world countries, Ericsson opened doors for its customers. The *quid pro quo* was orders in the hundreds of millions of dollars for Ericsson's products.

In our business, we encouraged our customers to consider our operations an extension of their own. Our company mission was simple: "to improve our customers' performance" regardless of whether to them that meant increasing sales or getting promoted. To help them improve, we shared with them the details of our research methodology and let them set our new product development plans. We trained them how to use our products better. We provided crackerjack telephone support; anyone and everyone could get drafted to man the phones, depending on the workload. At first we were afraid the "drop everything" approach would slow down our ongoing research schedule—we were worried about our own peace of mind. Instead it speeded our work, as we discovered what our customers really were interested in. What's more, we found out what we could *stop* doing that would never be missed. Best of all, once our customers got used to this higher level of support, they could only switch suppliers with difficulty. We had raised the barriers to entry in our market.

Selling peace of mind reaps huge rewards for any company, even if applied selectively. IBM wrote the book on selling relationships, and still leads its industry as a result. But as we have seen, IBM also has problems because it has been slow to decentralize and remains too committed to vertical integration. Perhaps, too, IBM has neglected the relationships built up over decades with its customers. When IBM became preoccupied with IBM's agenda, sales began to suffer. Any technical shortcomings are a symptom, not a cause of its problems. Besides, it is not the Japanese who are hurting IBM, it is the myriad American companies, big and small, that are serving IBM's customers better.

Your first step must be to review the account plans for your top ten customers (unless you are a retailer, your ten largest customers are probably other businesses, not consumers). They must address the operational problems that prevent your customers from meeting their goals. You must solve their most pressing problems; you must identify for them new opportunities; you must make their strategic goals your own. If your account plans so much as mention the importance of your technology, return to GO. If your company does not have account plans for its top ten customers, start reworking your résumé.

Retailers dealing exclusively with consumers must go through the same exercise. You must profile your customers statistically to understand their buying habits and life-style changes. But you must bring these statistics to life by dealing with customers directly. That means if you are Sears, your executives must spend time as floorwalkers; if Holiday Inn, they must work the front desk; if Burger King, flip hamburgers; and if Hess, pump gas. You must know: *What makes these people walk in the front door? What keeps them away?*

At home, Japan's industrial leaders have perfected the art of selling *anshinkan*. In the United States, Japanese car companies secured their position in the 1980s by selling peace of mind in the form of better quality, better value, and better service. Selling peace of mind can seem "fuzzy" compared with hard facts from the guys in white coats with clipboards, but it works. In many foreign markets (except for cars), Japan Inc.'s ambitions have been frustrated by vertical and horizontal integration, direct rule from Tokyo, and third-party sales. Best of all: many Japanese competitors are trying to sell technology, not what their overseas customers really value. For these customers, the result is *fuankan*—"anxiety." Your must seize this opportunity.

Action Item No. 13

Identify the most pressing business problems of your top ten accounts.

Rewrite your mission plan to solve these problems. Make their goals your goals.

Engineering Out Service

Raised on hardware exports, the Japanese believe service is something to be avoided. The idea is to engineer out problems so you don't need service, to make quality so high that products never need to be fixed. A worthy goal, to be sure, but service is more than fixing something that's broken. Your Japanese competitors think of quality as hardware reliability: reduce the number of defects per billion to the right level and you win the Deming Prize. By contrast, your customers think of quality as the entire experience from the first time they telephone you until they finally haul your product to the dump. The difference between these two ideas of quality is Service, with a capital S. Your Japanese competitors—unless you are in the car business—do not see this "big picture" definition.

Many products are so complex that they require ongoing support to be used properly. With communications systems and large computers, the need for training and support is neverending. Imagine Boeing delivering a 747 with a pat on the back, an instruction booklet, and a toll-free technical support number (manned from 9:00 A.M. to 5:00 P.M. Pacific Standard Time). Even with a relatively simple product like a refrigerator or a personal computer, an owner's manual may not do the trick. If your refrigerator goes on the blink after eleven years, you don't expect it to be fixed for free, but it's nice to get a little hand-holding from the GE Answer Center when you need it. One Sunday recently one of us called GE for help, and was walked through a minor repair with great patience. You can usually muddle your way through most PC software programs, but sometimes you need help. On the few occasions when we have had to telephone Microsoft with technical questions about its software, product developers took our calls right away. This is what "service" means today: maximizing the benefits your customers derive from your products.

Hardware quality alone will not sell, because quality is not a substitute for the service your customers expect. Successful application of your product may have little or nothing to do with its physical durability. Of course, great service is not a substitute for quality either! Today, extremely high quality levels are a *sine qua non*—largely thanks to the Japanese. Products that fail in the field will undermine the best of service strategies. If GE could just reduce the power consumption of its refrigerators by 75 percent it would be bulletproof.

Direct sales are no good without a strong service network. Your engineers must spend time with customers, finding out what's right and what's wrong with your products. If you have flattened your organization and shortened lines of communications, you need the direct customer contact that service provides. Otherwise you will be commissioning endless studies to figure out what people want. If the service infrastructure is not there, no amount of technology will turn your business around. Your Japanese competitors wrote the book on service—in Japan. But by defining service narrowly overseas, they kid themselves into thinking they can sell through distributors and avoid investing in a sales and service infrastructure overseas.

We recently saw advertised in a PC magazine a new NEC color computer monitor with all the features we were looking for and more; we were ready to buy. We called 1-800-NEC-INFO at 6:00 P.M. on a Friday afternoon to get: "sorry, gone for the day." At 9:00 A.M. on Monday, we started calling again, and got busy signals the first eleven tries; on the twelfth attempt we were greeted by a voice messaging system, then suffered five minutes on hold. Finally, an operator came on and gave us the number of a computer store in New York that sold the displays, adding, "Yes, the FG series works with your Macintosh, and I'll give you the name of an outlet in Chicago that sells the adapter cord you'll need." This is getting complicated: two purchases and special cords; what's next, screwdrivers, pliers, and a soldering iron? Clutching the persuasive ad copy we had torn out of the PC magazine, we decided to persevere. We made four calls to the dealer in New York; with each call we were put on hold at least twice; on the first three calls we ended up on somebody's voice mailbox. No one called back. On the fourth try we finally got a salesman who could help.

We have no doubt about the reliability of NEC hardware (which, by the way, is made in the United States), but if it's so difficult to buy from this company, God help anyone who needs something fixed. But don't laugh at NEC until you've tried calling your own company with a dumb sales question. And before you take a two-page spread in the national press, have a hard look at how you define service.

Nowhere has technology been so completely reduced to a commodity as in computers, where standards make everyone's hardware the same. You simply cannot differentiate yourself with technology; you have to go one better for your customers. Making it easier for them to do business with you is a step in the right direction; redefining the meaning of good service is probably the only chance you have of succeeding in a big way. You do not have to choose between service and manufacturing if making hardware is what you do. On the contrary, unless you can connect with your customers, you won't sell services, software, or hardware. There will always be a discount dealer selling computer equipment for less.

Build Service Into Your Products

Don't engineer service out, engineer it in! Hertz uses information technology to rent cars in the simplest possible way. Regular customers fill in a rental contract only once—when they sign on as Hertz Gold Service members. On arrival at major airports they find their cars waiting for them, backed into parking spaces, trunks open and ready for those heavy bags. The keys are in the ignition; the engine is running; the contract is hanging from the mirror already completed and authorized. Gold customers drive away, showing their driver's licenses to the parking attendant on the way out. When they return, they simply punch their contract numbers into a terminal in the parking lot and the machine generates their receipt. Hertz has built service into the process, and can slash costs and raise prices at the same time: its Gold customers are delighted to pay a little extra for the convenience of never being caught in an airport car rental line again. And unlikely to switch to another company unable to match Hertz service.

By making business flying less stressful than its competitors, American Airlines has taken the lead in its market. The whole front end of the airline is efficient and effective: pleasant, intelligent people answer the phones quickly; if the first person who answers has to make a handoff to another agent (e.g., for international flights), the transfer is done without a snag—no more please hang up and call another 800 number. Each of American's Admiral's Clubs located at airports around the world is an oasis where you can sit down and collect your thoughts for a few minutes before going on to an important meeting or pressing on to the next leg of a journey. The clubs are clean, tastefully decorated, and manned by efficient staff who know how to tackle the kinds of complex schedule changes that plague business travelers. Computers, fax machines, and photocopiers are freely available. Contrast American with Pan Am, which was so poor in everything from reservations to on-time departures that its demise was no surprise to anyone who flew it. Ironically, Pan Am had, in our experience, the most efficient and courteous on-board service—if you managed to get that far. Pan Am sold transportation and failed; American sells peace of mind and succeeds.

Otis Elevator turned back an assault on its business by the Japanese, among others, by raising the service stakes. Otis guarantees fast response anywhere in the United States, at any time, using a centralized service center to coordinate the activities of its field staff. For customers, Otis has eliminated a big headache; for its competitors, Otis has raised the barriers to entry and shifted competition away from technology; for itself, it has improved its performance in a market where service revenues are twice new-equipment sales.[2]

Procter & Gamble ties its computers to those of big retailers to keep their inventories low, since carrying costs (not leaky diapers) are what keep retailers awake at night. This keeps orders flowing smoothly from cash register to diaper plant. P&G is focused on its customers' concerns: keeping prices down and margins up. As an added benefit, P&G has fewer surprises on its order book, and a direct line to the consumers who buy its products.[3]

One small PC retailer we know was having trouble matching big discounters on price in its commercial accounts. So we advised the owner to carefully detail everything he would offer in his proposals, and to list separately all the services he now provides for free. "How many customers," we asked, "call up with questions after six months?" "Almost none," came the response. "Good, then offer two years of free telephone support. And add in that you will do an on-site visit every month. You can keep your customers loyal and discover a great deal about them that the discounters do not have the slightest interest in. When they are ready to buy again, these customers will think of you."

Building in service does not mean you have to give it away. During the 1980s, car dealers took a growing share of car repair business in the United States, largely by improving the quality of their work. Their investment paid off, since the service bays now account for the bulk of car dealer profits. Dealers charge more per hour for the labor of their mechanics, but customers are willing to pay a premium.[4] In 1990, DEC began billing customers for professional services they needed, rather than giving help for free or—much worse—relying on third parties to shave costs.[5] Of course, you can't always make your customers pay extra for service—sometimes they demand it for free. People who shop at Wal-Mart want low prices and good service; so do those who buy personal computers from Dell. If you're going to take on one of these two, you'd better make sure your costs are rock-bottom.

You cannot effectively combine service with your product unless you know your customers intimately. When working with salesmen we like to grill them about their customers' problems and strategies. It's shocking how few salesmen—and their bosses—have even read the annual reports of their biggest customers, let alone understand what makes them tick. You'd better get there before somebody else does.

Start by looking over the records from your service department; collect complaints from your salesmen. Be careful to work closely with your sales team to avoid conflicts, but any change that makes customers happier will delight them. Then start calling these customers to find out what's going on; find out why their customers complain to them. Once you understand the concerns of your top customers, you must redesign your service network around them. You will get nowhere if you set up a bureaucracy to "process the data"; you, and everyone else who makes decisions, must deal with it personally. And remember that every good idea from a customer that gets killed in a staff meeting takes a point off your market share.

Action Item No. 14

Assign responsibility for your top ten accounts to your top ten executives.

Each key player at your company must take full, personal responsibility for one key account. You'll see the roadblocks to better customer service disappear. And you'll discover what *anshinkan* means real quick.

The Technological Hunting License

Technology is like a hunting license. And that, to a large degree, is what many Japanese firms have in dozens of high-tech markets around the world. But a hunting license is no guarantee that you'll actually bring down that big buck. You might not even get a shot off. What's worse for Japan, the license is getting easier and easier to get, as Japan's new Asian competitors have shown. Anybody with a screwdriver and a soldering iron can enter the PC business, but nobody survives without strong service capabilities.

As long as your Japanese competitors are happy to hang out shingles that say "high technology, low prices," you command the advantage. Your customers have real, and very complicated, political, financial, social problems—to name just a few. One problem they don't have to worry about is how well your business does. And they don't give a damn about your technology—or that of your Japanese competitors. Forget about technology.

Look at the telephone companies. With digital technology, they have a huge array of features and capabilities to offer their customers. A few years ago, we approached New York Telephone about getting Centrex, a service that eliminates the need for us to buy an office switchboard. It took several calls to find out that what we wanted was available in our area only if we changed our telephone number; several more calls to find out that it would take three different N.Y. Tel organizations to get the complete job done; and a few more calls to find out that N.Y. Tel would give us no credit for our old system, which was not yet fully depreciated. Needless to say, we found somebody else to upgrade our telephones. N.Y. Tel has a technological hunting license, and it's shooting itself in the foot with it.

The Southern New England Telephone Company says its strategy is "building the intelligent network."[6] And SNET installed a state-of-the-art computerized exchange in 1990 in the small Connecticut town where one of us lives. He received notices offering the usual "custom calling features" (touch tone, call-waiting, call-forwarding, and speed-dialing) but what he had his heart set on was voice mail. For a few extra dollars per month, the service answers your calls when you are not there. It's like an answering machine but sounds much better and costs less. More than a dozen phone calls (all politely returned), two letters, and six months later he found out that (1) voice mail was not available through his brand-new local exchange, and (2) that SNET has no plans to offer such a service.

You can't sell technology if you don't train your people. The first person he called at SNET should have been able to answer a simple question with a simple "No, we don't have voice mail in your area, and I'm sorry but we don't have any plans to add it. However, we do sell answering machines that might meet your needs. Can I send you a brochure?" The first person we contacted at N.Y. Tel should have been able to handle all our needs—or at least coordinate the process. While with both of these phone companies we followed through to the bitter end out of professional (and perhaps slightly sadistic) curiosity, many potential customers must have given up in disgust after the first call. Your Japanese competitors are making the same mistakes, selling even supercomputers with little more concern about making life easy for customers. They will only get sales they can buy at rock-bottom prices from customers willing to suffer through the transaction. But don't think you can sit back and relax. Sooner or later your Japanese competitors will get the message. Librex, the notebook computer company set up by Nippon Steel, did. In 1992, *PC World* gave Librex top marks for service and support in a field of twenty-two suppliers.[7]

If you are selling to consumers, think of what's on your mind when you enter K Mart. You might be worried about your job or about money; you might be thinking about how you are going to keep your car on the road another year; you might even be thinking about what you are going to get your daughter for her birthday. You are certainly not thinking about K Mart's strategic goals for the next five years.

If you are selling to business, think of what motivates the people you work with. Imagine the sales pitch that would appeal to them; imagine what would make their lives easier. It probably doesn't have to do with initial price, and it certainly doesn't have anything to do with technology. It has to do with many concerns: their own careers, their budgets, and maybe even the profitability of their company. Consider the following scenario. Two companies sell computers to the accounting department. When the system goes down, the first sends in the techies to fix the hardware. The second sends its accountants to get the payroll out. Who's going to keep this customer?

On a recent television rerun of the 1960 U.S. Presidential election, the NBC team spent half the evening consulting the hot new RCA computer they were using to make projections. The technology was great—even though the candidates did not know until more than twelve hours after the polls had closed who had won, the very earliest computer projections showed Kennedy as the next President. The projections were accurate to within tenths of a percent. The machine worked, and to great effect. But where is RCA in computers now? Nobody knows or cares. If you don't want to suffer RCA's fate in computers, make sure your company knows how to use its technology to make life easier for its customers. You can start by reviewing your marketing materials and by tagging along on a sales presentation. If there is any talk of your products, technology, or engineering prowess, you have your work cut out for you.

The lesson is that technology sells, but only for those that can make it work. A new technology that answers real needs and gives real value will sell. Steve Jobs made Apple Computer a billion-dollar concern by making personal computers easy to use. Akio Morita made Sony the giant of consumer electronics by turning the transistor into something every teenager in America wanted: a small, battery-powered radio. In both cases, the catalyst was technology, but the result was much bigger than the sum of its technical parts. You can sell technology on its own merits to the thick-glasses-and-calculator set—plenty of Silicon Valley companies do so. But niche markets are not enough—Japan will not pay its way in the twenty-first century by selling PC upgrade boards and power-boosting gasoline additives. Japan Inc. wants to sell big, expensive products to everybody. These ambitions will be frustrated as long as Japan sells technology. Your job is to figure this out before your Japanese competitors do.

Action Item No. 15

Require all managers to spend one day per month manning your service desk.

Before they can be promoted to executive rank, managers must earn their "customer service wings."

Make It Easy to Do Business

Having the right products is not enough if you can't connect with your customers. One of us has been a loyal Sears shopper for years, never disappointed with the quality or value of any Sears purchase. Recently he called Sears to place a catalog order. As he went through his list, the sales agent said the order had to be broken in two: one for bulky items that had to be shipped to the local Sears store for pickup, another for the smaller ones that could be sent directly to his home by UPS. When he got to the last two items, which were replacement parts for a vacuum cleaner (one of the nice things about Sears is that you can always get spare parts), the sales agent said that these had to be ordered separately from a different Sears store nearby (not the same one where the bulky deliveries would be made). She went on, "I'll give you two numbers you can call in case one doesn't work; a lot of people tell me that this first number doesn't work." After six weeks, five calls, and three postcards, Sears had fulfilled his order. The merchandise was completely to his satisfaction, but once again he found himself asking, "Why do I do business with Sears?"

Our clients often ask us, "Why does ABC Co. do so well? It seems to have so many problems." The answer isn't about what ABC does right, but what everyone else does wrong. ABC makes plenty of mistakes, but fewer of them than its competitors. The first rule of the Hippocratic Oath for doctors is "Do no harm." So the first step to selling peace of mind is *Don't do any harm to what peace of mind your customer already has.*

How to make fewer mistakes? Where do you start? Start by making it easier for your customers to do business with you. Place a call to your sales office posing as a customer and find out what your customers go through. Follow the sales process from start to finish, and make sure you aren't punishing your customers for coming to you. Tag along on some sales calls. Spend a day on the service desk, and get an earful. Rectify some customer complaints personally. Start seeing your business from the customer's point of view, not your own. If you are really brave, give customers a toll-free number to the CEO's desk and tell them to call with any problem, anytime. Better yet, as we've said before, give the CEO a cellular telephone to carry with him everywhere.

The first problems you should help your customers with are the ones you have encountered—and surmounted—in your own business. Procter & Gamble knows how to control inventories of toothpaste and laundry detergent; K Mart and Wal-Mart benefit from that knowledge. Northern Telecom, with offices on five continents, can show its customers how to operate global networks. "We're sharing with our customers the expertise we've acquired in improving our own business processes," said one IBM manager.[8]

Once you have a feel for customer problems, institutionalize their solution. In discussion with your top customers, develop a monthly report card that tracks customer satisfaction levels based on what customers expect from you. Customers care about when their pizzas arrive; they do not care how fast orders are processed and sent to the kitchen. Customers care about when they arrive in Chicago and Frankfurt, not about when they pull away from the gate in New York or London. Customers care about how often their work gets interrupted by computer failures, not about how many defects per million your microprocessors have. Only customers can tell you how their satisfaction should be measured. Once these metrics have been established, *everyone's* performance evaluation and compensation should be tied to them.

Action Item No. 16

Find your toughest customer and make it your mission to make him happy.

The feistier and scrappier the better—your coworkers and competitors will want to avoid this demon. Exorcise him and you have turned your company around.

Cashing In on Japan's Crisis

You have a choice: you can sell your products at a discount or your company at a premium. If your business is run to solve problems for others, you'll command top dollar and drive a wedge between your customers and your Japanese competitors. If you run your business to solve your own problems, you will be discounting your way to an early grave.

Work closely with your customers, and you'll have nothing to fear from the Japanese or anybody else. But getting close to them is hard work, requiring changes in your organization, in your products, and—toughest of all—in yourself. Customer integration requires radical change in management thinking. "Customer" talk comes cheap: if every company in America that paid lip service to "serving the customer" really delivered, America's so-called decline would be a nonissue.

Companies that have gone through a real "customer" transformation are unrecognizable from their previous incarnations. And while the costs can be high, particularly human costs (since man is fundamentally resistant to change), the benefits are immediate. Problems that were intractable disappear; organizations are streamlined; company missions crystallize; sales and profits turn up. We know what happens because we did it. And as we abandoned our ivory tower approach to research, we lost many of our key players, who thought we were "selling out." We had to spend time with customers, neglecting our "real" work back at the office. At the time it seemed like chaos. In retrospect it was the resurrection of a moribund organization.

Japan is not reaching its customers—not even meeting them halfway. While well suited to Japan, management structures now in place travel poorly, or not at all. Until Japan can look outward—focusing on customer requirements, trusting local management, selling direct—performance in new markets will be poor. Technology at knockdown prices is not what customers want.

—11—

Japan's Wish List for the Year 2000

A century and a half ago, Japan was an insignificant feudal back-water in the northwestern Pacific. When Commodore Perry sailed into Tokyo Bay in 1853 and forced Japan at gunpoint to open its markets, he could not have imagined the consequences. A few decades later, Admiral Togo sailed the Japanese fleet into the Straits of Tsushima. There Japan sank its first Great Power. The Japan that sent the Russian Imperial Grand Fleet to the bottom in 1905 was already heavily industrialized. Soon afterward, Japan swallowed Korea and much of China and secured its position as a regional power to be reckoned with. By the time the Americans got the bad news in 1941, Japan had been at war in Asia, and winning, for decades.

In the late thirties and early forties, Japan honestly thought that it could go on to become the first real superpower. Instead it was humiliated. Less than a century after emerging from ob-scurity and only forty years after the victory of Tsushima, Japan was bombed back into obscurity. The destruction was so com-plete that many Japanese believed that Japan would never rise again. Yet today, Japan has achieved more than Admiral Togo could have dreamed. Without firing a single shot, Japan has emerged from complete subjugation to become the second most powerful economy on earth.

This resurgence has made businesses and governments all over the world nearly hysterical on the subject of Japan. The accepted wisdom is that Japan will core out one Western industry after another. This reaction is as inappropriate as it is wrong. Japan is a trading nation more like fifteenth-century Portugal and seventeenth-century Holland than nineteenth- and twentieth-century America, with its large landmass, natural resources, and powerful consumer and industrial base.

Like Portugal and Holland, whose day in the sun was relatively short-lived, Japan will rise and fall on its foreign markets, not its domestic ones. But foreign markets are notoriously fickle. They have no loyalty—the British had to solve this problem by outright conquest—and can shift quickly to cheaper sources of supply elsewhere. As the Portuguese and Dutch discovered, it doesn't take much to cut a trading nation from its markets. A war here, cheaper products and better terms there, and a commercial empire is gone, usually for good.

Japan is not another United States with its natural resources and vast internal markets. Nor is it a Great Britain at the height of empire, with its huge captive markets spanning the globe. Japan's options, like those of Portugal and Holland, are distinctly limited. And its hold on overseas customers is tenuous at best. The Japanese know this better than anyone. They also know that they have limited knowledge of foreign ways—and a limited desire to get to know foreign ways—and that the simplest method of keeping export markets loyal is an endless stream of cheaper and better products.

As the Japanese have learned, however, cheaper and better is not a barrier to market entry. So they spend much of their time looking over their shoulders at the Koreans, Taiwanese, and other Asian Tigers. These countries are at least as driven as the Japanese to join the ranks of the First Order of Nations. Japan's single biggest fear, apart from being deserted by loyal American customers, is that the Chinese will get their act together.

Japan's fanatical nationalist politician Shintaro Ishihara, in his book *The Japan That Can Say No,*[1] has tried to exploit worldwide fears of Japanese dominance. But Ishihara has not grasped the lessons of history (he wrote in the *Economist* that Pearl Harbor was an American *coup de main*!).[2] Few nations have ever been able to dominate markets they did not physically control. Moreover, the hardest lesson of imperial overreach is that conquered markets soon begin to exert powerful centrifugal forces and take control of events themselves. America turned the tables on Britain, and so did India. Ukraine and others are now doing the same to Russia. To keep its foreign customers, Japan must co-opt them, turning more American than the Americans, more Korean than the Koreans, and—here's the real challenge— more French than the French.

Japan was defeated in World War II by the potent American combination of two forces: high technology and multiculturalism, the strength America derives from the "melting pot." The Japanese have managed to absorb only the first half of this lesson, and they are completely committed to high technology as a result. Absorbing the second half will have incalculable consequences. Multiculturalism is the antithesis of Japan today.

Japan prides itself on its uniqueness and ability to avoid the integration with others that is necessary to sustain commercial or imperial expansion. You cannot spend more than an hour or two in Japan without having someone tell you how "different" Japan is supposed to be. And you cannot remain there much longer before discovering the significant barriers between foreigners and Japanese in everything from language—all foreigners must address any Japanese in honorific tones until invited to do otherwise—to which nightclubs visitors are allowed to enter.

To be successful over the long term, the Japanese must become more like their customers, to shed their self-imposed "uniqueness." This is a tall order, and will not happen without a

lot of turmoil, perhaps even social upheaval. Yoshimichi
Yamashita, who runs the consultant Arthur D. Little's Tokyo bu-
reau, made some very telling observations about the impact of
Japan's customers on his countrymen in the *Wall Street Journal*.
He said the big five in Japanese steel—Nippon, NKK, Kawasaki,
Sumitomo, and Kobe—have become "too 'Japanese' to survive
outside the closed system that has made them enormous."[3] He
believes Japanese firms will have to drop values that only the
Japanese can understand, start Westernizing their management,
give up the feudal "group ego" for individual initiative, and stop
ostracizing managers who speak English "too well." An entire
nation, however, cannot sort out its own cultural and business
management priorities and solve its customers' most pressing
problems *at the same time*. Customers will be put on hold, some
of them for decades, until the Japanese work this thing out.

No matter where the Japanese have chosen to invest in the
last half century, they have really succeeded only in commodities, like steel, textiles, and chemicals, and in consumer products,
like cars, cameras, and microwave ovens, which they have turned
into commodities. There is nothing wrong with any of these markets, of course, especially consumer goods. However, the Japanese, in their desperation to gain market share, have used an
endless stream of price and feature improvements to drive brand
loyalty out of consumer markets everywhere. Customers have
been so well trained by the Japanese to disregard brand for price
that they are buying from the Koreans and others instead.

The Japanese are in a tough spot: they need the loyalty of
foreign consumers but have no firm hold on them. To get closer
to their customers, they must overcome significant cultural differences. At the same time, the Japanese economic engine is running out of steam: the industries that powered its postwar
recovery are mature or in decline. New competition is emerging
elsewhere in Asia eager to imitate the Japanese and gobble up
the markets they fought so hard to win. A breakthrough source of

export energy is needed to keep the engine in high gear. Japan has not found that source.

Japan has tapped out the low-budget seam that has paid its way so far. Success in new markets will require changes in how Japanese companies do business—changes we just don't see happening anytime soon. Of course, you can expect your Japanese competitors to keep battering away at you on commodity hardware costs and quality. To win you had better meet them dollar for dollar, with higher quality. But if your customers are at the core of your business, you will be safe for the foreseeable future.

We cannot say for sure that Japan will not overcome the impediments before it. For some in Japan, the attitude is "If it ain't broke, don't fix it." Others know that growth will not continue without dramatic change. If the "four fatal flaws" are holding it back, why can't Japan change? After all, the Japanese are supposed to be "quick studies." Indeed, if galvanized, Japan can change. But we've dealt with all Japan's electronics giants, and in fifteen years, we have never seen a real decision-maker who was not Japanese, and never seen a real decision that was not made in Japan.

In many industries, anemic foreign demand, combined with the political liability of the country's trade surplus, has slowed exports to a halt, even put them into decline. Profits, always razor-thin in the cutthroat competitive environment of Japan, are running into a sea of red ink. Companies are increasing prices, lengthening product cycles, moving offshore, emphasizing more sophisticated products, and in some cases—like Diahatsu in cars—giving up.

Will this pressure be enough, though, to force Japanese companies to make the real changes needed to gain customer loyalty over the long term? In modern times, Japan has responded dramatically and quickly to external threats. But this time, Japan faces no powerful external threat, no Admiral Perry, no Russian fleet, and certainly no MacArthur. The Japanese must force themselves to change, which they have never done before.

In this chapter, we look at Japan's prospects in several strategic markets.

Industrial Products

A number of industrial markets feature prominently in Japan's plans to "break out" from cars and TVs.

One of the biggest prizes of all may be aerospace, a huge market with potential growth well into the next century. But Japan does poorly in markets that require high levels of customer service and cannot be addressed from afar. Industrial markets driven by American consumers, like commercial aviation, offer advantages to American companies like Boeing and McDonnell-Douglas. Airlines fighting it out for consumer dollars in the world's largest market for air travel place enormous pressures on their suppliers for the best in service and price. Companies that are well adapted to these demands are almost impossible to budge. It would be very hard for a Japanese company—say Mitsubishi—to sell commercial aircraft without quite literally being run by its customers, the airlines.

That being said, Japan has made no secret of its desire to pioneer hypersonic aviation.[4] Hypersonic commercial aircraft are a MITI priority. But no one succeeds in commercial aviation without control of the fundamentals: technology and markets. Japan controls neither. The United States, with the world's largest domestic markets, leads in defense and space technologies. The Europeans have, on paper at least, the same advantages: a large market of well-heeled consumers ready to fly. But the European Community has never understood markets. European air traffic control is a hodgepodge of overlapping and conflicting jurisdictions, all jealously guarded. Companies like Airbus are logistical nightmares designed to paper over clashing national interests rather than meet those of the flying public. Extortionate airfares are fixed by governments, which, because they own most of the airlines, prefer to gouge their citizen-consumers rather than serve them.

Isolated in the northwest Pacific, Japan is far from the other rich, consuming markets of the world. The Japanese islands themselves are mostly served by trains. For the international air traffic on which Japan's export machine depends, the entire Kanto/Tokyo area with its thirty million people relies on one small airport at Narita that the Japanese have the effrontery to call "New." We have been through the New Narita Airport many times: it's like a scaled-down version of the New York Port Authority Bus Terminal, only located forty miles away, somewhere in New Jersey. In short, the Japanese don't know from planes. Without this knowledge, it is very difficult to see how Japan could succeed in commercial aviation.

Could the Japanese build a competitive aerospace infrastructure? Last time we took a bus into Tokyo (not advisable; take the train) from the "New" Narita Airport, we counted sixty-five armored buses full of riot police on their way to do battle with Narita farmers demanding that Japan stop expanding airports onto their lands. In the twenty-five years since Japan's Ministry of Transport decided to build Narita, four police and one protester have been killed there; 10,000 have been injured and 3,400 arrested. Of three planned runways, only one has opened. This runway handles 360 flights a day, 50 percent more than planned. Eight families block Narita's expansion, and when intermediaries from five of them finally started talking to the government in November 1991, they did so surrounded by more than 6,000 riot police![5] Short of forced Elizabethan-style enclosures—like the Highland clearances in Scotland, the range wars in the United States, and collectivization in Stalinist Russia—Japan's farmers and their political clout will not go away. For all the talk about the power of the Japanese government bureaucracies, they have never successfully confronted Japan's farmers.

Regardless of its growing volume of international trade, Japan will never be able to build airlines on an infrastructure it doesn't have at home. JAL and All Nippon, Japan's principal carriers, ranked tenth and thirteenth respectively in terms of revenue passenger kilometers in 1990. The largest American carrier, American Airlines, had 40 percent more revenues than JAL and All Nippon combined and a fleet 2.7 times the size. The Japanese carriers are also growing their fleets more slowly. U.S. carriers United, Delta, and American have many more planes on order than JAL and All Nippon. William Kunske, a former VP of planning at Northwest, told the *Wall Street Journal* that the carriers "in the best position to become the Coke and Pepsi of [the world's] airlines" are American and United.[6]

Without a large common carrier base to sell to at home, Japanese aerospace manufacturers will have to look at their options carefully. Even though JAL has a small fleet, it is the single largest buyer of Boeing aircraft. Boeing expects to sell $35 billion worth of its aircraft there through 2005.[7] Even this is not enough to propel Japan into commercial aviation, however. It is far more likely that Japan will continue as a major subcontractor of aerospace components and subsystems. This eliminates the risks of primary contracting—and customer contact—and brings all the benefits of high value added.

The biggest threat to American and European companies, therefore, is in subsystems like aeroengines. General Electric has shown the way. In a concerted twenty-year effort to supplant United Technologies' near monopoly in jet engines—one of the costliest components of any aircraft and most expensive to develop—GE powered its way into a top position. Because airlines prefer to order airframes and engines separately in order to maximize their price leverage, however, competition is cutthroat and some suppliers have been weakened. This is just the signal the Japanese need. They could make a move now or wait until they have identified a technological discontinuity—a sudden shift in demand to hypersonic engines, for example—and pounce.

Another strategic industrial market that Japan has targeted is advanced materials. The Japanese see advanced materials as the oil of the future, the raw material on which all the world's products will depend. Self-sufficiency in raw materials has been Japan's obsession since its earliest contact with the Chinese in the sixth century showed what an advanced power with its own resources could do. If the Japanese are unanimous on one thing (and they are not often unanimous, despite appearances), it is on the need to protect supplies of raw materials. With advanced materials, Japan has a shot at ensuring complete self-sufficiency in a key area for the first time in its history. We expect Japan's competing *keiretsu* to move toward this goal in lock step, pumping out technological breakthroughs at a breathtaking pace.

Traditionally, the government of Japan orchestrates industry-government cooperation to develop technology it considers strategic. In superconductors, this group consists of 112 different Japanese companies, all pulling together in a single consortium to meet Japan's long-term goals. MITI figures that Japanese firms will consume $90 billion annually in advanced materials like polymers, metals, ceramics, and composites by 2000.[8] This agency gave Hitachi and Fujitsu $190 million in 1990 to develop superconductor technology[9] and has called for an "aggressive" research program. Says MITI's Kenusuke Yamamoto, "We want to make this [Tokyo's International Superconductivity Research Center] the Mecca of superconductivity research."[10]

The structure of its large industrial groups will help Japan to become world leader in advanced materials. The *keiretsu* are built a little bit like human beings. There are vital organs, like the brain, heart, and lungs, that sit at the center. Then there are peripheral elements, like hands and feet. In firms like NEC and Fujitsu, for instance, computer chips are the center. The peripherals are the line divisions, whose job it is to buy these chips and turn them into more valuable systems, like computers. NEC's legendary chief Koji Kobayashi described this interaction of parts as a spinning top (see chapter 4).[11] Today the NEC top spins on an axis of silicon, and NEC is the world's number one

Keiretsu Structure

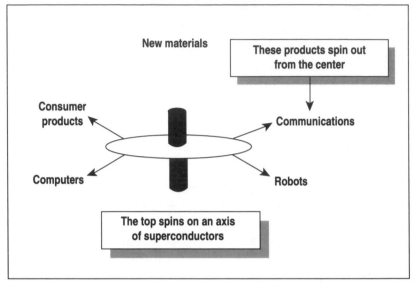

supplier of semiconductors. Tomorrow, the NEC top will spin on superconductors and other advanced materials. Indeed, Sumitomo Corp., the dominant member of NEC's *keiretsu,* has announced that it has already built a prototype superconductor magnet. This accomplishment put Japan ahead of the United States, even though companies like General Electric, Westinghouse Electric, and Du Pont have long planned to exploit superconductors.[12]

Materials supply, not customers, is at the heart of the *keiretsu;* as a result, Japan has done well in commodity silicon, especially computer memory chips. But the *keiretsu* structure reinforces Japan's highly centralized decision-making. Nothing significant can be done without the approval of the axis on which the top spins, and that axis is in Japan. Management has not figured out how to resolve the contention between overseas customers, the semiconductor foundries, and the line divisions (which use semiconductor raw materials). In short, the strains of vertical and horizontal integration are taking their toll. Japan may be able to dominate advanced materials, but it will have difficulty selling the products into which these materials are incorporated without major organizational change. Real change will require the inversion of the *keiretsu* system, putting customers at the center and making self-sufficiency in advanced materials secondary. A system designed to pump iron is incapable of solving real world customer problems.

Organizational inflexibility has been Japan's undoing in its most critical target market: information technology. Giants Fujitsu, Hitachi, NEC, Toshiba, and others have not been able to translate their strength in silicon into the kind of gains they hoped for in IT, despite what you might read in the press. The Semiconductor Industry Association has forecast that Japan's share of the world computer hardware market will rocket to 46 percent by 1994, more than four times its 11 percent share in 1984.[13] If such numbers panic the American public into supporting higher tariffs on Japanese chips, well, the SIA won't object.

The Prospects for Change

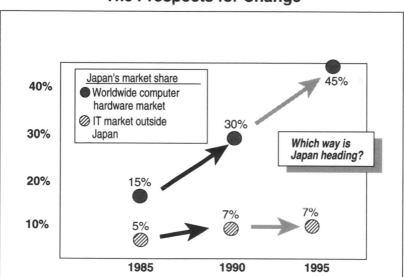

The fact is, the Japanese have done an excellent job in semi-conductors. And they have done just about everything they could to keep competitors out of Japan, one of the fastest-growing markets. Overseas, however, information system sales have been good, but not great. Japan Inc. had captured 7 percent of the international IT market by 1990, up from 5 percent in 1985. But we think Japan will have a tough time holding on to what it's already got. Even with acquisitions, we see Japan's 1995 international share of the IT market holding steady at 7 percent, and no better.

There has been a lot of panicky press about how the Japanese are about to destroy the U.S. software industry. A Massachusetts Institute of Technology study is quoted in *Business Week* as showing that Japanese "software factories" deliver 71 percent more debugged code per man-year than Americans do. And that failures per thousand lines are 56 percent fewer.[14] The theory is that by assembling code in well-tested modules, large amounts of bug-free code can be delivered. This may well work in a rigidly controlled environment where customers make no demands. But the experience of companies with large volumes of code, in say the tens of millions of lines, is quite different. Assembling modules to precise customer specifications can turn up a "day one" bug that no one has seen since the system was developed years before. Managing bugs and customers is a management problem of enormous proportions in which the software factory itself plays only a minimal role. Moreover, software factories located in Japan will be no comfort to customers whose system is down now, half a world away.

American companies now dominate the world's software market, employing 1.4 million people in the process.[15] But as Philippe Kahn, CEO of Borland International, a top-ranked publisher of off-the-shelf software for personal computers, says, "You have to be where the action is." The action is not in Japan, twelve time zones away from American customers. To get where the action is, some Japanese companies are investing in U.S.

software boutiques. CSK bought 100 percent of Micrognosis and 16 percent of Wavefront, ASCII bought 10 percent of database designer Informix and 70 percent of Hyperdesk, and the list goes on.[16] These acquisitions, however, are no substitute for complete corporate decentralization.

One large Japanese firm we worked with has a software lab in the United States. But the lab reports to Japan, not to its U.S. customers or even the U.S. line division. This means that when problems arise, the labs have to go through Tokyo to get permission to solve them. Also, because the people in the U.S. labs don't see themselves as playing an important role in the corporation—there is nowhere to get promoted to, for example—their approach to customer service is decidedly laid-back. A salesman for this company complained to us that "we're never going to get anywhere until our software people realize that this isn't a nine-to-five job." That says it all.

Without local control overseas, Japanese software will go nowhere. Already the most prominent American software houses have become thoroughly internationalized and will be hard to displace. Fully 60 percent of the sales of Microsoft come from abroad, for example, and 49 percent of Lotus Development's sales. Even Borland claims 34 percent of its sales offshore.[17] These are high export penetration rates for any firm and demonstrate a high degree of adaptability to local conditions.

Moreover, companies like Apple and Microsoft produce excellent Japanese software. Apple, for example, has pioneered the integration of its basic operating system—which can be laid out in almost any alphabetic language from English to Russian—with its *kanji*-based Japanese software. It is now possible to work simply and easily in both languages, even preparing multilingual documents that mix alphabets and *kanji*. This kind of adaptation to customer needs, when added to the enormous volume of applications available, is not easy to beat. Apple has rapidly become the machine of choice for those working in both Japanese and English and its sales growth in Japan has been stunning. NEC could have taken on this role, but by restricting itself to proprietary software in Japan, it has been virtually cut off from the growing world market for Japanese-vernacular computing.

Japan's industrial groups are well designed to exploit technological advances. But a Japan that lives by the technological sword can die by it. A new manufacturing technology or even a simpler way of doing complex and expensive things could allow competitors outside Japan to steal Japan's thunder. Today, for example, Sharp, Hitachi, and Toshiba dominate the $1.6 billion worldwide market for the flat displays used in calculators, portable computers, and similar devices. These are made from so-called active matrix liquid crystal displays. They are relatively expensive to make and use quite a bit of power. Production yield rates are poor and mass production is difficult.[18] Polyvision, a French division of a U.S.-based company, has developed a simpler, cheaper technology that could be used in small displays, like calculators, or in large ones, like televisions.[19] Polyvision produces crisp black-on-white images instead of the washed-out gray-on-gray typical of most calculator displays. With rapid commercialization, a technology like this could leapfrog years of work at domination of LCD markets by the Japanese. Some are even heralding this kind of breakthrough as the beginning of a prolonged decline in consumer electronics for the Japanese. (That assumes—and this is a big if—that American inventors don't opt to sell $10,000 products to the military and leave the $100 applications to the Japanese.) Similarly, as we have seen, American advances in parallel computing and workstations could set back three decades of Japanese advances in mainframe computers. Japan's domination of IT will remain a prediction, well publicized, never to arrive.

Consumer Products

Japan sees a big opportunity in the "digital revolution." Digital will blend consumer electronics, computers, communications, and entertainment into one unimaginably gigantic industry worth $1.3 trillion in 1990 and $3.0 trillion by 2000. That will be an extraordinary 17 percent of gross global product in 2000.[20] The advantage of digital is that it converts everything—music, pictures, words—into a simple, manageable computer code of ones and zeros. This means that movies, phone calls, faxes, photographs, books, records, cellular phones, home videos, and even home security systems can be blended into one set of identical numbers and manipulated at will. It is technically possible for images, sounds, and information from all these sources to be combined on your television or personal computer. Already, for example, Kodak sells cameras that store photos on compact disks for viewing on a TV or PC. Philips is now selling a multimedia product—part stereo, part videodisk, part everything else—under a name that suggests the limitless possibilities of digital, the "Imagination Machine." As Craig McCaw, chairman of McCaw cellular, says, "Everybody is in everybody's business today."[21]

For the Japanese, this is an extraordinarily risky time. Names like Panasonic, Kenwood, Pioneer, Denon, Sharp, and of course Sony are synonymous with consumer electronics. Each has a firm grip in one or several discrete markets. The digital blurring of their markets forces them to compete with each other on a host of new levels, and it introduces competitors, like Craig McCaw, that they never had to worry about before. Worse for Japan, digital is more than a blending of one product with another, it's the blending of products with software and services. That means, for example, that telephone and cable TV companies will compete with Canon in image development, with Minolta in fax machines, and with Panasonic in video entertainment. So will Apple Computer. Japan has not demonstrated the software, sales, and service skills necessary to meet these challenges, across so many fronts.

The substitution of service and software for hardware could actually shrink the market for consumer electronics. If consumers can pick up a single "information appliance" that does everything but wash the dishes for the price of today's television, they will. And the market will decline fast. Already a simple personal computer can eliminate thousands of dollars' worth of office hardware and ancillary services, like printing and layout work. And computers get cheaper by the day. When the same thing happens in consumer electronics, markets from answering machines to TVs and stereos could simply disappear. Look at the Japanese camera industry. High-end camera exports fell nearly 50 percent in the decade between 1981 and 1991 as consumers switched to hand-held videocameras instead. The autofocus low end is being replaced by no-tech disposables. An entire generation of Japan's photographic engineering has been made obsolete almost overnight. For some, like Canon, the answer has been to shift production overseas—80 percent of Canon's cameras are now made in China and Taiwan—and to look elsewhere for growth, like laser printers.[22] But laser printers are as vulnerable to technological discontinuity as cameras. The action is in software and services. Japan is not finding this shift so easy to master.

The digital revolution will stimulate a new generation of American entrepreneurs. This could prove the undoing of the Japanese in consumer electronics: they will face companies that are much more vigorous than the old industrial battlewagons overturned a generation ago. Worse, in most cases Japan's ruthless price cutting has bred brand loyalty out of the consumer markets in which Japan competes. This leaves little for Matsushita, say, if digital technology forces it to compete with Microsoft.

The hope that the digital revolution will force replacement of millions of old TVs and stereos out there is driving the Japanese hard in high-definition television (HDTV). In the rich countries, the market for standard televisions has long since matured: there are only so many VCRs and TVs that Americans and Europeans can buy. Unless, that is, all those VCRs and TVs suddenly become obsolete. The idea behind HDTV is to get every home to junk its existing TV, VCR, stereo, and personal computer, for a new technology that will keep those plants in Tokyo, Osaka, and Sendai humming. And keep the Koreans, like Goldstar, at bay.

To make sure their products are well enough priced to attract consumers, the Japanese are working furiously at driving the costs out of their analog technology and forcing down prices. Sharp cut its HDTV set prices by 70 percent to about $8,000 in the first few months after HDTV's introduction in Japan.[23] If Sharp can get its prices anywhere near the price of a standard TV set—and history says that someone in Japan will be able to do this—it hopes to precipitate an enormous wave of TV replacement before competitors can get to market.

Production is the culmination of years of work. But the Japanese have spent most of their time and effort on enhancing old-fashioned analog TV broadcasting. American companies, like AT&T, Zenith, and General Datacom, have leapfrogged the Japanese into a newer digital broadcast technology with cheaper and better transmission characteristics. But is the whole idea realistic? Asking consumers to replace their entire home entertainment investment, which may have been built up at some cost over many years and which works just fine, will not be easy. If the Japanese cannot persuade consumers to buy their HDTV sets, broadcasters, both over-the-air and cable, will not change the nature of the signals they transmit. Regulators could balk at the whole idea, leaving the Japanese out in the cold. At a minimum, regulators like the Federal Communications Commission and the European Commission are certain to reject Japanese broadcast standards for HDTV. Whatever standards are adopted, Japan's consumer electronics giants will continue to sell TVs, but the market may be much smaller than they anticipate.

The digital revolution may lead to counterrevolution in consumer electronics, giving Americans and Europeans a shot at reclaiming this lost territory. By contrast, American and European appliance manufacturers can only lose ground. The Japanese are uniquely qualified to make and sell consumer durables. There is absolutely nothing to stop them from pouring into the appliance market, adding to their dominance in microwave ovens by selling everything from washers, dryers, refrigerators, and stoves to air conditioners. Japanese companies already make all of these products, but they are often expensive and maladapted to Western consumer markets. These are the kind of technical shortcomings the Japanese have overcome before. Take Sanyo's "ductless air conditioning." The only obstacle to product takeoff is price.[24] At $5,000 it's just too expensive. But household names like Panasonic, Hitachi, Toshiba, and others could soon appear in America's and Europe's kitchens.

Services

Can Japan build a media empire capable of spanning the globe like Time Warner or Bertelsmann? At home the Japanese have no lack of publishing prowess, and the Japanese are quite as addicted to their TVs as Americans and Europeans, if not more so. Matsushita and Sony have bought their piece of the entertainment business. Does this mean that companies like Hachette, News Corporation, Paramount, Capital Cities/ABC, and International Thomson will be watching the exits?

The short answer is no: few markets are more consumer-driven than publishing, advertising, and films, and few businesses have to move more quickly to meet changing consumer tastes. This, in turn, means a lot of consumer input and very fast decision-making. An attractive alternative for Japanese companies, however, is the path taken by technical publishers like Elsevier in the Netherlands and Maxwell Scientific, the cash cow of the now defunct Maxwell group of companies in the United Kingdom. These firms are more easily centralized and customer relations are kept to a bare minimum. The Fukutake Publishing Company bought Berlitz International Inc., the language school, from the fast-dying Maxwell Communication Corporation. Fukutake is Japan's largest correspondence school company, among other things.[25]

Successful entertainment companies tend to be highly decentralized: good decisions are made locally. Moreover, the entertainment business is personality-driven rather than management-driven. The former head of Sony Music, Walter Yetnikoff, is said to have remarked that only prostitution is more of a people business.[26] Organic growth by Japan in the media business is unlikely, and success with acquisitions is elusive at best, in any industry. Japan will not take over entertainment; if you have any lingering doubts, just watch the children's movie *Otis and Milo,* about a dog and a cat on a long journey. Charming perhaps, but—well, slow. Disney is not at risk from Japan just yet.

Banking and finance are like entertainment in more ways than most bankers would like to admit. Mitsui has been banking for longer than the Old Lady of Threadneedle Street, the Bank of England itself. There is usually a bank close to the center of each *keiretsu* working to keep the entire organism liquid. The great names in Japanese banking, like Sumitomo and Mitsubishi, were built to serve the large commercial houses of the same name. Being at the heart of a *keiretsu* does not guarantee long-term growth and profitability, however. The *keiretsu* system may take the risks out of lending, but it also takes the judgment out of lending. In international banking, where judgment is everything, the lack of it is a major liability. Lately the judgment of Japanese banks has been seriously questioned. They rushed into California and by 1991 had 25 percent of banking assets there, including 20 percent of the property lending market. Much of this investment was funded offshore and booked at returns well below the cost of funds. And just in time for the biggest downturn in the California economy in a generation. The result has been large loan-loss provisions and even wholesale sackings at Mitsubishi Bank's Bank of California subsidiary.[27] So much for lifetime employment!

By some estimates the Japanese invested as much as $76 billion of their hard-earned money—much of it made selling to Americans—in U.S. properties between 1986 and 1991. Most of these investments have been made at the top of markets that are now worth 20 to 30 percent less than at their peak. In 1990, a Japanese investor paid $841 million for California's celebrated Pebble Beach Golf Club. Seventeen months later he sold it for $500 million.[28]

As if their investments abroad weren't bad enough, Japan itself has been rocked by a series of banking scandals that have touched some of the most revered banking names in the country.

Japanese decision-making makes good judgment difficult. Large groups at home and abroad must approve loans at every stage. Thus big, complex deals being hammered out in London or New York can be held up for days or even weeks while local Japanese managers burn the midnight fax transmitting clauses back and forth from Tokyo for further clarification. For European and American bankers used to instant decisions, working with Japanese bankers can be very frustrating. Japanese bankers have tried to get around this by prequalifying loans through months of studying prospective customers and agreeing on what the bank might do if that customer came to the market.

Cash without customer service will not play, either. The Japanese banks' idea of customer service is curious (though anything would be an improvement for the service-starved American banking public). Cashing a simple traveler's check in Japan has the trappings of an ancient animist worship ritualized over the millennia into a highly stylized Noh drama.

First, you must enter the bank. In Japan this means entering the temple of the august and requires careful mental preparation. Once inside the temple precincts you approach the counter: a long table running the length of the banking hall that separates bankers from their customers. There are comfortable chairs on either side of the counter for its full length. This makes the counter both intimidating—you can't just saunter up and plunk yourself down—and inviting. Getting served means asking, carefully, for permission to be seated. Once permission is granted and you are seated, you may ask to cash your check. At which point you will almost certainly be told very politely by a nice young woman in uniform wearing impeccably clean white gloves that she is very sorry but you must go up any number of flights to the foreign exchange department.

Once upstairs—if you don't read Japanese you may have to repeat this little inquiry on each floor till you reach the inner sanctum—you must go through this ritual all over again. This time, though, you will be proffered a small basket into which you will be invited to deposit your passport, countersigned checks, and a detailed form showing your name, address in Japan, and various other details. The teller will then pass this on to someone else, who will disappear with your passport to review the whole procedure with great care. The basket and contents will be passed on again at least one more time, usually to a man (the real authority in this transaction). Once everything is approved, the bank's chop (its seal, in effect) is applied, the cash is deposited in the basket, and the basket, cash, passport, and receipt are returned.

We have timed this process in many banks around Tokyo, chosen more or less at random to see if one bank has any service advantage over the other. In no case did we leave the bank in under twenty minutes, and we never saw fewer than four people handle the transaction. Nor did we see a single computer. For all this handling, however, everyone had to wear white gloves to ensure that the proper amount of physical detachment was maintained.

So long as their industry booms at home and abroad, generating lendable savings, Japanese institutions can lend money. But when the scissors effect of a domestic downturn and a recession in key foreign markets combines with poor lending judgment and an inability to gauge foreign markets, Japanese banks become highly vulnerable. It is not safe to bet on Japan's long-term strength in international banking.

The Telltale Signs

Suppose the Japanese do decide to make real changes. How will you know? Will you just wake up one day to find that they are all over you? That the business you have spent your life in, that held such promise, is sinking fast?

If you are wise, you will watch your Japanese competitors closely, looking for the series of warning signs outlined here. Good intelligence has to be systematic. We have based our telltale signs on Japan's four fatal flaws. Once you see these flaws being fixed, you know you've got problems.

You've got problems if your customers are seeing real decision-makers from Japan on a regular basis. Direct sales indicate that change is taking place, and in fact a number of Japanese companies have started to sell direct outside Japan. But most important, if your customers have instant access to decision-makers, it means that your competitors aren't holed up in Japan anymore and that they are listening. It won't be long before they start reacting to what they are listening to at your expense.

Once you know that decision-makers from Japan have relocated, along with their staff, into long-term assignments in your territory, you probably don't have long before being hit with something big.

You've got problems if your Japanese competitor moves one of its divisional headquarters out of Japan. NEC, for example, transferred control over its offshore PC business to the United

States. If real decisions are made overseas, by local managers, major change is underway.

How do you know that these executives are real executives and not "shadow" ones? You'll see foreigners in important line and staff roles in Japan itself. You'll see the central bureaucracies in Tokyo shedding employees by the tens of thousands. No less than a radical shift in the power structure will be necessary to make customers integral to their decision-making. Mass layoffs in Tokyo and Osaka would certainly be news, and layoffs are not out of the question—eventually Japan Inc. must deal with its overmanned staff organizations. More likely, Japan Inc. will "restructure" its excess managers into early retirement, suppliers, or new divisions. Since such reorganizations take a good two years before effecting change in the field, you can start counting off the months once the process begins.

You've got problems if your Japanese competitors start eliminating extraneous products. It means that they are focusing on what their customers think they do best, not what the company agenda in Tokyo calls for. In electronics, for example, all the big *keiretsu* currently manufacture virtually everything conceivable that plugs into the wall or runs on batteries. Once they specialize, these companies will be dangerous. Specialization is easy to track because it will be accompanied by a series of market exits, mergers, acquisitions, and so on. One early indicator: Matsushita said in 1992 that it would cut its fifty-thousand-item product line by up to 30 percent.[29]

When outsourcing to foreign companies takes place in a big way, you will know that *keiretsu* obligations are weakening and customer bonds are tightening. This is a certain sign that your Japanese competitors have decided to take the needs of their customers seriously. A shift away from vertical integration may be hard to identify. Many Japanese companies still brag in their ads about how they use all their own parts to assure quality (although NEC and Toshiba, among others, are sporting the "Intel Inside" logo in their PC ads). By the time your Japanese competitors have abandoned unnecessary activities in order to concentrate on the people who pay the freight, their customers, you will be in trouble if you are not ready. This is a change you must detect early.

You've got problems if Japanese engineers are all over your customers. It means that your competitors are trying to solve real customer problems, not shoehorn the latest technology into the market. People from the labs working with salesmen means customers, not high-tech pipe dreams, come first. When technological visions are abandoned for real frontline work, watch out!

The Clock Is Running

How much time do you have? A revolution in how Japan does business will take time, lots of time. Already leading-edge American and European companies are implementing the lessons of this book. These lessons are hard ones, to be sure, requiring the dismantling and rebuilding of your business. The answer is: act as if you don't have much time, get to work now, and you'll have a head start, regardless of what the Japanese do.

Should the Japanese commit themselves to change, they will act fast. They don't do things by halves. If the change comes, it will not take place incrementally, as do Japanese product refinements. If it happens, you will suddenly realize that your Japanese competitors are closer to your customers than you are. When faced with irresistible outside pressures, Japan has changed before. The most recent example occurred in 1985, when the dollar collapsed and a revolution in Japanese manufacturing took place in a few short years. Unfortunately for Japan, most of its problems today are internal, not external. As we have said before, the Japanese have no tradition of responding effectively to internal forces.

Building commitment is what will take time. Right now the symptoms have been identified by most Japanese managers we have met. They know they are not doing as well as they should in the industries they have targeted to replace cars. They are unsure of the causes, but they are learning. Forward-thinkers in Japan are moving in the right direction. Normally in Japanese business "nails that stick out get hammered down," but when the consensus is that customer integration is essential, everyone will be behind the change.

If Japan Fails

If Japan fails to develop its new target markets, the effects will be felt around the world.

In Japan, serious economic fallout will result. Japan has squandered much of its national treasure on financial speculation in the 1980s, and pressured by the United States to reduce its trade deficit it will spend much of the rest on infrastructure in the 1990s. Without large amounts of cash generated by the industries of the future, Japan will not be able to support its rapidly aging population. After the turn of the century, living standards could suffer. Stagnation at home would have an impact on every industry in which Japan now competes and significantly alter the competitive outlook in the industries it has yet to enter.

For its third world competitors, Japan's failure would reveal as bankrupt the *dirigiste* approach to industrial development. Japan would become an example of what not to do. For these countries, considerable opportunities will remain for commodity hardware sales. But higher-value activities will shift to the newly industrializing countries as well. India, for example, could become a major exporter of software during the next decade. To do so, Indian companies must learn from Japan's mistakes.

Europe, preoccupied with internal policies, will be least affected of all the world's regions. Europeans are unlikely to learn from Japan's mistakes—even to recognize them. They are even less likely to capitalize on the opportunities Japan misses.

America has the most to win and lose from Japan's failure. For a while, the preeminence of American high-tech leaders will go unchallenged if Japan pulls back. But without serious competition, American business will grow fat. Once the fins start sprouting, decline will not be far off, as the American car business so ignominiously demonstrated. The fact is, America needs Japan to keep from losing its edge. Japan is all that stands between America and decline. It's like the wolves and the caribou in the Canadian Arctic: the caribou feed the wolves, and the wolves keep the caribou strong.

—12—

Building the Customer-Driven Organization

You have seen all those headlines screaming that the Japanese are launching so many Pearl Harbor attacks on American and European industry. This kind of talk is scary. It is also misleading.

True, Pearl Harbor is one of those scars in American life that will never really heal. It was devastating, and it was delivered without warning. Every time someone says "cars" and "Pearl Harbor" in the same sentence, you are meant to draw the immediate inference that Japanese commanders Genda and Fuchida are flying again and that you are lying in your bunk on the *Arizona,* catching a few winks early on a Sunday morning. The Pearl Harbor talk is meant to terrify. And it does.

But no one can honestly say that the dismantling of the American and European auto industries by the Japanese is a sneak attack. The battering of General Motors, Chrysler, and Ford, and soon Renault, Fiat, and Mercedes, is not a "day that will live in infamy." Rather it is the result of several decades of mismanagement.

This chapter is about avoiding similar mismanagement, and in a curious way, about the real lessons of Pearl Harbor.

The first lesson is that Pearl Harbor was not a success. At Pearl Harbor the Japanese created, with their own hands, the atom bomb. This taught them a lesson they have not forgotten: they were defeated by a technology. They are now fanatical about exploiting promising technology.

Second, Pearl Harbor and all Japan's surprise attacks throughout Southeast Asia happened because the United States and Britain made two mistakes: they ignored all the small signs that had been gathering for months in advance; and they did not have a systematic way of interpreting Japanese military actions and intentions. Revisionism, which has had an inexplicably common appeal in recent years, confuses conspiracy ("Roosevelt knew all along!" or "Churchill planned the whole thing!") with stupidity. The same can be said for Western competitiveness today. If we had heeded the signs and had carefully and systematically interpreted them instead of spending our time in self-absorption, our automotive industries would not now be so troubled.

Pearl Harbor was, in effect, a spectacular failure of American management. In the half century since, we have had plenty of opportunity to examine Japanese industrial actions and intentions and do something about them. But many American managers are heading straight for Battleship Row twice in the same century. And the Europeans are lining up for whatever berths are left over.

Finally, the biggest lesson of Pearl Harbor is that it may not have been an altogether bad thing, in strictly military terms. Nagumo and his pilots took away even the possibility that U.S. commanders could rely on a battleship fleet ever again. This forced "management" to use its collective imagination and to completely rebuild itself around what was left—aircraft carriers. American carrier fleets still control the high seas a half century later.

In the same way, Japan is now saving Western managers from themselves. During the last two decades, Japan has targeted and eliminated our industrial battlewagons, one by one. Once again, we will have to use our imaginations and rebuild ourselves completely.

The job of Western management now is how to turn such radical restructuring into industrial leadership. This is what our book is all about. In this chapter we will review the steps you must take to translate the lessons of this book into action, to revamp your company's strategy, and to protect and enhance your own career. We will outline step by step what you need to do to integrate quickly and effectively with your customers and cut the Japanese, and your other competitors, off from theirs.

As you will have seen by now, our rules are simple; it doesn't take a Harvard MBA to figure them out. But it will take a lot of stamina and enduring corporate commitment to make sure that they are followed vigorously and consistently. You will have to change fast if you arc going to succeed. If not, your company is likely to sacrifice you in thc time-honored way—with the ax.

Managing Management

How do you completely restructure a company? The place to start is with corporate organization. Companies are put together like airframes. At low speeds an airframe made of plywood and canvas works fine. At supersonic speeds it simply falls apart. Competing successfully with the Japanese is like going through the sound barrier. Companies will have to be redesigned from the ground up, made of new materials, and powered with different engines to withstand the supersonic pressures of modern competition.

Plain-Vanilla Company

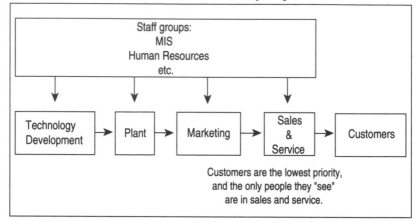

Shown here is a model of a plain-vanilla firm—the kind of propeller-driven plywood-and-canvas job that is common today—made of a few basic components: the labs, the plant (operations in a service company), the salespeople, and after-sales customer service. The overhead that ties our firm together is general management, including staff functions like accounting, human resources, and management information systems (MIS). Each part of the firm adds something—the labs design a product, the plant makes it, and salespeople sell it. To compete successfully against the Japanese, each part must be reengineered. Individually, these changes may seem minor, but the cumulative effect is a revolution in company management.

The best way to start rethinking your company's management is to identify your customer's biggest problem. This is not as easy as it sounds. VCR manufacturers think consumers want hand-held computers and give them palm-size devices with dozens of tiny buttons and cryptic codes. VCR Plus recognizes that all they really want is a simple, one-step way of recording shows they like.

What if you are selling to United Parcel Service? UPS sells the speedy and cost-effective movement of parcels across vast expanses of geography, or just next door. But how many of UPS's suppliers understand the impact of even a small change in the price of fuel on UPS's bottom line? Selling to UPS means helping UPS control fuel consumption.

Once you have figured out what your customers' biggest problems are, rewrite your corporate mission to solve this problem. Sounds simple, doesn't it? Just rewrite a few words based on what your customers want. Take a look at your current mission. It is probably as vague and undirected as that of BellSouth. BellSouth provides telephone service to millions of people in the U.S. Southeast. In its annual report it says that its mission is "meeting customer needs through investments in a dynamic, ubiquitous, efficient network." This is all very nice, but it says absolutely nothing about what these needs are and how, exactly, BellSouth will meet them except by spending a lot of money.

Just as likely, your mission is not undirected. It is misdirected. Here is an example of something we saw recently: an industrial company with a very precise mission that is entirely self-absorbed. On the left is what the company thinks of itself; on the right is what customers think. The comparison is painful.

Company Mission	Customer Response
We want to be number one.	We couldn't care less.
Company Values	**Customer Response**
Excellence is our only standard.	Their products failed and we lost business. We will sue.
We are a team.	We were promised a new product yesterday that they dropped today.
We do more for our customers than anyone else.	We have strict cost goals; we don't want fancy gizmos we don't need.
What we promise, we deliver.	We have made promises to our customers based on what they said we would get last quarter. They just delayed it for another year.
We are innovative and willing to change fast.	They are pushing us to buy things we don't need just to meet their sales goals.
Our people are our strength.	They are mismanaged.

Almost every company has a similar litany of goals and values in its mission statements. The problem for most firms is that they don't understand that all these platitudes do nothing for their customers.

The smartest thing you can do, we advised one company, is to take your customer's biggest problem and post it somewhere in your shop where everyone who works for you can see it. Next to this, show your solution to this problem: what you are committed to doing to make your customers' lives easier. This way you know, and your customers know, exactly what you will do for them. Everyone will see how well you measure up to your commitments. This must be your first step. Unless your firm consistently does something useful for its customers, it cannot long be profitable. Everyone must know what this "something" is supposed to be. Imagine walking into your local bank and seeing its commitment to clear all deposited checks overnight.

Making such a public promise is risky. If you fail, everyone—customers, competitors, employees, and shareholders—knows about it. But making a public promise forces you to establish clearly what it is that bothers your customers most. This way you create a mission that everyone in the firm can hang on to, and you avoid goals like "increase earnings per share by 15 percent annually" that have no day-to-day application. Better still, a public promise creates a simple philosophy for people management. "This," it says, "is what we are supposed to be doing." If someone isn't helping meet that goal, he or she should be reassigned, even fired.

If you don't make promises in public, no one in the company—and certainly none of your customers—will understand the purpose of all your hard work. Sales will suffer. Also, people will be hired and fired for reasons that are not clear to them, making customer interaction more difficult than ever. One company we worked with had big customer service problems. Without first asking itself what it really does for its customers and therefore what the customer service VP should be doing, the company simply fired the guy. Maybe it was the right move. But who's to know? Without a commitment everyone can work with, firing someone is a meaningless gesture. The service problems, by the way, got worse.

Retired New York mayor Ed Koch used to walk up to crowds and while the TV cameras were rolling he'd ask, "How am I doing?" (Actually, it was more like "How'm I doin'?") Being New Yorkers, they told him, loudly and on TV for everyone to see. Koch took a risk. The public could have given him the Bronx cheer. But he knew that if he waited for the elections to come around, it would be too late to find out. So don't wait for the quarterlies. Ask your customers, "How are we doing?"

Have monthly staff meetings to discuss the discrepancy between your mission and how your customers say you are doing. Use the results of these meetings to set monthly priorities for your team.

You can't make this work unless all real decisions are made in the line. Corporate staff must be eliminated. As quoted by American economist Milton Friedman, Gammon's Law says that bureaucracies are "like 'black holes' in the economic universe, simultaneously sucking in resources and shrinking in terms of 'emitted' production."[1] This law applies equally to government and business bureaucracies. The best staff organizations are lean, and focused on improved customer relations. The worst are fat and bloated and spend their time on internal meddling.

This is a problem for many companies. In most, staff groups bind the firm together. They manage relationships between divisions, they plan, and they manage the corporate culture. This is a costly exercise with no measurable output. With no way to measure their effectiveness, staff easily become bloated and inefficient. Then they get cut, sometimes tens of thousands of them at a time. It makes more sense to put these people to work doing something useful where it really counts: with customers. They can do more from the front lines than by trying to lead from the rear at HQ. What's more, they will be forever loyal, and so will your customers.

Traditionally managed companies operate somewhat like a child's game of telephone.

Service gets a call from a customer describing his desperate need for a doorknob that he can't seem to find anywhere.

Service tells sales. Sales dismisses the matter—"We don't carry the product"—until service explains that this is for a very important door, the bathroom door.

Sales tells sales management. Sales management has a meeting to discuss the sales potential of bathroom doors. Sales management calls marketing and tells marketing that it really ought to research the market for bathrooms. It's booming and we're missing a big opportunity.

Marketing management has several meetings. It discusses the marginal propensity of baby boomers to bathe and concludes that there really is something here. Marketing calls manufacturing.

Manufacturing doesn't have time for this and calls the labs. It tells the labs that there has been an unexplained increase in bathing and that the labs really ought to get on the case.

The labs have many, many meetings over the next two years and report to management that the firm's customers are particularly unclean and need a bath, very badly by all accounts.

But, the labs report, we just happen to be developing a new soap for the job and it will be ready in three years.

Delighted to see a customer need so well matched with the firm's ability to develop new products, management is convinced. Soap it is, management rules, but let's allow four years, just to be safe.

In these companies that play telephone, everyone learns only one thing about customers: they stink!

The company's staff, of course, is managing by the numbers, by objectives, by necromancy, by anything that doesn't really involve customers. Companies built like this suffer from two major disadvantages. First, the only people who are accountable to customers—the folks in sales and service—are far removed from anyone with any real authority. Second, a large staff organization keeps it that way. Thus management is insulated both from its customers and from the process of solving customer problems. With disadvantages like these, it is not too hard for the Japanese to compete.

The best way to compete with the Japanese is to make sure that everyone, not just sales, deals with customers all the time. Do this in several steps. To begin with, turn the company on its head so that all employees have the authority to make changes. This way the company hears from its customers everywhere and all at once. Everyone must respond.

There are plenty of people who will think they should be spared the unpleasant duty of actually having to work with your customers. They never see the light of day and prefer it that way. No firm can compete successfully over the long term, however,

The Company on Its Head

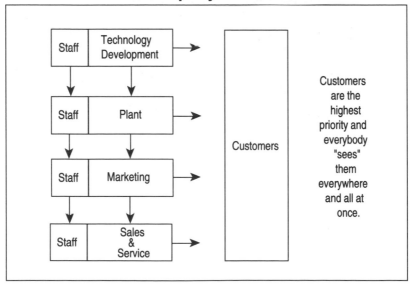

unless everybody is exposed to customers. Nothing good can come from a firm where there are managers who don't know who signs the paycheck and why. Redo the organization chart to ensure that everyone understands his or her new role. Follow a simple rule: employees who don't design, make, or sell a product or service *and* work with customers should be reassigned. Even human resources people, for example, must spend time with customers, to understand their priorities and, by extension, your employment requirements.

Next, get rid of the biggest barrier to customer integration: management clutter. Too many firms are overstaffed or undermanaged or both. The key to success is a flat, four-layered matrix. In the matrix, everyone reports to a superior and to a customer.

You will find that this matrix imposes strict size limitations on the firm. A firm can only grow as large as the number of direct reports the managers in each layer can handle. If ten direct reports are manageable, a firm can't grow much beyond ten thousand peo-

Keep Close to Your Customers

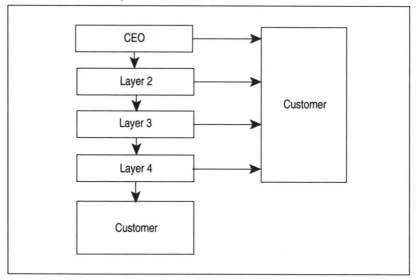

ple. Some companies are experimenting with close to twenty direct reports, and that may be the limit of the envelope—about 160,000 employees. It is also worth noting that there are not many companies bigger than 160,000 who have much to brag about these days.

Now the organization is connected to customers in just about every way. Since all employees, no matter where they work and no matter how they rank in the company, are only a phone call away from a customer, the firm's responsiveness is maximized. Moreover, since the entire operation is only four layers deep, decision-making should be fast, efficient, and effective.

Next, list all the issues now on your desk. How many are customer-related issues? If you are like most managers, very little of what you do on a daily basis has anything to do with customers. Make customer service your priority. Insist that the only decisions you will make will be those dealing with customer satisfaction. Should someone be promoted? Yes, if this promotion demonstrably improves customer service. If not, well . . .

Doing the Organization Chart

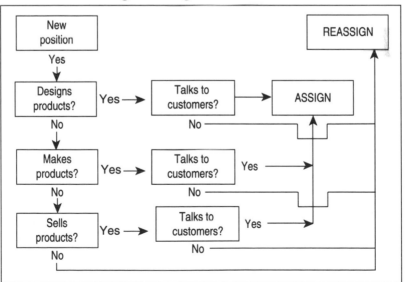

Soon you will find that no one will ask you to decide anything that has nothing to do with customer service improvement. Before long, customer service will be the sole criteria for all internal decisions. Here's a decision we *know* will be painful: should you play golf with your customers? Only if you can measure the resulting service improvement, and we doubt that you can!

Whatever you do, you can't get away from the basics of administration. But you can change the context in which administrative issues are decided, and you can delegate a lot. Make it a rule to pass all administrative questions to subordinates—they will love the challenge.

Now that you have made over your organization, double-check to see that everything is in order. Key customer problems have been identified. Every person in the company does one of three things—design products and services, make them, or sell them. There are no more than four management layers. Customers are well integrated into each layer and into each functional element of the organization. Finally, make sure that *everybody* sells. Your company is now ready to compete against the Japanese. It is simpler and more directed than before, and ready to move fast to cut your Japanese competition off from their customers.

Managing Your Design Process

The farther your design center from your customers, the worse your products will be. When the development people are a great distance—measured in miles or layers of organization—from customers, decisions will be right only by accident, not by design. If you run your communications like our game of telephone, you will be vulnerable to anyone who can connect with your customers more easily than you can. And once your competition figures out how to manage that relationship, you'll be dead.

Just jump into the box and fold your hands neatly so the competition can nail the lid down good and tight.

To prevent this from happening, use two tools: customer oversight and sign-off.

For customer oversight, put your customers in your design center. If you are selling industrial products, give customers a permanent home there, with offices they can go to, passes allowing unescorted access to your facilities, and the ability to work directly with your people when, where, and how they want to. You will reap immeasurable benefits. If you sell to consumers, offer them all-expense-paid trips to your design center to discuss future products. Get people from the community—try school trips—to go through the place regularly. However you do it, get people through your operations every single day. It keeps the place on its toes and forces you to identify what your customers really like about what you do. It's also a great way to find out what they don't like and to change it. If this makes you nervous, remember that if your design center isn't worth seeing, your product isn't worth buying.

Take a selected group of important customers and turn them into an oversight committee to "manage" your design center. This gives them an opportunity to tell you what they do and don't like about your products but also what they think of your operations and way of doing business. You will learn lots, very inexpensively.

Try co-location. Locate design centers near customers, where possible, and always integrate design centers into your manufacturing operations. This way they are close to the people who matter: their customers and the people who make what they design.

Your design centers will not be insulated and will have no excuse for developing products that your customers neither want nor need. If your customers don't want it, don't design it. Don't set technological direction *a priori;* set it as a result of clearly stated customer requirements. Use customer oversight to get customers to approve development plans. Have them formally approve your product and service ideas before you start. If your people cannot get customer approval for what they are doing, there is clearly little value in the exercise.

Use customer sign-off: Everywhere on your product development flow charts where you now have a periodic internal review, put in a customer review instead. If the lab people say this is too difficult to do, redesign the process. If customers don't approve of your progress, stop development immediately.

Customer oversight and customer sign-off ensure that developers can justify their plans to real customers every step of the way. And it ensures that everyone gets the message: if your customers don't want it, you don't do it.

You won't have to worry that your customers will leak your good product ideas. Customers have too much leverage to lose by doing this. They want to increase their control over what you are doing, not lessen it.

You will benefit significantly. You will not waste money on what customers don't want, and when your ideas materialize, your customers will already have budgeted for them. We were once shown a top-secret project that a company had spent tens of millions to develop. This project, we were told, would turn around the company's fortunes and pry the competition loose from several key markets around the world. But when we asked the product managers how the company knew that its customers actually wanted what it had spent so much money to develop, they assured us that market research told them so. No one in the firm had actually talked to a customer directly. The project failed, and the company's fortunes plummeted.

Managing Your Production and Operations

Like your design process, production and operations are often isolated far from customers. Most companies believe that their factories have nothing directly to do with their customers and that there is no obvious reason for integrating customers into them. We believe that as with laboratories, anything that can be done to integrate customers into the process should be done.

Start by making workers responsible for the cleanliness of their place of work. To welcome customers, your plants should be spotless. Visitors should feel, quite literally, that they can eat off the floors with more confidence than they can eat in your company's cafeteria. In our experience, as we have said, market share is directly proportional to plant cleanliness. We are also convinced that if the plant is a mess, everything else is too.

If you are making industrial products, make your customers your "virtual" plant managers, having plants report, in effect, to them and not to you. Start by listing your top ten customers. Give some of their top people unescorted twenty-four-hour-a-day access to your operations. Have them set your customer service goals. Post these goals, and the names of the customers who set them, widely throughout your plant. Next to these goals, post large, easy-to-understand charts showing how well you are doing. Measure plant performance, for bonuses, raises, and promotions, *exclusively* by how well the plant meets these goals.

If you are making cars, do the same thing. Instead of posting production numbers so that everyone can see them, show after-sales service problems instead. Get everyone on the plant floor to work to the one thing that will bring customers back to the showrooms: how well the car ran after it was bought. This forces the plant to accept responsibility for real customer problems.

Consider Disney World. This is the ultimate in customer integration into the "plant." At Disney World, customers experience Disney products and services hands-on. They even pay for the privilege. Disney does everything possible to make customer experiences of Disney, in all its manifestations, so enthralling that they will be brand-loyal forever. Is there a business in the

world that could not benefit from applying Disney's lessons to its
business?

Very often customer service problems can be solved more
quickly by changing your operations and procedures than by anything else. Speed of delivery is a perfect example. Nobody likes
to wait. Every operation should work like retail: the moment customers order, they take delivery. To improve your performance,
you will have to change how you make and deliver your products. Customer satisfaction may be significantly improved if
order-to-ship intervals are shortened. What's more, faster delivery will do wonders for your cash flow.

We recently had an illuminating experience with delivery
speeds. We wanted to buy a scanner to scan pictures from books
and so on for use with one of our personal computers. Having
dutifully read up on the best buys, we ranked three—one from
Xerox, one from Hewlett-Packard, and one from LaCie.

Xerox got the best press but we couldn't find a dealer. Xerox people in the Yellow Pages had never heard of the device.
We finally got a toll-free 800 number from somewhere and
called. A machine answered and asked us to leave our name and
number. And that was the last we heard from Xerox.

Hewlett-Packard had done a lot of advertising for a new
model that was also favorably reviewed, though not as well, in
our view, as Xerox. But, with no joy from Xerox, we went after
Hewlett. H-P has plenty of dealers, but none of them could
promise a product in less than a month. And they didn't seem too
worried about it either.

So we called our third choice, LaCie. They took our call and
credit card number right away and shipped us the scanner overnight.

Here is a simple example of how a buyer's third choice can
become a first choice simply because one company understood
the impact of order-to-ship intervals on customer service and the
others, with supposedly better products, did not. Our scanner was
up and running within twenty-four hours. And *our* customer in

turn was delighted with the new service that we were able to provide. Within forty-eight hours of our call to LaCie, we had paid for our scanner many, many times over.

Once you have decided to manage your plant to meet customer service requirements, it is important to disclose these goals to your suppliers. They need to know how your customers are measuring you and how they too will be measured. Then rate suppliers every month on how well you do. Make sure they know that failure to make the grade every month means serious problems in your business relationship.

You will be pleasantly surprised by how quickly suppliers can add imaginative solutions to customer problems that seem intractable. Most companies are nervous about saying too much to suppliers for fear that it increases their leverage, especially over price. But they miss the advantages that they can gain with their customers by giving their suppliers a chance to solve their most trying problems. The improvement in customer service and market share will far outweigh any loss in leverage over price.

Cut costs continually. Cost-cutting is not a once-a-business-cycle thing. The firms that get into trouble are the ones that have not drawn the relationship between high customer service and low costs. They wait until it is too late and then have to take a machete to their organization. Then the *Wall Street Journal* does a story on their sorry shape, which gets even sorrier. Especially if shareholders don't like what they read.

Smart companies make cost-cutting a way of life. They cut costs all the time. They don't wait for competitors to do it for them. And they don't wait for business to slow down, forcing their hands before the shareholders do.

Continual cost-cutting raises quality and improves customer service. No scrap, as Japanese car companies are discovering, means no defects. Scrap costs, therefore, are functionally related to quality. As one goes down, the other goes up. Also, no product defects means no returns, recalls, or withdrawals. In short, push down costs and customer service will go up. It pays, therefore, to push costs down every day. Cost reduction should be a continuous process and the full responsibility of everyone.

As we mentioned in chapter 6, one Japanese car manufacturer in the United States is doing more than reducing costs, it is turning "green," something else that should be of concern to every manufacturer in Europe and the United States. According to this company's theory, a high-quality, low-cost plant with no waste also eliminates environmental costs and associated contingent liabilities. Here is a classic case of a Japanese manufacturer cutting right through issues that Western manufacturers spend untold billions worrying about. The company wants suppliers to take back everything it doesn't use, like packaging. The only output of its plant should be cars.

Not only does this mean fewer defects and therefore lower costs than for competitors, it also means a sharp drop in interference from environmental authorities and a lessened likelihood of being sued. Nobody wants to be the next Johns-Manville, meeting all today's standards but failing to anticipate tomorrow's.

The most important decision you will make in speeding up your operations is what to outsource. Our rule here is simple: if someone else can do it better, let him. The only things you should be making in your plants are those things that have a measurable impact on customer service. If you can't demonstrate precisely how your customer can benefit from an internally sourced component or process, subcontract it.

We were thoroughly shaken once on a tour of a Deming Prize–winning operation in Japan to see that the company had convinced itself that maximizing internal sources of supply somehow guaranteed quality. Well, the quality was there, and the company had the prize to show for it. But sales were evaporating and costs were extremely uncompetitive. No one had made the connection between costs and quality or between customer service levels and costs. In fact, the plant had no customer service information at all to go by. And management couldn't understand why its costs were so out of line.

The problem was easy to diagnose: excessive vertical integration had forced the plant to use internal sources regardless of cost. Outsourcing the lot would have given the plant the cost and quality leverage it needed to do something useful for its customers. But, working to the agenda of its sister divisions, this company had few meaningful alternatives. Had management taken control of the situation and insisted that product design and manufacturing procedures be run to strict customer criteria, this company would have had its Deming Prize *and* sales leadership. As it is, it has the prize and not much else.

Rearrange production lines frequently. Every six months, if possible. Production lines should be flexible enough to be rearranged by plant personnel whenever they think they can improve customer service by doing so. People on the floor know how to get the most out of the process, so the process must be able to accommodate their ideas. If the system is too rigid, all the small innovations that raise customer service levels will be stifled.

Rebuild production lines every twenty-four months. There are few industries left where two-year-old processes are still cost-effective. It is better, therefore, to plan on change every two years than to wait for a competitor to schedule changes for you.

This way you are never out of the change "mode." Change will become a way of life for your plants, and they will always be reinvigorated. Allan Toomer, formerly a vice president at Northern Telecom and one of America's leading manufacturers, said to us, "It's not the cost of parts; it's the process, the process, the process."

Managing Sales and Service

High customer service levels are self-correcting: once your customers know who to call and how loud to scream, human nature takes over. They won't give you the opportunity to forget the lessons they have taught you. Thus, customer integration is risky.

Even a small drop in customer service levels will result in a sharp drop in sales.

To make sure that service stays top-notch and that customers don't defect, corporate officers have to be in the front lines, not back at headquarters, where they aren't doing any good for customers. All executives should be moved forward, into sales and service. At one Japanese firm looking for answers to collapsing market share worldwide, we asked each senior executive in turn when he had last spoken to an American customer. One could recall a bit of banter at a trade show six months previously. The embarrassment was acute, to say the least.

To make forward positioning work, the organization has to be flat and responsive.

One retailer we know fired a store manager when she changed a store window display to attract local customers. The retailer, a small but national chain, had decided that all its window displays should conform precisely to the company image. The manager, put in charge of a new outlet in New York's trendy SoHo district, noticed that sales in her store were going nowhere. So she took the initiative and started changing the window displays to see what would bring in customers. Sales started to increase. But the chain preferred lower sales to local initiative and got rid of the manager. The store has since closed and the chain has been sold.

In another case, a specialty retailer with dozens of outlets wouldn't let its store managers make buying decisions. Every store coast to coast had to take the same merchandise, like it or not. Indeed, company buyers never asked store managers what their customers wanted, nor did they ever visit stores or see customers. Since taste varies widely between, and even within, regions, the retailer was stuck with mixed sales performance and lots of inventory. Their solution to this problem was to give managers more discounting flexibility to get rid of the stuff. When this didn't work they simply closed a third of their outlets. A better approach would have been to fire the buyers and let store managers buy what their customers wanted.

Firms selling to commercial and industrial accounts have the same problem. Take the case of American Express. Amex believes that it offers better service to the merchants who accept its American Express cards than competitors Visa and MasterCard. This, it believes, justifies charging merchants a higher sales commission on card use than either Visa or MasterCard charges.

Try telling this to an American Express account representative. These Amex employees know that their customers' biggest problem is cash flow. They also know that most merchants believe that because Visa and MasterCard ask for smaller commissions, Visa and MasterCard do more for merchant cash flow than American Express does. To the sales rep this translates into the unpleasant task of chasing down merchants who try to boost their margins by "suppressing" the Amex card and asking customers for Visa and MasterCard instead. The more chasing they do, the less selling they do and the harder it is to make their numbers. The short of this is that American Express is frustrating its customers and the Amex people who work with those customers.

In effect, American Express is asking its customers to act against what they see as their own best interests. This is just the kind of weakness in corporate policy that the Japanese home in on with deadly accuracy. Amex has magnified this weakness by telling sales reps to talk merchants out of their dissatisfaction rather than simply fixing the problem.

Because American Express account representatives are at the bottom of the corporate pecking order, they have little influence on company policy. Customer service decisions are made far from the front lines and, as a result, are often wrong. Recently, for example, American Express has started picking fights with merchants, publicly cutting off some of them. This simply angers the rest and convinces them that Amex has little understanding of what customer service is all about. As this war between American Express and its customers goes on over their heads, the morale of the sales force declines and so too does their ability to position American Express as an exclusive and valuable service.

Cutting off customers is like cutting off your nose to spite your face. Amex could easily solve its problems by giving account reps in the field the discretion to offer competitive rates. Once its merchants were convinced that American Express's primary mission is to improve their cash flows and help preserve their margins, the Amex account reps would be well positioned to pour on attractive extras at lucrative rates. However, as long as American Express deprives account reps of the authority to solve customer problems, the company will be increasingly vulnerable.

The example of American Express and the example of the two retailers teach an important lesson: the only people who should make policy decisions are those who work with customers daily. This means giving sales people executive power. It also means flattening the organization to push executives out into the field. Indeed, even talking to your sales people will be beneficial. It will boost morale and you will learn a lot more about what is really going on.

Flattening the organization is vital to your interests because, as we have seen, your Japanese competition suffers the Amex problem in megadoses. It pays therefore to reorganize sales and service operations to hit the Japanese where they are most vulnerable—with customers.

The key to flattening the organization is making sure that *all* officers are assigned to customers, not just those responsible for marketing and sales. Management's mission in the flat organization is twofold. First, management must understand the difference between its idea of service excellence and customers' needs. Second, management must support salesmen directly, going out on important calls, assisting at presentations, and piloting customer problems through the corporation.

We recently visited a firm where "communication" was all the rage. Because management wasn't getting its message across and customer complaints had risen to alarming levels, just about all personnel had been assigned "communications schedules" on which they had to report how they communicated, to whom, and how often. This monumental waste of time also meant having people who collected and monitored all this useless paper. In short, this company was making its problem worse, not better. The solution is to organize the company so that communication is built in. "Organize to communicate," we told them, "don't communicate to organize." Keep the company flat and make management accountability clear for customers to see, and use.

One experience sticks with us. A CEO we know prided himself on his somewhat grand role, never going anywhere without an entourage. He was good at "entrances" in the style of the kings of France. Soon his customers began complaining. He even got in a fight with one of them by bragging to its chairman—who was frantically trying to reverse an earnings slide—about an acquisition he had just made. This CEO was constitutionally incapable of going out on a simple sales call and would never have deigned to answer the complaint line. This attitude cost him at least $500 million worth of business, and the story isn't over yet.

In a flat organization, an executive can take the customers' position and win, even if he must force a confrontation. When the manager wins, the customer wins. In a hierarchical organization, it is common for the manager to lose, which means that customers will soon have one fewer supplier to mess up their plans. For this reason, deep, hierarchical organizations are easy pickings for Japanese competition: they are not designed to serve customers and can be neutralized quickly by a firm with a better product. A flat organization, by contrast, is next to impossible to dislodge.

Our rule, as we have said, is that the only people who should make decisions are those who work with customers every day. To make any decisions worthy of the name, therefore, every manager should spend one week a month with customers. This means going out with sales and service people on regular calls and working the front counter, not doing a round of golf or going to lunch.

If you are a senior manager selling to large companies, save peer-to-peer executive meetings for those times when you are on a sales campaign and have arranged meetings for this purpose. Visit sales offices unannounced. These visits should be low-key, enabling you to concentrate on the type of grass-roots problems that might get covered over by worried sales and service people. Go on sales calls. During these calls, keep your mouth shut. Let sales people sell and service people service. Ill-timed comments, especially by those untrained in sales, can be damaging. So just listen. Listen very carefully. If you have problems with the presentation, let your people know after the customer meeting, not during it. This way you will gain the kind of access to low-and middle-level people in the buying organization that is essential to building customer confidence.

Upside - down Organization

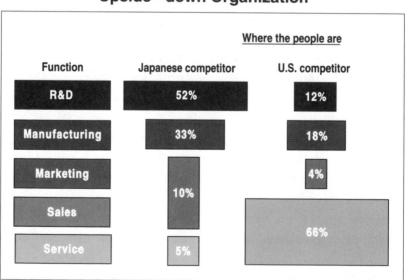

Avoid the upside-down organization. Since most of your Japanese competitors are technology-oriented, they will hire lots of engineers. In the chart here, we have compared two companies we examined, one Japanese and one American, in the same industry.

The Japanese organization in this example is upside-down. Its resources are all placed upstream, where they can have little impact on customers. In this case, Japanese sales are falling, technology is lagging, and the company has begun to consider market exit. The antidote is to do what the American competitor has done: put at least two thirds of your people in sales and service.

Have executives develop account plans. Too many account plans are developed by salespeople without the authority to offer customers what they really need. The result is that customers don't get what they want, opportunities are missed, and the competition takes the business. *This work must not be delegated to staff.* The best way to make sure that senior management understands customers is to have each manager sit down at a personal computer and work up an account plan. Executives who personally prepare detailed, easily updated, and computer-based account plans are more responsive to customer needs than those who wait for their minions to submit sheets of useless paper.

For commercial customers, account plans cannot be done in a vacuum. Each executive must meet with senior and middle customer management from every functional area—technology, manufacturing, marketing, sales, and service—to determine customer goals.

Then managers must take three steps. First, they must determine the deepest business needs of customer management—exactly what the chief executive officer is trying to do with the company. Second, they must carefully assess obstacles preventing the customer from achieving those goals. Finally, they must identify what they can do to help customers reach these goals.

Having done this, managers will take customer concerns seriously and develop a battle plan that really works. To paraphrase Dr. Johnson, "Depend upon it, sir, when an executive knows he is to be hung by his customer upon the morrow, it concentrates his mind wonderfully." At budget time, management's direct responsibility for accounts will give it a clear idea of what will work and what will not. It will know what can be squeezed out of the budget. Nothing is better guaranteed to drive customers insane than service-level cutbacks in the name of budgetary restraint. One company we worked with decided as soon as sales began to slide that its customer service desk had to go! Its customers went too.

Every manager should try this: follow a random shipment from the plant floor to the customer's door, then stick around to see what happens. We once ordered some personal computers. They arrived and we got them all up and running in an hour or so. A week later the manufacturer sent three guys over to install them! With the expense of this useless service call, the manufacturer lost whatever it had hoped to make. Imagine what would have happened if the finance VP had turned up for this.

Nothing beats seeing for yourself how real products are installed by real service people for real customers. You can see what is done, and more revealing, what is not done.

If you make washers and dryers, go out with an order to see this process firsthand. Get a good handle on how your products are used and the problems people have getting them to work. What you learn will do more to cut down on service problems than anything else. Not only will problems be obvious to you, but when people see that the boss is hopping off the back of a delivery truck to find out how customers like the product, they are going to make damn sure that the boss has a nice day.

One of us once ordered a set of four home air conditioners. Because they were for rooms of different sizes, each machine came from a different supplier best rated for each room. Now, you would think that all air conditioners are more or less the same. Not so. Some were poorly packed and hard to install. Others were difficult to use and had instructions designed for Ph.D.'s. The moral of the story is to make it easy to install, easy to turn on, and easy to use. Like Campbell's Soup, you just warm it up. Making your products as easy to use as Campbell's Soup will give you great respect for Campbell's. Its soup uses simple packaging that hasn't changed in living memory. You can cook it over a campfire or on a $6,000 Garland range.

Take your top customers, or, if you are selling retail, your top stores. Then create a "buddy" system. Take all the top managers in the firm and assign one to each customer. This way your top people will have to take personal responsibility for the performance of a significant part of your business. The accounting people will almost certainly scream, as will the legal department, the human resource types, and others. How they do will be a measure of their real capabilities and of whether they know the firm well enough to solve its customers' real problems. Having finance managers work cash registers every now and then will give them a new perspective on running the company's point-of-sale system to maximum effect.

If you are like most people, you avoid the customers who are hardest to deal with. This is a serious mistake. Your toughest customers have the biggest monkeys on their backs. They probably have the most difficult time working with you because they are doing things no one else has thought of, yet.

Serve them and you will manage to kill two birds with one stone: you will improve your customer service by focusing on the hardest customers, and you will gain invaluable competition-beating insights into future uses for your products.

To serve your "worst" customers best, twin the CEO with the meanest, nastiest customer the firm has and make it the CEO's personal goal to turn that customer into a pussycat within a year. Meet monthly. *You* may not have any agenda items. *They* certainly will. There is no trick here: just talk to customers about their problems. Many companies are terrified of talking frankly to their customers. Usually with reason. They would take a beating. Our philosophy is different. If you're not taking a beating from your customers every single day, you're not close enough to know what their real problems are. And you're in no position to solve them.

So be open. Let customers tell you what you're doing wrong. Don't argue with them. Don't defend your firm—that's fruitless. And don't make promises about what you will deliver and at what price—that's the salesman's job. Several years ago the makers of the popular analgesic Tylenol discovered to their horror that someone was tampering with their packaging, replacing Tylenol with cyanide and killing customers. The makers moved rapidly to clear the shelves of their product and to cooperate fully with health authorities, retailers, and the general public. The Tylenol case proved that there is only one way to deal with customer problems: head on. Market share was preserved and Tylenol's reputation fully restored. Don't wait for the competition to poison your relations with your customers. Listen to your customers carefully and solve their problems, now. Get the full picture. Don't flinch.

If you manage a grocery store or a chain of grocery stores, exchange your suit for a smock and spend at least half a day every week running a till. Chat with all your customers, and not about the weather. Spend another half day a week working the service desk. At least twice a quarter, target a neighborhood near one of your stores. Take a stroll. Knock on doors. Talk to people. "Do you shop at my store?... Tell me what's right with it. What's wrong with it. I'm the boss, I want your business, tell me what you would like me to do to improve." And don't tell anyone in the company you are in his area. The shock to store employees when they find out will have a salutary effect. You will be pleased with the results!

One of the most impressive things we have ever seen is Paul Feiner's Help Desk. Feiner is a politician in Westchester County, just outside New York, who regularly sets up a Help Desk in supermarkets in his district. If you have something to say to Feiner, just walk up and say it. He runs newspaper advertisements inviting people to call him at home, anytime, day or night. He's there with his constituents, he's accessible, and he's popular. The striking thing is that the owners of the supermarkets that Feiner uses to such effect are nowhere to be seen. And the service levels in most of these places is what you would expect from hide-and-seek management.

Our advice is, set up your own help desk. Put a big sign above it: "I'm the boss—talk to me." See what happens. Your customers will give you plenty of smart ideas on how to run your business. You won't get this kind of feedback from artfully worded customer surveys and carefully staged focus groups.

Every executive in the company—from every department, including MIS, legal, public relations, finance, and human resources—should spend one day each month taking calls from customers with problems. Everybody needs to know who signs the paycheck and what his problems with your firm are. No one can be spared this duty. If customers stop buying, everyone loses his or her job. That means that everyone owes allegiance to the firm's customers and everyone had better have a clear idea of what those customers want and why. There is no better place to start than the service desk. Take this one step further. On all performance evaluation forms, regardless of position, have a space showing the number of days on the service desk each quarter.

If all senior managers answer the phones Roger Penske–style, it won't take long for people throughout the firm to get the message. When the lowest-ranked employees see the highest-ranked roll up their sleeves to take calls, morale will improve, and so will service levels. If management has been getting its lights punched out regularly by customers, few in the firm will doubt that management knows what it is talking about.

Trying to fix customer problems is a great way of learning what is really wrong with your company. It will give you a finer appreciation of your customers' needs and of the employees charged with meeting those needs. And when you review the latest in statistical measures of customer service quality, the numbers will mean something to you.

Make customer service the key to management rank. Once you get all your managers working with customers, you can begin working on a new corporate culture. Since no one can function effectively in your company without spending time in the trenches with your customers, no one can expect to be promoted without excelling at customer service. If you have restructured your entire system of corporate rewards and promotions to do this, as we have suggested, your job should be fairly easy. To fix it in stone, we recommend making customer service goals the priority item in performance reviews. It doesn't matter what else Jones does so well. If Jones can't manage customer issues, Jones isn't promotable. It's that simple.

Once your customers have told you the things you must do, let them rank these to show you what you must do first. They know what is most important; you do not. Give your customers a clear signal that you will meet their most important needs first, not last. This isn't just talk or customer service hot air spouted by your PR department.

Good service does not mean promising the moon. By letting your customer set priorities and due dates for meeting them, you are also helping your customer understand the limits of the doable. We all have customers who want everything done yesterday. Bringing them into the process lets them understand that, like them, you too have operational problems that cannot be solved overnight. If customers understand these problems, they will have a fuller appreciation of what you can do and a better understanding of what they, in turn, can expect.

If you run a department store and you know that your customers are unhappy, take your customers' priorities and post them where all your customers can read them, in big, bold red letters. Next to them post your target dates for solving these problems. And next to these track your performance. Do the whole thing in public. You won't have to do this exercise too often before you find that you are no longer listing problems up there for all to see but leading-edge customer service goals for the future.

Once everyone knows what customers expect, set up a system of awards for exceeding—not meeting—these expectations. This way everybody—you, your employees, and your customers—knows who comes first and why. The whole company will be working from the same set of rules: customer rules.

To ensure maximum impact all around, have your customers present awards to your employees for beating the service goals customers have set. Invite your customers in, make a big deal of it, and show your appreciation by giving real awards for real accomplishments. Try a trip to the Caribbean instead of plastic things from the local sports shop dolled up with the corporate logo. Your people will get the message, loud and clear. So will your customers. So will your cash register.

Give customers twenty-four-hour access to executives. Put a toll-free phone number on all your receipts, for example 1-800-THE-BOSS, and give each executive a portable cellular phone so that he or she will have to answer no matter what happens or where. Not only will this shorten up lines of communication between you and your customers, it will do a lot to reinforce customer faith in your company. It will also do something for your employees. Once they know that their customers can and will call the most senior people in your company at any time of day or night, they will, you can be sure, fully appreciate the consequences of such a call.

They will move heaven and earth to ensure that Mr. Big isn't dragged out of his bed in the middle of the night by a furious customer with a problem that has to be solved *now*. Customer service levels will increase. So will sales. Also, if customers know that when they have a problem it is Mr. Big who strides into their office a few hours later, they will take your commitment very seriously. And they will reward you with their business.

Whatever else you do, you must have an outside opinion. Get an independent party to audit customer satisfaction levels every quarter. Ask your customers how they would like to see your performance measured. Live by what they tell you. Make the audit results item one of every company meeting. The amount you will save in improved customer satisfaction will more than pay for the cost of the audit.

Make the standards set by your customers your criteria for corporate success. Integrate them into everything the firm does. Build them into all components of corporate planning. Tie promotions, salary increases, and bonuses to meeting these service goals. Make sure that all personnel in the firm know that their customers' welfare will be accurately reflected in their paychecks. Build account plans around service goals, and make meeting them the sole criterion for capital acquisitions. Bob Crandall, CEO of American Airlines, is supposed to have said that he won't buy a single piece of equipment from an airplane to a computer unless it measurably improves customer service. He is right. A piece of machinery may have this or that rate of return. But if it doesn't do something for your customers you are probably wasting the company's valuable resources.

The same goes for mergers and acquisitions. Mergers are pointless unless customer service will improve in a clearly measurable way. Assessing acquisitions on financial criteria—future cash flows and so on—is useful, of course. But it is not a necessary and sufficient condition for justifying a deal. If acquiring another company will not increase customer service, there is a high likelihood of acquisition failure. Indeed, using yardsticks other than customer service for buying a company means you are ignoring the one component essential to making the acquisition work: your customers. Too many times, as a result, deals that are long on so-called synergy fall short on customer service and collapse after relatively short periods.

Use War Games

We had a customer that had a hard time translating our advice into action. Just telling the customer what was wrong and what to do about it didn't seem to work. All the senior and middle management agreed with our diagnosis, but the firm just couldn't get it together. This made implementing our recommendations impossible. Moreover, even though sales were starting to fall off in important accounts, the inertia was so great that the firm seemed almost paralyzed and incapable of an adequate response. We puzzled over this problem for a while and then tried something new. We put a sales team and its executives in a room for a couple of days just before they had to begin bidding on a major contract. We broke them into small teams and gave them name tags—with the real names of customers and competitors. For the next forty-eight hours we umpired a war game as they fought it out for the business. Two days of this and everyone from executive to junior salesman knew *exactly* what the customer wanted and why. Within six months this sales team brought in a deal worth $975 million!

This war game identified almost all the customer's major concerns and demonstrated clearly what the company was not doing to alleviate them. Rather as in our American Express example earlier in this chapter, it doesn't take much to figure out what keeps customers awake at night once you are wearing your customer's name tag and carrying around your customer's baggage. Had American Express pulled together a slice of the company, including the CEO and some middle managers and account reps, and put them in a room for a day or so to simulate a competition for the business of even the smallest clothing store or pizza parlor, Amex wouldn't be fighting customers on the pages of the *Wall Street Journal*. In the game we ran, the company had a chance to correct its course *before* asking its customer for the business. The changes made were the right ones, and the company was handsomely rewarded.

So, if you want to bring all these lessons home fast, and make money doing it, try a war game. Your people will reach conclusions quickly, they'll effectively get management sign-off as part of the process, and they'll bring in the business.

What We Would Do at General Motors

For all its assertions to the contrary, General Motors does not have problems with Japanese competitors. Its problems, big ones, are with its customers. General Motors is simply too far removed from car buyers and too complex for them to influence.

This weakness is what the Japanese car manufacturers long ago recognized. What, they asked themselves, do we have to do to serve American car buyers better than General Motors? Having resolved that question to their customers' satisfaction, Toyota, Nissan, and the others took large amounts of market share away from GM in GM's home market and in doing so then significantly weakened its ability to hold on to other important markets, like Europe.

To us, the solution is clear-cut: GM should get closer to its car buyers than the Japanese. The best way to do this is to use our four rules of counterstrategy: disintegrate, decentralize, sell direct, and sell peace of mind.

GM is simply too large and unwieldy to compete in any market, let alone one as cutthroat and fast-paced as automobiles. We would divest everything not directly related to making and selling cars, starting with Hughes Aircraft and Electronic Data Systems. Next, we would sell off all factories making subassemblies and parts—to the Japanese, if necessary. We see no advantage to designing and making car engines, for example, not to mention headlights and radios. These can and should be made by someone else.

Next, we would decentralize the firm by breaking it into several smaller ones using well-established marques—Pontiac,

Buick, Chevrolet, Opel, GMC Trucks, and so on—and float each as an independent company. We would offer shareholders shares in all the new firms, in the same way that the Bell System was distributed to shareholders in the 1980s. Each new company would have to survive on its own. Instead of just being fired, all HQ staff would be invited to bid for a role in one of the divested firms. Those who could find a role would, in effect, have moved into the line. Doing this would eliminate headquarters staff, of which GM now has 91,000 in the U.S. alone.[2] And it would cut loose GM's operations in Europe, where the company is a profitable leader with a lot of forward momentum.[3]

We would flatten these organizations, leaving only four levels between CEOs and customers. This would make them small, quick on their feet, and capable of winning customer loyalty and keeping it.

As GM is currently organized, it sells to dealers, not to car buyers. It is natural, therefore, for GM to respond more quickly to dealers, whose only interest is moving cars, than to the car-buying public. So our next move would be to start selling direct to the public, acquiring a chain of repair shops for after-sales service, and eliminating car dealers as quickly as possible. We would launch a strategy of consultative selling, door-to-door, if necessary. Manufacturing would be restructured to drop-ship individual cars to customer homes anywhere in the country within forty-eight hours. For this service we would talk to shipping companies like Federal Express. This is just the kind of thing they might be interested in and could probably do very well.

To give customers piece of mind, we would encourage employees to buy competitors' cars and give them a bonus for determining what it is about these cars that is better than GM's and what improvements should be made. We would also pay employees to report on competitor customer service and what GM has to do to lead the market. We would send all executives out on our door-to-door sales campaigns and have them randomly follow car orders right to customer homes. All managers, whatever their department, would be charged with following up with individual customers every six months for the entire period in which they owned the GM car, *no matter how long that was*. All customers would be furnished with a toll-free number to the CEO's office and would be encouraged to use it, no matter how small their complaint.

In addition, we would require GM's service centers to call every customer once a quarter to inquire about his or her car, and about any problems the customer is having both with the car and with the company. These calls would also be used to invite sample groups to local discussions on the model they have bought. Lab people would bring ideas for improvements to these sessions and have the owners go over the vehicle showing what is wrong with it and what works well.

Within twenty-four months, we are certain, the divested GM companies as a group would be outperforming the old GM in a big way. Within thirty-six months, Japanese companies would be forced to make enormously expensive changes in service and distribution. The American car industry would be on the road to recovery.

Where to Start

You can regain ground lost to your Japanese competitors. Do it by hitting them where it hurts: at the customer level. Here's how to start:

Focus, focus, focus your efforts. List all your company's activities in order of value to your customers, and make your goal to outsource the bottom two thirds of the list. If you are vertically integrated, internal production of components should be cut in half within two years, by three quarters within three years, and by 95 percent within five years. Use our outsourcing rule: *if it can be outsourced, it should be outsourced.*

Nothing should be sourced to a sister organization unless

cost and quality are clearly better than what's available outside. Place the obligation on the sister company to prove this. Don't just take it for granted that a sister company's products can serve your customers just because company policy says that it must be true.

Next, take a list of your products and rank them from best to worst. Start knocking the bottom ones off the list: your customers won't miss them, and you will be better able to serve customers with the products they really want. Within three years, the only thing you will still be making yourself are those things that you are certain add real value for your customers.

Flatten and disperse your organization. Count the number of layers of management, from factory worker or salesman to CEO. There should be no more than four. Eliminate all headquarters line and staff planning functions: any planning worth doing should be done in field sales offices. Wherever possible, locate sales and service offices directly across the street from big accounts. All R&D, manufacturing, and headquarters activities should also be near key customers. This way, everybody feels the heat. No one is too remote to know exactly what customers want and when they want it. Remember: customers like to influence their suppliers. Make sure that you are close enough to them that they can make their voices heard effectively and that your organization is flat enough to make your responses count.

Make everybody sell. Assign each of your top ten executives to one of your top ten accounts. Make them work personally with account managers to identify and meet customer goals. These goals should include those not directly related to the performance of your product. Fast-track promotions, at all levels in your company, must be related to how well managers excel at customer service. Ideally all, but at a minimum two thirds, of your employees must deal with customers on a *daily* basis. Even your plants should be open to customers and should be a showplace for your company, spotless and efficient. Manufacturing employees who know that customers come through the plant daily will take great pride in their work, especially when they are regularly called on to explain what they do and why it improves levels of service to your customers.

Sell peace of mind. List the biggest problems faced by your top ten customers. Redefine your company mission to solve them. Take the bottom half of your customer list (in terms of sales) and stop selling to them or find another distribution channel. Establish a customer advisory committee so your customers, not you, originate new product ideas and approve them as they progress. Give your customers sign-off authority on all stages of product development; if they don't approve, cancel the product. Have all executives spend one day a month on the service desk taking calls. In discussion with your customers, establish key service criteria and track your performance monthly against these metrics. Compensation for *all* staff should be based on this performance.

America's Biggest Threat Is Not from Japan

Half a millennium after the German printer, Johannes Guten-
berg, developed movable type, a few of us would meet one eve-
ning a week in a grimy little brick building in the middle of a city
parking lot. There, a tall, middle-aged, and slightly avuncular
man began each meeting by carefully prodding us for evidence of
Gutenberg in the commonplaces of everyday life. Marshall
McLuhan's point was simple: When Gutenberg's tools changed
the way we moved information, it changed the information as
well and unleashed powerful social forces. Spot the new tool, he
urged, and you will quickly spot changes as cataclysmic as the
Reformation that followed Gutenberg's press.

Like movable type, the microprocessor is just such a tool. Its introduction has been followed by Reformation-sized changes that
are restructuring businesses, governments, even whole societies
worldwide.

Microprocessors and movable type share one formidable
characteristic. They slash the cost of information to fractions of
what it had been before their introduction. Any time the cost of

information falls even slightly, power shifts from the few who can amass enough wealth to control it to the many who previously could not. But when something like movable type comes along, there is a major, one-time, cost discontinuity. When this happens, the power shift is seismic.

When Japan tried to capitalize on these changes to propel itself to dominance in information technology, something went wrong. Japan understood what was happening to information costs all right. It specializes in producing more stuff, cheaper. But Japan misdiagnosed the underlying historic forces driving information costs down and therefore the impact of lower costs on its IT customer base. To beat Japan, it is essential that you do not make the same mistake.

If you get caught on the wrong side of this power shift, nothing will save you—neither technology nor organization skills nor corporate culture. This is what happened to the Japanese in information technology. They stayed ahead of the falling information cost curve but were unwilling to share power with their customers. Even today they have not recognized that those who derive power from microprocessors are not those who make them but those who use them.

Overnight, microprocessors empowered consumers at the expense of business and government. Companies, even states, built over this fault line are coming down fast. What has happened to the American auto industry, and to countless other American firms, is no different from what is happening to the Soviet Union or to riot-torn central Los Angeles. All these organizations were on the wrong side of the information cost curve when it dropped.

Cheap information in the form of a home video put police beatings in Los Angeles on every TV set in America, stunning the Los Angeles Police Department and ruining its credibility in a few short seconds. Riots followed in which dozens died and billions' worth of investments were lost. Within moments Los Angeles slipped from the First World to the Third.

Cheap information swept the Soviet Union from superpower to beggary in months. The Soviets wanted to be the top industrial power but refused their citizens access to cheap photocopiers, telephones, and personal computers. The photocopiers won, and the Soviet Union has ceased to exist.

The sudden collapse in the cost of information ushered in by microprocessors will swallow any individual, corporation, or government standing in the way. Cheap information killed demand for IBM's flagship products, very big computers. The company is desperately trying to restructure before it is too late. Japanese companies have been slow to respond to the empowerment of their customers and, as we have pointed out many times in this book, may even be incapable of response. Your mission is to ensure that you do respond, effectively and profitably.

The Information Cost Curve

Japan Inc. recognized the most obvious feature of the information cost curve: it is not linear. For most of written history, information costs have fallen almost imperceptibly. Long periods passed between major cost discontinuities. From the invention of writing to the printing press took many thousands of years. But once discontinuities, like movable type, began to occur, they occurred with increasing rapidity.

From the printing press to the bill of exchange and other commercial instruments took only hundreds of years. From this commercial revolution to the industrial revolution took only a century. From the industrial revolution to the telegraph, only half a century. And from the commercial computer to the personal computer, only twenty-five years passed.

Now, seemingly daily announcements double the power of previous generations of microprocessors and associated hardware and software. Information costs are in complete freefall. A large part of Japan's industrial strategy has been designed to exploit this phenomenon with ever more rapid product introductions. This fast pace was intended to keep the country ahead of the cost curve. Indeed, Japan, better than any other country, understands that success means building enduring profitability during a time when quantum information-cost declines are a daily, not a millenarian, experience. Being on the wrong side of this cost curve can wipe out whole industries, as companies around the world are finding out to their cost.

From the Holy to the Banal: A Short History of the Cost of Information

What Japanese strategists did not understand about the history of falling information costs, however, is that it is also the history of shifting power. With each decline in the cost of information, power moves from producers, like the *keiretsu,* to consumers. The sharper the decline in information costs, the more radical the power shift. Some shifts are so radical that social upheavals erupt on a broad scale. We are in such a period now, much of it driven by Japanese costs strategies, and to understand what will happen and how to profit from it, we have to understand that it has happened before.

Information was once so precious it was sacred. Information on how to grow crops, when to plant them, and when the seasons were expected to change was painstakingly collected. Commonly it was reposited in temples and controlled by the religious elite with the full authority of the state.

Scarce and very expensive to acquire, information had great value to those who controlled it. From the earliest Mesopotamian king to Lenin and the *shacho* of Japan's industrial giants, rulers have recognized that information is power. Controlling it meant keeping power. Giving it away meant relinquishing power.

At the same time, high-cost information also made early civilizations vulnerable. Nothing more devastated these societies than the sacking of their temples: with the loss of that building went the loss of all knowledge from when to plant crops to how to rebuild the temple itself. A crude predator could eliminate thousands of years of carefully collected information at a stroke—and often did. Such "lost" civilizations are still being unearthed.

For millennia information costs didn't fall by much. Information was expensive to collect, expensive to store, and without machinery, it was even expensive to use. Empires and city-states rose and fell and knowledge increased, but the costs of acquiring, managing, and disseminating information stayed pretty much the same. Large empires in China, India, and Italy used bureaucratic and administrative skills to bring down information costs and widen information dissemination, but these efforts had little lasting impact. Information was managed in Rome pretty much as it had been in the earliest Sumerian cities thousands of years before.

Rome did, however, divorce the management of knowledge from temples by creating large libraries for civil administration and learning. But information was still tied to geography: you had to go to the library; it didn't come to you. Information dissemination remained a problem until relatively recent times.

Christianity made several important strides forward. The accepted wisdom is that Christianity's great gift to civilization was the monastic system that preserved information following the collapse of the Roman Empire in the West. Monasticism did preserve information, but this didn't do much to cut the costs of acquiring it or increasing its dissemination. Indeed, for a time monasticism may even have increased these costs: illuminated texts were extremely laborious to copy.

The cost discontinuity in Christianity was the invention of the portable temple. When a priest can say a mass anywhere, the temple goes to the people. Information, for the first time, was on the move, and Christianity became a portable, go-anywhere, cross-any-ocean phenomenon. This cut the cost of information dramatically.

It was also a major change in "software." Making the temple portable and information mobile was a change in thought, not technology. The next major software change, the translation of the Bible into the vernacular, allowed people to have the temple to themselves, as it were. This too brought down the cost of information. However, information still had to be collected manually and recorded by hand, a very slow and expensive process. But the first hesitant steps in the secularization of information had been taken: information no longer had to reside in temples. It was losing its sacred character.

What followed was explosive. Gutenberg's fifteenth-century invention of movable type was the most dramatic drop in the cost of information since handwriting was developed. It made books commonplace and universally available. People could leave the priest behind and take the book with them, anywhere.

Information, and with it immense amounts of power that had resided with the church and state, moved suddenly into the hands of individuals. Cheap books literally made the library at Alexandria available to anyone. Common people gained access not just to religious knowledge but to scientific knowledge and political ideas as well. For the first time individuals appropriated the power to interpret information and to create it: they could print books. The power shift that followed movable type was indeed cataclysmic.

The Reformation spread across Europe like wildfire. It flourished especially along major trade routes, following the business paper trail across Northern Europe. This shift in control over information was naturally resisted by incumbent rulers, and dueling books were soon followed by dueling nations. Religious wars tore Europe apart for centuries.

But with the discovery of the New World, perhaps the most

important event in history, the printing press had further consequences that we are still feeling today.

The combination of portable, secular information in the
hands of the newly empowered and "reformed" colonists created
a force that raced through the New World. These colonists saw
their rights as "self-evident" and not bestowed on them by a
church or a state. Low-cost information enabled them to create a
political process of their own and to assume, for the first time, an
educated electorate. The secularization of information was complete. Low-cost information, in effect, created America.

By substituting information for craftsmanship the industrial
revolution made literacy a mass phenomenon. In the nineteenth
century improvements in printing technology came that, among
other things, lowered the cost of newspapers and made mass cir-
culation achievable on a daily basis. With the invention of the
telegraph, information became available everywhere instantly.
Marx might have said that in the nineteenth century the masses
began to take "control of the means of information production."

Social upheavals followed: revolutions swept Europe; the
United States was engulfed in a civil war of a gruesomeness
never before seen.

By the mid-twentieth century, the burgeoning volume of information needed management, and the computer age began.
Computers cut the costs of information further than ever. Soon
the microprocessor was developed, and the opening shots of the
personal-computer revolution were fired.

What makes PCs different than any other tool of information cost reduction is that people aren't on the receiving end anymore. They can buy information, sell information, and most
important, create information. Personal computers are the ultimate information-generating machine. The PC completes the
shift of power from producers to consumers. The personal computer is a social force of unprecedented magnitude.

From the holy to the banal, the falling cost of information

has meant the growing empowerment of consumers at the expense of producers.

Japan did not realize that this power shift was as old as civilization itself. By jumping on the information technology bandwagon after World War II, Japan imagined itself in the vanguard of the information revolution. Instead, Japan engineered an information strategy that contained the seeds of its own destruction. Working hard to stay ahead of the falling information cost curve, Japan pushed the curve down faster than ever. What Japan failed to realize, however, was that in a process that has been going on for millennia, falling information costs empower consumers, not producers. Japanese memory chips, PCs, and faxes helped empower customers as never before. They were liberated from their Japanese suppliers, free to buy from Americans, Koreans, Taiwanese, or anybody else. Japan's industrial structure, particularly the *keiretsu,* was completely maladapted to this shift. Their customers got away from them, finding more responsive competitors behind every PC and telephone set.

The Iron Laws of Information

The challenge for business, government, and labor is to exploit the power shift to consumers, not to get slam-dunked by it. This means observing what we call the Iron Laws of Information. The Iron Laws make the process of consumer empowerment predictable, even manageable.

The First Iron Law: Cheap information *always* chases out expensive information.
The Second Iron Law: In information, disorder is *always* increasing.
The Third Iron Law: Information *always* flows to the least regulated economy.

The First Iron Law says, in effect, that you must count on information getting cheaper and on losing control over markets.

Japanese-style vertical integration designed to give you more power as a producer is a mistake. Your customers will appropriate this power faster than you can. The First Iron Law warns governments that policies designed to raise the price of information far above costs (for example, by regulating long-distance telephone traffic) will almost certainly collapse as cheaper information rushes in to replace costly, regulated information.

The Second Iron Law says that as information is more widely disseminated, disorder increases. This makes neat market segmentation based on long-term trends impossible: the segments change too fast. It also makes regulation impossible. As power moves away from government to consumers, the number of people that have to be regulated increases exponentially and thus the power of governments to regulate them evaporates. Trying to regulate business, governments will be left regulating the powerless, not the powerful. Regulating the telephone industry is futile, for example, when anybody with a PC and a modem can build a worldwide telephone network within minutes.

The Third Iron Law says that information, and therefore market power, always flows from the most regulated to the least regulated economy. Misguided government control (whether industrial policies, protectionism, or Soviet-style planning) simply chases information—and with it, market power—to other, less regulated countries. In the machine age, high tariffs and other import barriers could, for a while, keep jobs at home. In the information age, by contrast, the only beggar-thy-neighbor strategy that works is free trade. If you open your economy, you can suck your neighbor's information base dry. Trade in goods and services will follow the free flow of information. Hong Kong today, not Japan in the 1960s, is the model of effective government policy.

The biggest challenge of the next century will be to exploit the Iron Laws successfully. For business, this means ensuring enduring profitability as market power moves to customers. For government it means creating good jobs by facilitating information flows. For labor, it means increasing the bargaining power of unions by improving worker productivity.

These are not complex goals in themselves. But for many companies, governments, and unions around the world, there will be painful transitions to make.

For Japan, this transition will not be easy, if it can be made at all. The entire structure of Japanese industry is based on the premise that information, and therefore market power, can be controlled by business. The *keiretsu* and their elaborate horizontal and vertical interworkings are about control. So are Japan's preferences for centralization and consensus-based decision-making. As we have pointed out many times, very little of what Japanese companies do, from their hiring practices to their product design and manufacturing philosophies, are designed to subordinate themselves to customer direction.

Centralized control is not consistent with a process of continual consumer empowerment that has been going on worldwide for thousands of years—a process from which Japan has been largely isolated and for which it is ill prepared. Just how ill prepared is demonstrated by the bankruptcy of Japan's strategy in all of its targeted information technology markets.

What the Iron Laws of Information Mean for Business

Only a few years ago, a widely published text on business strategy suggested that there were many competitive forces determining industry profitability, including suppliers, potential new entrants, substitute products, competitors, and customers. Except for customers, none of these remain today. With the shift in power from producers to consumers, customers are now the only criteria for all market activity.

What is happening to business today is no different than

what happened to all the governments of Europe once Luther nailed his manifesto on the doors of Würtemberg Cathedral. Like the Church in the sixteenth century, companies the world over are being convulsed as control shifts to customers. The naive blame the recession, the Japanese, their governments, anyone. But the Iron Laws of Information are at work. Today's Protestants are the new, flat, disintegrated organizations we have described in this book. Our model of the disintegrated, decentralized, customer-driven, service-oriented company is designed to take advantage of the falling information cost curve and to profit from the consumer power that results from it. These organizations are well adapted to the new realities of consumer control over their operations. They will sweep their competitors from the best markets, just as Protestantism swept Catholicism from the hot sixteenth-century markets of Northern Europe and the Baltics.

Japanese businesses have failed to grasp the lessons of history. If they want to profit from falling information costs, they will have to reform themselves just as Luther reformed the Church. This is unlikely as long as power remains in the temple, that is in Tokyo. Japan is hoping for a Counter-Reformation, but it is unlikely to occur. Besides, the Jesuits understood better than anyone else that you can't build market share without going to your customers.

What the Iron Laws of Information Mean for Governments

The Iron Laws of Information make virtually every kind of economic intervention not only futile but counterproductive. Governments have always taken great comfort in increasing their control over markets. They don't like giving up power any more than anyone else. When policies for "managing" industries, "stabilizing" markets, and "protecting" employment are combined with Gammon's Law of Bureaucracies, the result is usually an immeasurably unproductive and expensive mess.

Broadcast regulation, a favorite of governments everywhere, is an excellent example. Broadcast policies control who can transmit what, and when, to whom. Soon, however, consumers will be able to transmit their own videos *into* the network, making every home a television station. Regulation therefore means controlling the output of every home in the nation. If cable TV and telephone technology merge as expected, people will be able to broadcast anything they want, from high science to pornography, to anyone, anywhere, who has a telephone. Broadcast regulation in one country would mean regulating everyone in the world with a telephone, something that is clearly impossible. This is a perfect example of the First and Second Iron Laws. As information costs come down, disorder increases rapidly, and policies built up over decades simply disappear.

The Soviet Union shows what happens to governments that make the wrong decision. The Soviets tried by force to maintain the price of information far above its costs and created an elaborate Communist Party structure to administer its information policy. The ultimate result of this policy was the end of the Soviet state.

The United States is farthest ahead in loosening barriers between citizens. It is less regulated than most of its trading partners; it has fewer government-owned companies, and is probably less protectionist (though this is arguable). Serious barriers remain, however. Farm subsidies and protectionism are major threats to increased empowerment of individuals. And there is as yet no clear understanding of the impact of a failed health care and education system on consumer empowerment. Indeed, in our view the most serious threat to growth in any market is illiteracy: the illiterate cannot access, manage, or disseminate information.

Where the Soviets resisted the Iron Laws and the Americans have followed them, the Europeans have tried to split the difference. With notable exceptions like the United Kingdom, most European governments believe that the good of the state is best served if state-owned companies keep the price of information well above costs and extort monopoly rents from their citizens. Germany, for example, extorts billions this way from telephone customers. Far from doing Germany any good, however, this policy (as the Third Iron Law predicts) keeps down telephone penetration and forces German companies to move their computer services to other countries, like the United Kingdom.

In the European Community as a whole, market unification plans usually mean extending German and French policies of state control to other countries, like the United Kingdom, that don't want to get caught behind the information cost curve. This, the Germans and the French seem to think, will level the playing field.

The United Kingdom sees great advantages to Franco-German policy. So long as France and Germany keep the price of information high, the United Kingdom can use the First Iron Law to siphon off their information business. As a result, the United Kingdom is becoming the information entrepôt of Europe. All of Britain is the Heathrow Airport of the European information business, the place where European information is sent to be collected, managed, and then redistributed piecemeal to the other members of the European Community.

The consequences of the United Kingdom's policy for the continentals is incalculable. Riding its low-cost information strategy, Britain is emerging as the dominant force in services in the Community. It could easily wind up controlling Community banking, advertising, accounting, and insurance markets by early in the next century. A new age of British imperialism will have begun. Britain's information costs are lower and its overseas connections are wider and deeper, giving it significant economies. Using the Third Iron Law, Britain is less regulated than its neighbors and is better adapted to exploiting the markets of the next century.

Continental governments are trying desperately to regain control. In everything from the Common Agricultural Policy to high-tech R&D programs like JESSI and RACE, the European Community is pouring money behind a dyke that simply cannot hold. All the while, European industry is losing its competitive position; flagship high-tech companies are falling by the wayside despite rising government R&D expenditures. There is something Quixotic in Community policies.

Japan is really no better off than Europe. Indeed, this whole book is a litany of Japanese government misdirections. From its corporate organizations to its industry-government cabals, Japan has done just about everything the Iron Laws say that it should not do. The results, which we have chronicled at length in previous chapters, should therefore surprise no one.

Smart governments get ahead of the falling information cost curve. We were once asked to advise the industry ministry of an OECD member state on its information policy. This country had established formidable barriers to keep out the low-cost information of neighboring countries. It had gone to great lengths to build large national monopolies that were either state owned or so tightly regulated that, in the words of government guidelines, they were "managed" by the state. This country believed that the only way to gain a greater share of the information market in the next century was to build on these policy foundations and expand its control of industry. The ministry was preparing to seize control of the R&D labs of the country's major information technology manufacturers and apply Japanese-style direction and guidance. The ministry asked us what benefits they could expect by doing this.

Senior bureaucrats at the ministry knew that they were losing control, and that low-cost information from neighboring countries was devastating their economy. Completely oblivious to the Iron Laws of Information, they blamed neighboring governments, maintaining that their free-trade policies constituted cultural imperialism.

We pointed out that the problem wasn't with their neighbors or predatory foreign companies. The problem was with their own electorate. Ordinary citizens had become powerful enough to ignore their government. They were voting with their pocketbooks for foreign goods and services. Without policing every household in the nation, their policies would fail. And, we added, policing every household would hardly be acceptable in a democracy.

Our advice was to rebuild public policy not on intervention, but on an aggressive strategy of driving domestic information costs far below those of neighboring states. To do this, we advised a program of rapid deregulation and privatization and a series of tax and other fiscal incentives to push costs lower still. This, we pointed out, would make the nation's other assets, its education system and physical infrastructure, attractive. It would begin to reverse the information flow to neighboring countries that government bureaucrats had already observed. Within the decade, we predicted, our client would be well on the way to success in information markets worldwide.

Anywhere they are resisted, the Iron Laws of Information will sweep governments from power and destroy established political, social, and economic structures. Third world governments, especially, risk being toppled. They will want all the benefits of the First World's economic power. But they will not want to face the consequences of letting every citizen use a personal computer.

First world governments will also have to get used to sharing power with the Third World, where the number of consumers is growing most quickly. By positioning themselves as bitstream entrepôts, relatively small nations, like Singapore and Hong Kong, will be able to exert power beyond all proportion to their size. This will have significant foreign policy implications for the United States, in particular. Indeed, the Iron Laws of Information predict that the New World Order we hear so much about will not be the United States in concert with a few powerful allies but a complex web of power-sharing between the newly empowered consuming nations of the Third World and those of the First.

Perhaps the most troublesome issue facing governments in the information age is illiteracy. The illiterate are powerless, not relatively, but absolutely. Illiteracy is the new slavery. As the middle class gains more control over information, the poor will be left farther and farther behind. In the industrial age, any able-bodied person, regardless of race, sex, or ability to read could find work. Only the literate, however, can control and process information. All the advantages of the falling information cost curve go to the educated.

For drop-outs, there will be fewer and fewer alternatives: blue-collar jobs are evaporating. Inner cities are a special problem (especially in America) because they have large concentrations of illiterates. Their situation is hopeless, and the faster information costs come down, the more hopeless they will become. We called this a new slavery, but our language may not have been strong enough. Even slaves worked and produced. What we are seeing in our inner-city illiterates is a new class of the permanently unemployable. Governments therefore ignore illiteracy at their peril. Those who cannot work at a simple computer keyboard will be forever cut out of the benefits of the information age. Their existence will become destabilizing, and social upheaval will almost certainly result. The Los Angeles riots are just a warning.

What the Iron Laws of Information Mean for Labor

The Iron Laws of Information are also devastating labor. In the machine age, the role of unions was to extract monopoly rents from capital by withholding labor. In the information age, however, labor has learned the hard way that withholding services is greeted as an opportunity to move production offshore. Power is now so diffuse and machine-age jobs are declining so fast that unions offer little or nothing to their members. Unions try futilely to bargain with companies that are themselves being whipsawed by the shift of power to the consumer. The struggle between labor and capital has become a sideshow, occasionally inconvenient but rarely of any consequence. The exception that proves the rule is unions of public employees. Governments with monopoly control over services can still extract concessions from their "customers" to meet labor demands.

Labor has to reestablish its bargaining power and its ability to guarantee high-wage jobs. Since the standard of living of workers depends on their ability to improve their productivity, labor needs to get into the productivity-enhancement business. Unions can regain their bargaining leverage by filling the void left by government and employers; they can make their workers valuable by making them knowledgeable and well trained. Such a strategy would give labor real political clout for the first time in a generation, making it an agency of the upwardly mobile, instead of a rearguard action in an industrial Dunkirk.

—14—

Japan Tomorrow: The Big Green Tsunami

Imagine a car manufacturing plant with five million square feet, one mile across, employing five thousand workers, turning out half a million cars a year. Imagine this factory generating no waste: no smoke up the chimney, no fifty-five-gallon drums of toxic wastes, no dumpsters of garbage to landfill. Zero emissions. Is this an environmentalist's dream? A nonnegotiable demand from Greenpeace at Rio de Janeiro? A factory-of-the-future publicity film from Detroit? Not at all: this facility is a reality today, operated by one of Japan's big car manufacturers.

To improve its competitive position, not incrementally but radically, this car company has embraced the ultimate environmental goal of any manufacturer, zero emissions. What drives management to this goal is continual, relentless cost reduction and quality improvement. At the factory there are no gimmicks, no "Environmental Leadership" programs and no Vice Presidents of Environmental Affairs. Employees, especially executives, will tell you that going "green" is the right thing to do. But zero emissions is not about feeling good about yourself. Nor is it a one-time quick-fix.

Zero emissions requires what we call "lean management." Unlike lean manufacturing, the system of production perfected by the Japanese car companies to reduce costs, lean management requires rethinking your business well beyond the factory walls, embracing all activities from product conception, to design, supplier relations, production, sales, service, and final disposal. Squeezing out all waste lowers costs and improves quality, but also improves customer service. With lean management you must redefine your business in light of genuine customer expectations. In part these changes require the judicious application of new technologies and new investment, and they result from many incremental improvements in processes, but mostly they demand new ways of *thinking*. Reducing waste is a way of life.

Through their governments and their spending habits, consumers everywhere are forcing companies to shoulder the environmental consequences of their activities. Throughout the world, people—citizens, voters, customers—have become "green." They are concerned about the environment, and they expect their governments do something about it. They also expect the companies they buy from to meet their environmental obligations in ways that go beyond public relations. Biodegradable trash bags and compostable diapers are no longer enough. We call this environmental trend the "Green Wave."

Smelling big opportunity, Japan Inc. has decided to ride the Green Wave. Export sales are always on its agenda, of course, but Japan wants much more from the Green Wave. Japan will use environmentalism as a catalyst to propel itself to the next stage of industrial development. If successful, Japan will completely redefine business and production for the next century. The threat to America's future is profound.

In American industry, environmental responsibilities are primarily viewed as a burden, a not-so-hidden tax imposed by a vocal, granola-eating minority. While Japanese managers are galvanized by this new challenge, their American competitors too often hope in vain for the good old days when men were men, and a little pollution was a small price to pay for jobs. If the United States does not adapt lean management as its goal, the "coring out" of American industry which took place in the past twenty years will seem like a mere prelude. On its present course, America will get swamped by the Green Wave—or more ominously the big Green Tsunami. Will your company rise to this challenge, or will it be swept away with the other industrial flotsam of American business?

Natural Resources and the Postindustrial Economy

During the past generation, industrial growth has been "dematerialized," or uncoupled from the consumption of the earth's natural resources. What we buy today, from cars to soda cans, is made with less metal, oil, and water; what we turn on, from light bulbs to refrigerators, uses less electricity; our cars run on less gas. Better technology and more efficient production is partially responsible for this dematerialization of the economy. But in addition, as consumers have grown richer, they have spent more and more of their income on services, like entertainment, travel, and dining out. Clearly, fewer natural resources go into $15 worth of cable TV shows, than into $15 worth of charcoal for the barbecue. Perhaps most important of all, the "information economy" has swelled, as computers have found their way into virtually every aspect of human activity. The raw material content of a $250 computer microprocessor or a $500 computer program can be measured in cents. Their value derives not from any materials they contain, but from the knowledge of the producers who make them—and the people who use them.

Concern about the environment—and wasteful consumption, for that matter—is not new. But real pressure to use our natural resources more carefully began only twenty years ago. The first

OPEC oil embargo in 1972 delivered a striking lesson to the world's consumers. While this event was entirely manmade, it was seized by environmentalists and neo-Malthusians as an object lesson on the limits to growth. Waiting in gas lines, everyone could consider the fragile link between industrial growth and the environment.

Around the world, governments, businesses, and consumers reacted often with fear, then with action. Dramatic changes resulted that greatly reduced the use of natural resources, particularly energy. Voluntarily, and in response to price increases and government regulation, people turned out the lights, turned down the thermostat, and started thinking about structural changes. Homeowners invested in attic insulation and storm windows, not to mention more fuel-efficient cars (as often as not Japanese). Industry upgraded inefficient electric motors, incandescent lights, and old trucks. The amount of energy required to produce another dollar's worth of production began to fall, in some countries quite sharply. In the 1970s, as oil prices rose rapidly, this reduction in "energy intensity" of the world's economy was sharp. In the 1980s, when oil prices declined, efficiency improvements slowed, but continued nevertheless.

During the past generation, pollution control laws have also had a dramatic effect on air and water quality. In the industrialized world, for example, air emissions of sulfur oxides, particulates, and lead have fallen dramatically, despite increased industrial activity.[1] In the United States, the power industry generates two and one-half times as much electricity for each unit of pollution they produce as they did in 1970.[2] After the Love Canal disaster publicized the potential ill effects of small quantities of industrial byproducts, toxic waste disposal was recognized as a serious problem, and the result was tighter controls. Then hysteria about garbage disposal problems resulted in new recycling requirements around the world.

Pollution laws have forced industry to reduce its use of natural resources, hastening the process of dematerialization. Less lead is used in gasoline, less mercury in batteries, less coal is needed to produce a kilowatt-hour of electricity. In the 1970s, many predicted that the world would run out of key commodities if we didn't change. Well, we did change, and most raw materials are now in surplus. Industry continues to wean itself from the consumption of natural resources. "Sustainable growth," the current mantra of the environmental community, is becoming a reality.

"Global warming" became the apocalypse of choice in the late 1980s. Carbon dioxide is not in itself harmful, but its growing concentration in the atmosphere is apparently causing the earth's average temperature to rise. While other pollutants have been controlled in large measure, CO_2 emissions have persistently increased over the past twenty years, raising questions about the cumulative effect of human activity on the planet as a whole. The global warming frenzy reached its peak at the United Nations–organized Conference on Environment and Development (better known as the "Earth Summit") which took place in Rio de Janeiro in 1992.

In preparation for the Earth Summit, the European Community proposed a new tax on hydrocarbon fuels (primarily coal, oil, and natural gas) based on their carbon content (that is, their ability to cause global warming). While the U.S. response was lukewarm, to say the least, Japan also indicated its willingness to levy a carbon tax in order to reduce CO_2 emissions. The thin end of a long wedge has been inserted between consumers and their fuels of choice, even if it takes some years before a "carbon tax" is widely adopted. The carbon tax will eventually sever growth from oil and coal once and for all.

What Dematerialization Means for Japan

The dematerialization of industrial production has had a dramatic effect on Japan. While many benefit from this shift (and some, particularly the third world producers of raw materials have suffered remorselessly from falling commodity prices), Japan may benefit the most.

As we have noted, Japan is an isolated island nation without natural resources, driven since the mid-nineteenth century by its need to secure raw materials for production. With the rapid industrialization that followed Commodore Perry's arrival in 1853, Japan's leaders first became obsessed with their lines of supply. For the past 50 years, Japan has maintained an aggressive export strategy to cover its huge imports of everything from wood to fish, iron ore, and oil.

Unlike the United States, which is richly endowed with natural resources, Japan has nothing. As we have said before, Japan is a trading nation which must sell its wares (most of which are luxuries like cars and cameras) to buy necessities (without which Japan cannot survive). Nobody ever froze to death because he didn't have a cassette tape player. Americans don't appreciate Japan's predicament, and Japan is often surprised that we are unwilling to take their exports so they can pay their oil bill.

The truth is, Japan must export to pay for oil and other natural resources. That is why the Japanese are extremely sensitive to protectionist sentiments in the United States. Pressure to reduce its trade surplus persists and will only get worse. But no amount of Structural Impediment Initiatives and jawboning at the GATT talks about rice imports will change the facts. Japan cannot abruptly shift production overseas (even if plants need to be closer to customers) or open its markets to a flood of imports without threatening its security. Admittedly its current trade position leaves quite a bit of room for error, but given what is at stake, Japan needs a healthy buffer.

The only alternative Japan has is to cut raw material imports. The less Japan imports, the less it will need to export. In this way "harmony" with its trading partners can be achieved. Dematerialized industrial production offers Japan a way out.

Perhaps more than any of its Western competitors, Japan

needs to sever oil consumption from growth. The oil *shokku* of 1973 brought the Japanese industrial juggernaut to a screeching halt. The Japanese saw themselves running on empty, the eventual losers in a *Mad Max*–like scramble for the few remaining drops of oil in the world. That's why the greatest advances in fuel efficiency in the industrialized world during the past two decades have been in Japan.

If their track records for drift net fishing, whale killing, and rain forest destruction are anything to go by, the Japanese are not particularly concerned about the environment, especially outside of Japan. And anyone who has witnessed Japan's historical treasures surrounded by seas of vending machines, its postwar construction (truly horrible even by the standards of modern architecture), or Tokyo's beautiful Imperial Palace grounds bisected by a six-lane superhighway, knows that environment aesthetics have not been a top priority.

Indeed, Japan seems willing to take grave environmental risks to secure its energy independence. The country has embarked on the world's most ambitious plan to generate nuclear power, stockpiling plutonium (a byproduct of conventional nuclear reactors and one of the deadliest substances known) in the hope that a fusion power breakthrough can be achieved.

Whatever its "green" credentials, Japan will only eliminate its trade problem if it can reduce its raw material consumption and imports. In other words, get rid of oil and the trade problem will take care of itself. Exports could even decline without reducing Japan's wealth. Japan could then move production overseas to get closer to its customers without upsetting the house of cards on which its prosperity is now based.

So Japan will ride the Green Wave. With the running start that began in the oil crisis of the 1970s, Japan already sets energy efficiency standards in many areas. Its challenge now is to squeeze the waste out of its other products and processes. Japan's overseas customers are ready for these changes; its American competitors are not.

After Failure in Information Technology, Japan Is Even More Desperate

Japan's successes in getting the resource monkey off its back have been mixed. After the U.S. oil embargo in 1941, Japan attacked Pearl Harbor and grabbed the rich oil fields of Indonesia—a strategy which ultimately proved futile. In response to the Arab oil embargoes of the 1970s, Japan truly made energy efficiency the "moral equivalent of war" (in the immortal words of Jimmy Carter). In a tactical sense, Japan's efficiency drive paid significant dividends, wringing more steel and cars out of every barrel of oil. But so far, Japan's grand strategy to move up the industrial "food chain" has not worked well.

Poor results in information technology—as close to resource-free as you can get—have left Japan chugging along in the same resource-intensive industries it first staked out thirty and forty years ago. There is plenty of room to make its low-tech manufacturing more efficient and to increase the "knowledge intensity" of its cameras, bread cookers, and pickup trucks. But to use the analogy with which we began this book, Japan still needs another home run to come after cars. Base hits will no longer do.

In response to customer needs and pressure from its trading partners, Japan will continue to move its factories overseas. What's more, Japan Inc. needs new labor as much as natural resources. With little natural growth, Japan's population will age rapidly over the next two decades. Since large-scale immigration is out of the question in racially conscious Japan, its industrial giants must move overseas to find new workers. To do so without hurting domestic living standards, Japan must shift low-value-added production offshore and focus on capital-and knowledge-intensive opportunities at home.

Information technology was going to make all this happen. But IT, which at the crack of the bat sounded like it might be a grand slam for Japan, has started looking like a double at best.

Environmental opportunities are now Japan's best shot at bringing everyone in before the inning is over.

How Japan Will Ride the Big Green Wave

Japan will develop its environmental opportunities the way it attacked information technology—mobilizing government and industry from top to bottom toward a single, well-defined objective.

Japan is driven by efficiency, not environmentalism. Fortunately for Japan, efficiency is almost always better for the environment than any alternative. While its GNP has continued to expand rapidly, Japan's oil imports have fallen steadily since 1975, as have emissions of most pollutants.[3] Throughout the past twenty years, the Japanese government has kept up the pressure on industry. This drive for efficiency is what makes Japan so dangerous to its competitors: efficiency means lower costs and higher quality.

Many observers are rightly fixated on Japan's concern with R&D and technology. But a survey taken by Dentsu Institute asked Japanese CEOs what they expected their main concerns to be in the future. At large companies, the environment headed the list, along with R&D.[4] Technology plus efficiency make a powerful combination.

After the energy shocks of the 1970s, the government of Japan turned the screws down on big business, particularly the heavy users of energy, like railroads, steel mills, and electric utilities. MITI also added energy efficiency projects to its R&D investment list. Since then, MITI has broadened its environmental portfolio from energy efficiency and pollution abatement to sustainable development. Indeed MITI has a *one-hundred-year* environmental plan for Japan, which places much emphasis on energy-related technologies.[5] Perhaps more to the point, MITI has the bankroll to make these dreams a reality. You can be sure any new technologies that result from these programs will be available for export. Japan got a big shot in the arm in the 1970s when its fuel-efficient cars were suddenly in demand in the United States; green exports could provide the next burst of growth.

Taking its cue from MITI, Japan Inc. will spread the green gospel down through the *keiretsu*. Strong intergroup relationships allow manufacturers to exert pressure on suppliers to meet their standards for environmental efficiency. If Toyota wants its sister companies to switch to water-based paints and returnable shipping containers, they will do what they are told. Close contact also makes it easier to find new uses for industrial byproducts. The financial resources of the group make any investments that may be necessary easier to swallow. Because of these relationships, the Green Wave is likely to roll over all Japanese industry faster than it might elsewhere.

In 1991, the Keidanren, Japan's club for major corporations, released its "Global Environmental Charter," guidelines to encourage good environmental behavior among its members. Japan's business leaders can see that its overseas consumers are looking for change. Being green is good for business.

Japan will also wring whatever it can out of international organizations. At the Earth Summit in Rio in 1992, Japan had an unusually high profile, clearly indicating that the environmental wave is one that Japan would like to ride. While the Japanese government was fanning the "technology transfer" flames, Japanese companies were front-and-center flogging their wares. And who can object to Japan's self-serving calls for the transfer of environmental technology to the Third World when the ends are so worthy? Japan is investing heavily in environmental technology and wants to exploit its advantage.

Japan is likely to use development aid aggressively to build environmental markets. The Third World and Eastern Europe (the region most in need of environmental cleanup) can expect a helping hand—if they buy Japanese. If the Japanese get there first, they win. And there's nothing sinister about it: this is the name of the game in foreign relations. Elsewhere, Japan Inc. is likely to use a combination of joint ventures and strategic alliances to build market share.

For all their achievements, the Japanese know very well that they do not have a monopoly on good ideas in the environmental area (or anywhere else). At overseas listening posts throughout the world, amplifiers will be on full. Your Japanese competitors will be gathering information on environmental technology and methods as vigorously as they fed Western information technology back to HQ in the seventies and eighties.

Don't be fooled by the public relations wiffle-waffle of which Japanese business is so enamored. You will be reading such hard facts as "the harmonious coexistence of our product and nature." One ad we saw spoke of "new links within families, new links between businesses, new flows of information between people and the environment, a new sense of connection between our individuality and the world we inhabit."[6] This may sound like terminal California-style New Age dementia, but it is not. Japan means business.

What the Opportunities Are

Environmental opportunities are vast, covering markets as diverse as cars that get better gas mileage and processes that remove toxins from contaminated soil. At the core is environmental technology: techniques, products, and services that reduce pollution before it is generated, save energy, or clean up environmental messes that have already occurred.

On pollution controls, the OECD estimates that the large industrial countries spend about 1% of their GNP every year, pushing this market well above $100 billion in the United States alone.[7] We estimate that total worldwide expenditures on environmentally related products and services in 1991 were $300 billion, some two-thirds the size of the car market and half the size of the information technology market. By some measures, the environmental industry is growing faster than biotechnology, telecommunications, or computer software.[8] Every new government regulation makes this market bigger, and one resource the world will never run short of is government regulations.

Many companies are trying to increase the "green content" of products to appeal to consumers, eliminating toxic ingredients and excess packaging, as well as making them recyclable, returnable, more energy-efficient, or simply relabeling them "environmentally friendly."

With at least three-quarters of consumers calling themselves environmentalists, the green appeal is a natural for consumer product manufacturers and their retailers.[9] While there has been something of a backlash against green marketing which got out of control in the late 1980s (with biodegradable trash bags, compostable diapers, ozone-friendly deodorants, and "Supergreen" gasoline), appealing to the environmental concerns of consumers can help sell products if done judiciously.[10] Many products like mercury-free batteries and small fluorescent lights meet real needs. Often, mature products can be repositioned for growth in this fashion.

Japan is addressing these opportunities, to be sure. Honda, Nissan, and Toyota are investing heavily in high-performance, high-efficiency, low-emission engines—perhaps the most practical purchase any environmentally minded consumer can make is a high-mileage car. Sony and NEC are eliminating CFCs from their production processes. Hitachi and Toshiba are trying to reduce the CO_2 emissions of their power plants. Japan is maintaining a strong position in technologies for eliminating, treating, and preventing industrial and municipal pollution. The country is also investing heavily in alternate energy sources like solar panels and hydrogen cells.

But these are not the real opportunities the Green Wave offers Japan. The relentless pursuit of cost reduction and quality improvement, in response to environmental pressures from many quarters, will reinforce Japan's commanding position in its traditional markets and offset the setbacks suffered in information technology.

In a sense, Japan's accomplishments to date are based on re-exported American inventions like the transistor and statistical quality control. Achieving the goals of zero emissions will require completely rethinking management and manufacturing strategy, akin to the challenges of "zero defects" production but much more difficult. If Japan Inc. embraces zero emissions as its target for the next decade, a genuinely Japanese accomplishment will have been achieved.

For decades, direct labor costs have been a declining share of total costs for most manufacturers, to the point where in some industries, like semiconductors, it is a minor consideration. Material costs are often high, particularly if semifinished goods are purchased for further processing. In many industries, carrying costs for work-in-progress and finished goods is greater than for labor or raw materials. Speeding the flow of goods from suppliers, through the factory, and on to customers is what really reduces costs today. In other words, the low-cost producer is the one with the highest inventory turns.

Like inventory control, zero emissions requires new thinking about how materials are handled throughout the manufacturing process. For example, to reduce its use of CFCs to clean computer-printed circuit boards, one manufacturer first tried water-based cleaners, but then settled on no cleaning at all, instead installing the parts more precisely in the first place. More accurate handling of computer parts was required, but several steps in the manufacturing process were eliminated, as were all solvents (CFC or water based). Furthermore, production was sped up and fewer parts were damaged by rough handling. In another case, a car manufacturer required its suppliers to send parts in reusable plastic crates. Not only were fewer workers required to unpack parts, but parts went more quickly to the production line. What's more, the plastic crates were designed to deliver smaller quantities to the line more frequently. Line workers had fewer steps to take to reach the parts they needed, because the crates were smaller. Parts inventory carrying costs declined. Quality improved because the parts were handled by fewer people.

Redoubling its efforts to reduce emissions will enable Japan Inc. to set new standards in manufacturing. Many competitors remain focused on quality alone (measured in defective parts per million, for example), which all too often ignores the waste involved in achieving high levels of quality. Which war are you fighting—this one or the last one? We visited one electronics factory in Germany which prides itself on quality; this quality was achieved by rigorous inspection. Defective pieces were simply junked or reworked by hand at great expense. Even the Deming Prize, the apex of achievement in manufacturing in Japan, recognizes quality without regard to the waste it may take to get there. In future, this quality must be achieved without waste. For the smartest competitors, first-rate quality will be the *result* of eliminating waste.

Waste reduction does not end at the factory gate. Japan Inc. has fine-tuned just-in-time delivery like a Stradivarius. Not only are parts delivered to factories exactly when they are needed, but even convenience stores in Japan receive their deliveries many times a day, moments before consumers are expected in the store. All these trucks delivering everything from spark plugs to *sushi* are choking Japan's highways—and its air. A significant challenge, to which the Japanese will no doubt rise, is to eliminate the environmental byproducts of the just-in-time system.

Pollution prevention doesn't always pay when measured in conventional terms. Looked at in isolation or evaluated by strict financial standards, waste reduction can look like a poor investment. But with a philosophy of lean management, waste-free production will *always* produce results. For a car company to require its suppliers to deliver parts in reusable containers may seem like eco-nuttiness, and indeed handling all those container returns is expensive and complicated. But the resulting improvement in materials handling and process control is revolutionary.

Can Japan Succeed?

Unendowed with natural resources, destroyed by defeat in World War II, Japan has always run "lean" compared to its industrial competitors. Furthermore, as a densely populated island, Japan felt the ill effects of industrial pollution early, enacting a number of significant environmental regulations in the 1960s. The oil *shokku* of 1973 and 1979 destroyed whatever illusions Japan had about its ability to squander energy. Japan maintained its momentum during the 1980s, with relatively little backsliding compared to its competitors, particularly the United States. So Japan has a running start at riding the Green Wave.

Environmental pressure, particularly the risk of dependence on the Middle East for oil, is largely external. During its history, Japan has responded most effectively to external pressures, rather than internal forces. Waste reduction and industrial efficiency is the kind of agenda that MITI can get behind foursquare. By comparison, improving customer relations is too amorphous and has no technological component. After the war, Japan's government and industrial leaders mobilized the country for reconstruction. A clear, new goal is needed, and environmentalism fits the bill perfectly.

Information technology was not the right challenge. While it achieved certain well-focused objectives, like the VLSI project, MITI could not drive all of Japan on a forced march to information technology leadership. The reason was simple: Japan wanted to solve the problems of its U.S. customers from afar, without talking to them. Riding the Green Wave, Japan will be solving its *own* environmental problems, dealing with matters over which it has control. The automobile industry met Japan's need for small, fuel-efficient cars, for which there was a ready market overseas. This scenario can be replayed on the environmental stage. The next "Fifth-Generation Project" will involve energy and resource efficiency and may well succeed.

Many of Japan's industrial giants diversified with unrestrained gusto into information technology during the 1970s and 1980s. Most of these investments have been disasters, because they served the needs of Japan Inc., not its customers. Nippon Steel finds it much easier to sell efficient steel production processes, with which it is intimately familiar, than laptop computers, about which it knows nothing more than scores of faceless competitors. Japan Inc. will be serving real customer needs in environmental technology—its own. A short step will take these companies and their expertise into the open market, at home and abroad.

Much of Japan's success in manufacturing has been attributed to *kaizen,* the art of incremental improvements. Focused on quality and efficiency, *kaizen* has produced successive generations of better and cheaper cars, TVs, and cameras. While *kaizen* improvements have not been able to correct problems with customers, this philosophy is well suited to the Green Wave. Waste reduction and resource efficiency are natural extensions of *kaizen*. Companies which reduce their emissions to zero do so through the relentless pursuit of small improvements, not the application of blockbuster ideas or technologies.

The financial *shokku* of the early 1990s forced Japan to reconsider the freewheeling years of the 1980s. Extravagant living is not the Japanese way, and many were uncomfortable with the excesses of the previous decade. They come much more naturally by economy; their country has already proven its capacity to reduce waste and to operate efficiently. The Japanese can turn the slogan "less is more" into reality if anyone can.

Why America Can't Respond

Americans like to think of cheap oil as a competitive advantage. Since John D. Rockefeller struck oil in Pennsylvania a century ago, government policy has been to keep oil plentiful and cheap. At one time (before World War II perhaps), cheap oil may have given us a competitive advantage. Today, cheap oil enslaves American business.

Like Japan, the United States made great strides after the oil crises of the 1970s in reducing the energy intensity of its economy. Between 1970 and 1990, the amount of energy it took to produce each dollar of output fell by a quarter. Nevertheless, Americans consume twice as much energy (and other natural resources) as the Japanese for everything they do.[11] In other words, every dollar of output generated in the United States requires twice as much coal, oil, steel, timber, and other raw materials. During the past twenty years, the gap between American and Japanese energy efficiency actually widened!

It's no wonder the Japanese use less energy: electricity and gasoline cost two to three times as much in Japan as in the United States.[12] Gas costs $1.25 per gallon in New York, so we squander our natural resources and run up our trade deficit. Gas costs $3.75 per gallon in Tokyo, so Japan runs energy-lean and turns a trade surplus year in, year out.

As long as prices were rising quickly (in the 1970s) or people were afraid they would start rising again (in the early 1980s), Americans did increase energy efficiency. But by the late 1980s, when real prices had fallen to postwar lows, the country was backsliding. After the sharp recession of the early 1980s was over, total energy use again began climbing quickly.[13] Along with the 1950s gas prices went the 1950s attitude toward waste: we're talking constitutional rights here! Without the correct price signals, American industry has little incentive to run lean.

The government has tried to overcome the disadvantages of cheap energy prices through regulation, for example by setting standards for car fuel economy and large appliance power consumption. These changes have worked—but only on *new* cars and refrigerators. Incredibly, by the late 1980s, the average new car sold in the United States got better gas mileage than the one rolling off the show room floor in Japan. But because high performance standards do not affect the millions of clunkers still on the road, the average car in the United States consumes nearly two and one-half times as much gas as in Japan.[14]

After the big push of legislation in the 1970s, the U.S. government did not keep up the pressure on industry to be more efficient. In Japan (and Germany) the pressure was relentless. As a result, Japan produces nearly two-thirds less CO_2, the bête noire of the global warming doom and gloomers. Each kilowatt-hour generated in Japan results in one-eighth as much sulfur oxide and one-fifth as much nitrogen oxide as in the United States.[15] There is a lack of political will here that is going to catch up with American business very soon.

The Clean Air Act of 1990 provides plenty of new incentives for industry to reduce emissions, but little to galvanize industry or revolutionize efficiency. The U.S. Environmental Protection Agency challenged big business with its "33/50" program, a voluntary effort to cut toxic emissions by 33 percent by 1992 and 50 percent by 1995. About 250 companies, accounting for a large share of the country's toxic output, signed on. Meeting this "challenge" will make great press release copy, but if your Japanese competitor cuts all waste right to zero when you have achieved a 50 percent reduction, your cost position will be undercut by a wide margin, perhaps fatally so. If you want to talk about "saving the whales" in your annual report, meet the EPA's challenge. If you want to save your company, meet Japan's—or go one better.

In resisting environmental regulations every step of the way, American industry turned an unprecedented opportunity into financial burden. When the Clean Air Act of 1990 was passed, the cost of compliance for industry was estimated at a crippling $25 billion per year. The auto industry successfully resisted tougher emissions standards than originally proposed, calculating the additional costs in the billions.[16] Similarly, Detroit resisted higher mileage standards (although in fairness GM, at least, advocated higher gas taxes as a better means of reducing fuel consumption). If Japan embraces these changes, Japanese companies will be the ones that benefit, whether they manufacture in Japan, the United States, or elsewhere.

By EPA estimates, total real outlays for pollution control activities will rise from $115 billion in 1990 to $185 billion in the year 2000.[17] These figures may be accurate, but each business chooses whether to consider the pollution control laws as a tax or as an incentive. By exceeding its legal environmental responsibilities, your company can make the investment necessary to be the low-cost producer in its field, to make "lean management" its new philosophy.

One man's burden is another's opportunity. Many companies continue to look for ways to "fix" their pollution problems, buying environmental technology rather than changing how they do business. As a result, legal burdens like the new Clean Air Act are make-work schemes for those selling environmental solutions. But where will the technology come from? The United States already buys nearly three quarters of some types of pollution control equipment from foreign suppliers.[18] Add that to our oil bill, and you can see where we are headed. Other countries, notably Japan and Germany, are using tough regulation to drive environmental technology development. Our burden is becoming their opportunity.

For many companies, the environment remains a public relations or legal problem, or both. Environmental affairs are a significant share of big business's legal costs in America.[19] Environmental regulations (like everything else) in America seem designed to generate the maximum amount of legal conflict (with attendant paper work). By some accounts, more is spent on legal fights about who is responsible for the so-called Superfund toxic waste sites, than on actual cleanup. As a result, it is only the fear of another Bhopal that gets some companies to spend real money. For others, public opinion is what matters. Some have gone to patently absurd lengths to demonstrate the environmentally benign qualities of their products. For a while, the favorite technique of the public relations strategy was to hire a well-known consulting or accounting firm to do an elaborately detailed "life-cycle cost" analysis which "proved" what common sense tells you cannot be so. For example, you might tally the environmental costs of manufacturing a titanium frame mountain bike, Kevlar tires, Spandex racing shorts, and SPF-30 suntan lotion (not to mention the nuclear energy needed to heat the hot water for showers) and conclude that driving to work is the ecologically correct thing to do. Wouldn't this money have been better spent on real efficiency improvements?

Officially, at least, few if any companies make environmental affairs a public relations function. Many join health, safety, and environmental affairs into one staff group. Elsewhere, environmental managers report to the legal department, and occasionally to human resources. In Japan, by contrast, environmental matters are normally considered a line engineering function—in other words, they take it seriously. When American companies realized that quality was important, many rushed lemming-like to appoint a new "V.P. for Quality," as if quality was something to be grafted onto an organization. In Japan, quality is everyone's job, and it looks like the environment will be too.

Counterbalancing the foot-dragging contingent, a number of forward-looking American companies, particularly chemical producers, have decided to rise to the environmental challenge before them. But all too often, their goals are far too modest. Hailed for their foresight are companies with goals like "reduce the generation of all waste 50 percent by the year 2000 (from 1992)" or "reduce manufacturing waste 25 percent by 1994 (from 1991)." Frequently reductions like this can be achieved by simple housekeeping improvements and by operating machines within closer tolerances. If you reduce waste by only 50 percent over the next ten years, you're probably falling behind industry averages—even in the United States. Your toughest competitors are looking for this kind of cost improvement *every year*. If you want to succeed, set your sights high, so you can really challenge your people. You don't want them to be retired or dead before your "50 percent by 2001" plan reaches its grand finale in a flurry of press releases.

By the early 1990s, exposure to foreign competition and deregulation ended the days of cheap financial capital in Japan. So too the days of cheap cnvironmental capital must eventually end in the United States. How long can the U.S. government insulate your company from world energy price levels? And how long can you compete with those for whom abandoning trailer loads of toxic chemicals in fifty-five-gallon drums on the New Jersey Turnpike is not an option?

Some of the companies now seen as part of the environmental vanguard have warned that the salad days are over: pollution prevention pays during the early stages, but later you have to spend real money. No surprises here. The difficulty in reducing waste increases logarithmically as you approach the limit. In other words, going from 90 percent to 99 percent on your zero emissions program may be tougher than going from 1 percent to 90 percent. Similarly, going from 99.0 percent to 99.7 percent may be tougher than the first 99 percent. At the beginning, simple changes will produce dramatic results; later you have to ask the tough questions: How are we organized? Why do we make this product? What is our business? What do our customers really value? The process is very similar to approaching zero defects in manufacturing, except to produce zero waste, you must reexamine all activities, in and out of the factory.

Technology and the Green Wave

Although MITI has targeted environmental technology for investment, American companies are on the leading edge in many areas. Innumerable processes and technologies (frequently from small and medium-sized companies) are reaching the market in the United States in response to the new Clean Air Act and other legislation. In the early 1990s, venture capitalists and mutual funds began scouring the field for investment opportunities, facilitating the development of new ideas.

Over the next decade, the prospects are bright for new products and companies addressing the environmental market. But companies looking for a technical "fix," a dose of Yankee ingenuity, to solve their environmental problems will be disappointed. Zero emissions is achieved through better management (better thinking, really), not better technology. As in information technology, leadership will go not to those with the best hardware, but to those who can solve customer problems. America may have the hardware, but Japan is developing the "software," the new thinking, necessary to make zero emissions a reality. Environmental technology hardware will eventually become a commodity as it has in IT.

Losing high-end opportunities to Japan will be a dramatic reversal from IT, where the United States made software and systems (and money) and Japan made commodity chips (and losses). Will we then raise tariffs and countervailing duties on efficient, environmentally friendly products? Will we put special surcharges on cars that get 100 miles per gallon? Or will we simply go broke paying for ever more foreign oil?

The After-Effects of the Green Tsunami

A uniquely Japanese system of management, well adapted to their lack of natural resources and concomitant need to be frugal, may do for Japan what thirty years of exports have not achieved. The Green Wave could reduce Japan's dependence on unstable sources of oil and other raw materials, improve its antagonistic trade relations, enable production and management to move overseas, and finally allow Japan to embrace its customers.

If it can successfully ride the Green Wave, for the first time in its history, Japan will be secure, able to act with confidence, free to find a new role commensurate with its economic achievements. Riding the Green Wave may be this new role, a part scripted just for Japan to play on the new world stage.

The potential is there for the Japanese to become the "non-oil barons" of the postindustrial era, shifting the center of gravity in the energy world from Riyadh to Tokyo. As the environmental leader, Japan can have real political clout without threatening anyone. At the moment, Japan finds it difficult to flex its muscles militarily, or even politically, because of its history and fragile position as a trading nation. Japan understandably did not want to rock the boat during the Gulf War, for example, since 50 percent or more of its oil comes from the Middle East.

Better management, not environmental equipment and service sales, will be the real dividend for Japan. Nevertheless, as Japan improves its manufacturing, techniques and equipment developed for internal uses will find ready markets overseas.

Environmental technology has big sales potential around the world. In addition, Japan can reinforce its position in key industries, especially cars, by driving down costs with a zero-emissions strategy. Even in information technology, relentless cost reduction will pay the best dividends in the commodity hardware markets that Japan has staked out. "Lean and green" management will open up new markets in countries with tough environmental standards and will give Japan Inc. a leg up with many new products and technologies not yet fully developed. Finally, as suppliers of advanced green components and processes, Japanese vendors can get their hooks into customer companies that need "environmentally correct" suppliers to help meet their own legal or market requirements.

As waste is eliminated from all activities, Japan has an opportunity to revolutionize its service industries. Poor productivity in services is a problem in all countries, but in Japan more than most. An obsession with waste elimination may be the catalyst needed to shift service productivity onto a new plane.

By substituting information for energy and raw materials, Japan will further increase in the value of knowledge. With zero waste, sustainable development will be a reality. Japan will have ushered in the age of information, but in a way perhaps even the Japanese have not anticipated. For the past twenty years it has been Japan's hope to serve the information age with computer hardware, a strategy that has produced mixed results at best. Riding the Green Wave Japanese industry can serve overseas and domestic customers across a much broader range of markets.

Will America Finally Get What It Wants?

"We've got it all, and it's ours to squander," the credo that served American industry for two hundred years, has now become heresy. No amount of wishful thinking and low gas prices will protect American business from wasteful practices when foreign competitors turn to lean management. And don't forget, many markets will be closed to those unable to meet very high green standards. In fact, you can expect environmental laws to be the nontariff barrier of the 1990s.

In the zero emissions game, "50 percent better than we were in 1990" won't cut it. Even the emissions targets set by leading-edge American companies have the hollow ring of Detroit pronunciamentos from the 1980s: "the best-built cars in America." Customers wanted the best-built cars in the world—and the best service too. Wasteful production means wasteful thinking means high costs (and almost always poor quality). Few survive as high cost producers in their markets.

Ironically, America may yet get what it seems to want: manufacturing jobs, by becoming Japan's sweat shop. With cheap energy, relatively lax pollution standards, low-cost wages and abundant—if poorly educated—labor, the United States may be the perfect location for low-tech manufacturing that Japan no longer wants. But we may find ourselves competing with Mexico and Indonesia for these jobs, while the opportunities needed to support a large middle class shift to Japan, Western Europe, and even industrializing countries, like Singapore, that are getting with the green program. Wasteful industrial practices are associated with the Third World, not the First. We must choose the direction we wish to take. The Green Tsunami draws near.

ACKNOWLEDGMENTS

John Celentano, for thoughtful advice on information technology. Betsy Howard and Bob Easton of The Wilkerson Group, Inc. in New York, for their generous time and valuable insight into the pharmaceutical industry. Lisa Indovino, for many hard lessons on customer needs. Juri Jurjevics, who gave us early encouragement and advice on writing and selling this book. Kathi Paton, our agent, for believing in our idea. Bill Rich, who reviewed an early manuscript and contributed materially to its improvement. David Rottman, for patient encouragement, for helping us frame our proposal, and for explaining the inner workings of the publishing world. Al Toomer, for inspiration over many years on the integration of manufacturing and customer service. Truman Talley, for sharing our enthusiasm, and focusing our efforts. Brian White, for helping to shape the ideas in this book through many discussions.

APPENDIX

Japan's Technologies Share

	World Market		U.S. Market		Japanese Market		World (Ex. Japan)	
	Size 1990 $b	Japan's share	Size 1990 $b	Japan's share	Size 1990 $b	Japan's share	Size 1990 $b	Japan's share
Computers								
Supercomputers	2	30%	1	1%	1	87%	1	1%
Mainframes	41	20%	13	15%	8	63%	33	10%
Minicomputers	34	15%	12	3%	7	70%	28	2%
Workstations	15	11%	8	5%	3	40%	12	4%
PCs	75	19%	31	8%	11	90%	64	7%
LANs	23	1%	14	0%	0	40%	23	0%
Peripherals	83	34%	34	28%	12	67%	71	28%
Software	72	9%	30	1%	14	45%	58	1%
Services	115	13%	85	2%	22	60%	93	2%
Total	460	17%	228	7%	78	63%	383	8%
Semiconductors								
Total	58	49%	17	22%	23	88%	35	23%
Telecommunications								
Public switching	21	15%	7	1%	3	98%	18	3%
Transmission	17	21%	5	8%	2	99%	15	12%
PBXs	9	18%	4	15%	1	85%	8	9%
Terminals	28	55%	12	30%	8	99%	20	38%
Outside plant	11	5%	3	1%	0	90%	11	2%
Network services	341	16%	126	0%	58	96%	283	0%
Total	427	20%	157	3%	72	96%	355	4%
Information Technologies								
Total	945	20%	402	6%	173	80%	773	7%
Cars	450	27%	135	28%	55	97%	395	17%

Source: North River Ventures estimates.

NOTES

Introduction: Cracks in the Facade

1. Japan's great entrepreneur-industrialist Konosuke Matsushita's still-fresh maxims on this subject, best summed up by "The customer is God," are recommended reading for any manager bent on better customer service. See, for example, Konosuke Matsushita, *Quest for Prosperity* (PHP Institute, 1988).
2. *The Competitive Status of the U.S. Electronics Sector* (U.S. Department of Commerce, 1990).

Chapter 1: Facing the Threat

1. See *The U.S. Computer and Semiconductor Industries: A Partnership for Success* (Semiconductor Industry Association, 1990); *The Competitive Status of the U.S. Electronics Sector* (U.S. Department of Commerce, 1990).
2. In 1989, for example, Japan had a trade surplus of $45 billion with the United States; its total fuel imports in the same year were $43 billion. *Japan Economic Almanac 1990.*
3. "The silvering of Japan," *Economist,* October 7, 1989, p. 81; "Gone fishing," *Economist,* January 6, 1990, p. 61.
4. "Together under the sun," *Economist,* July 15, 1989, p. S9.
5. For a stunningly iconoclastic view of Japan, see Karel van Wolferen, *The Enigma of Japanese Power* (Vintage Books, 1990), p. 429.
6. "Japan's auto industry may soon consolidate as competition grows," *Wall Street Journal,* April 24, 1990, p. A1; "So far, Nissan's catch up plan hasn't caught on," *Business Week,* September 17, 1990, p. 59; "Daihatsu planning to halt imports to U.S.," *New York Times,* February 14, 1992, p. D4; Honda, Nissan, and Toyota annual reports.

7. "Video hangover," *Economist*, January 13, 1990, p. 69.
8. "Will DAT become the next household name?" *New York Times*, December 2, 1990, Section 3, p. 6.
9. "Will tackle it soon, honest," *Economist*, September 2, 1989, p. 69; "Ready, steady . . ." *Economist*, September 23, 1989, p. 79.
10. "Paris boosts aid to electronics groups by FFr 6bn," *Financial Times*, April 4, 1991, p. 1.
11. "The planners strike back," *Economist*, February 16, 1991, p. 57; "EC electronics companies ask Brussels for extra protection," *Financial Times*, April 23, 1991, p. 18.
12. "Who are the copy cats now," *Economist*, May 20, 1989, p. 91.
13. "A McDonnell deal in Asia would jolt the airliner industry," *Wall Street Journal*, November 15, 1991, p. A1.
14. "A split over machine tool imports," *New York Times*, October 7, 1991, p. D1.
15. U.S. hysteria about the trade deficit has resulted in calls to action against Japan. But there is three times as much trade between Canada and the United States as there is between Japan and the United States. Trade with Japan is remarkable only in that it is so unbalanced. Even America's trade deficit is, in one sense, illusory. On the basis of ownership, not location of manufacture, America has a trade surplus with the world and a balance of trade with Japan. See "The myth of economic sovereignty," *Economist*, June 23, 1990, p. 67.
16. "Noted Japanese retailer plans Ritz Tower store," *New York Times*, June 19, 1991, p. D6.
17. Carl von Clausewitz, *On War* (Penguin, 1968), pp. 276, 282.

Chapter 2: The Information Technology Fiasco

1. Japan's exports of computers and peripheral equipment rose from ¥10 billion in 1971 to ¥2,108 billion (approximately $15 billion) in 1988; see *Information and Communications in Japan* (InfoCom Research, 1990), p. 169.
2. Koji Kobayashi, *Computers and Communications* (MIT Press, 1985).
3. NEC 1991 Annual Report, p. 3; IBM 1990 Annual Report, p. 34.
4. *Business Week Innovation 1990*, p. 102.
5. Marie Anchordouguy, *Computers Inc.* (Harvard University Press, 1989), pp. 174–75.
6. "Japan sets sights on winning lead in new computers," *New York Times*, April 30, 1990, p. A1; "Japan asks aid on new computers," *New York Times*, March 15, 1991, p. D1.
7. "Japan seeks SI expertise through joint research," *Computer Systems News*, June 4, 1990, p. 6.
8. "South Korea's semiconductor makers seek transition to sophisticated chips," *Wall Street Journal*, July 29, 1991, p. A5G.
9. "Boom in manufactured exports provides hope for U.S. economy," *New York Times*, April 21, 1991, p. A1.
10. "Flat out in Japan," *Economist*, February 1, 1992, p. 79.
11. "Future technology bright for 'flash' chips," *Wall Street Journal*, February 6, 1992, p. B1.
12. "Motorola: one step backward, two steps forward," *Business Week*, June 24, 1991, p. 42.

13. "Falling off the learning curve," *Economist,* February 23, 1991, p. 64; "On their shoulders," *Economist,* July 14, 1990, p. 72.
14. "Inferiority complex," *Economist,* February 1, 1992, p. 78.
15. "Slump hits Japanese electronics," *New York Times,* February 24, 1991, p. D1.
16. "Tweaking Big Blue's beard," *Economist,* October 28, 1989, p. 71.
17. "Japan agrees to measures to aid sales of U.S. goods," *Wall Street Journal,* January 10, 1992, p. A3.
18. "Advancing on many fronts," *Financial Times,* April 23, 1991, "Computer Industry," p. 4.
19. "Toshiba warns of 58% profits fall," *Financial Times,* February 21, 1992, p. 19.
20. "Client/server craze driving growth in software market," *Computerworld,* March 11, 1991, p. 8.
21. "Codex adds network services," *Computer Systems News,* November 19, 1990, p. 37; "Brace yourself for a fourth wave," *TPT/Networking Management,* March 1989, p. 11.
22. Professional service expenditures will grow from $15 billion in 1990 to nearly $50 billion in 1995; see "Service forecast: bullish on SI," *Computer Systems News,* October 1, 1990, p. 1.
23. "How computers can choke companies," *Economist,* June 9, 1990, p. 66.
24. "Subcontracts that work well," *Computerworld,* February 4, 1991, p. 61.
25. "Outsourcing boom over? You ain't seen nothin," *Computerworld,* January 13, 1992, p. 8.
26. "WYSIWYG," *Computerworld,* June 24, 1991, p. 126.
27. "One high-tech race where U.S. leads: personal computers," *Wall Street Journal,* October 31, 1989, p. A1.
28. "Japan opens up—slowly," *Communications Week,* December 24, 1990, p. 31.
29. "Five chip-makers become competitors," *Financial Times,* December 3, 1990, "Japanese Industry," p. 4.

Chapter 3: Jack of All Trades and Master of None

1. Sony 1990 Annual Report, p. 50.
2. Sony 1990 Annual Report, p. 4; "Stalking another hit like the Walkman," *New York Times,* February 23, 1992, Section 3, p. 8; "Media colossus," *Business Week,* March 25, 1991, p. 66.
3. "Sony to market digital tape decks in U.S.," *Wall Street Journal,* June 5, 1990; "Cacophony," *Economist,* June 1, 1991, p. 63; "In harmony," *Economist,* July 20, 1991, p. 83; "Tape wars: how Philips beat Sony," *Financial Times of Canada,* February 25, 1991, p. 1.
4. "Sony to market digital tape decks in U.S.," *Wall Street Journal,* June 5, 1990; "Philips and Sony tout endorsements of products," *Wall Street Journal,* September 4, 1991, p. B6; "A compact disk advance starts a new battle," *New York Times,* June 19, 1991, p. D1; "Cacophony," *Economist,* June 1, 1991, p. 63.
5. Sony 1990 Annual Report, p. 6; "Camcorders: sweet revenge for Sony," *Business Week,* December 23, 1991; "Counterpunch," *Economist,* June 30, 1990, p. 66.
6. "Adventures in Wonderland," *Barron's,* October 7, 1991, p. 8; "Sony to raise up to $3 billion in Japan, U.S.," *Wall Street Journal,* August 8, 1991, p. A3;

"Will intramural squabbling derail debt-ridden Sony," *New York Times,* August 11, 1991, Section 3, p. 5; Edward Klein, "A yen for Hollywood," *Vanity Fair,* September 1991, p. 200.

7. "How lean production can change the world," *New York Times Magazine,* September 23, 1990, p. 38.
8. "Japanese automotive industry," *Financial Times,* December 20, 1990, p. 10.
9. "Building smaller, buying bigger," *New York Times Magazine,* February 18, 1990, p. 68.
10. Interview, John Celentano, Samuel & Co., Inc., Randallstown, MD.
11. Interview, Chrysler Corp. Public Relations Dept.
12. "Kubota forges ahead on high-tech push," *Wall Street Journal,* July 19, 1990, p. A6.
13. "Texas Instruments, Kobe Steel form venture," *Wall Street Journal,* March 20, 1990, p. B4.
14. "Japan's smokestack fire-sale," *Economist,* August 19, 1989, p. 51; "Japanese find U.S. high tech a risky venture," *Wall Street Journal,* November 8, 1991, p. B1.
15. Hitachi advertisement, *Wall Street Journal,* March 14, 1991, p. A10.
16. "Stalking another hit like the Walkman," *New York Times,* February 23, 1992, Section 3, p. 8; "Sony is turning more cautious after reverses," *Wall Street Journal,* January 7, 1992, p. B1.
17. NEC 1989 Annual Report, p. 22.
18. "Japan/U.S. Challenge of the 1990's: Achieving a Balance," special *Business Week* advertising supplement, p. 76.
19. "NEC to resell Stratus gear," *Computerworld,* April 22, 1991, p. 104.
20. "NEC licenses chip technology to AT&T," *Wall Street Journal,* March 8, 1990, p. B4.
21. "IBM gears up for battle over mainframe disk drives," *New York Times,* August 25, 1991, Section 3, p. 9.
22. IBM First Quarter 1991 Report to Shareholders.
23. "Scenting extinction," *Economist,* December 14, 1991, p. 69.
24. "Noted Japanese retailer plans Ritz Tower store," *New York Times,* June 19, 1991, p. D6.
25. Interview, Chrysler Corp. Public Relations Dept.
26. "Chrysler minivan regains momentum," *Wall Street Journal,* June 20, 1991, p. B1.
27. "Components to order," *Financial Times,* December 4, 1989, "Japanese Industry," p. 8.
28. "Global PC outlook," *Wall Street Journal,* February 11, 1992, p. B8.
29. "Can a keiretsu work in America?" *Harvard Business Review,* September–October 1990, p. 181.
30. Confidential Interview with Fujitsu executive.
31. "Matsushita sets pact with sun on technology," *Wall Street Journal,* December 6, 1990, p. B3.
32. "Why Sony is hoping that the world will thrill to Michael Jackson," *Financial Times,* March 28, 1991, p. 15.
33. "NCR sets up meeting with big holders to lobby for support to fight AT&T bid," *Wall Street Journal,* December 13, 1990, p. A5.
34. "Cross-border alliances become favorite way to crack new markets," *Wall Street Journal,* March 26, 1990, p. A4.

35. "Intel announces a line of workstations using its 386 and 486 microprocessors," *Wall Street Journal,* January 23, 1990, p. B4.; "Motorola, taking on rivals, to launch line of multi-user business computers," *Wall Street Journal,* March 5, 1990, p. B4.
36. "Compaq narrows search for supplier of microprocessors," *Wall Street Journal,* October 1, 1990, p. B18.
37. "The rival Japan respects," *Business Week,* November 13, 1989, p. 108.
38. "The truth about big business in Japan," *Business Tokyo,* April 1990, p. 27.
39. "Making foreigners cross," *Economist,* August 19, 1989, p. 62; "Big business in Japan," *Business Tokyo,* April 1990, p. 27.
40. "Japanese automotive industry," *Financial Times,* December 20, 1990, p. 10.

Chapter 4: When Tokyo Calls the Shots, Japan Comes First

1. Koji Kobayashi, *Rising to the Challenge* (Harcourt Brace Jovanovich Japan, 1989), p. 41.
2. Koji Kobayashi, *Computers and Communications* (MIT Press, 1985) p. 47.
3. Koji Kobayashi, *Rising to the Challenge,* pp. 17, 59, 61.
4. "NEC in the U.S.: a detour on the road to the big time," *Business Week,* August 5, 1991.
5. NEC 1991 Annual Report, pp. 17, 27.
6. "Under Japanese bosses, Americans find work both better and worse," *Wall Street Journal,* November 27, 1991, p. A1.
7. "Japanese influx 'helps the EC,' " *European,* November 22, 1991, p. 22.
8. "Japanese are unfazed by U.S. downturn," *Wall Street Journal,* November 30, 1990, p. A2.
9. "Japanese start to shop more cautiously abroad," *Financial Times,* January 2, 1991, p. 13.
10. "Zenith is shifting Taiwan jobs to Mexico, signaling trend in other manufacturers," *Wall Street Journal,* November 12, 1991, p. A4; Matsushita Electric special *Fortune* advertising supplement, p. S-6; "Sony said ready to build TV sets in Pennsylvania," *Wall Street Journal,* April 17, 1990, p. B4.
11. Albert Alletzhauser, *The House of Nomura* (Harper Perennial, 1990), p. 254.
12. "Like Japan, but different," *Economist,* November 3, 1990, p. 76.
13. "Nintendo is ruling out a new home in Seattle," *New York Times,* February 11, 1992, p. D2.
14. "Where will Japan strike next," *Fortune,* September 25, 1989, p. 44.
15. "Do it my way," *Economist,* November 24, 1990, p. 74.
16. "The irony behind Japan's insularity," *Financial Times of Canada,* July 16, 1990, p. 34.
17. "Some indignities to end for Koreans in Japan," *New York Times,* May 2, 1990, p. 5.
18. Confidential interview with Fujitsu executive.
19. "Some 7-Elevens try selling a new image," *Wall Street Journal,* October 25, 1991, p. B1.
20. "Impact of Japan's EC auto deal," *Financial Times,* September 16, 1991, p. 7.
21. "Japanese systematically invest in Europe prior to 1992 changes," *Wall Street Journal,* December 10, 1990, p. A7D.
22. "Emphasis on design," *Financial Times,* June 4, 1991, p. 9.

23. "Collaboration in the lab," *Financial Times,* September 20, 1991, p. xi.
24. "Japanese spoken here," *Economist,* September 14, 1991, p. 67.
25. Confidential interview with Fujitsu executive.
26. "It's a shakier perch for Toshiba's laptops," *Business Week,* August 5, 1991, p. 64.
27. "NEC: a growing commitment to America," 1988 *Fortune* advertising supplement.
28. Fujitsu Network Switching of America, Inc., company backgrounder, March 1991, p. 2.
29. "It's a shakier perch for Toshiba's laptops," *Business Week,* August 5, 1991, p. 64.
30. See also Gary Katzenstein, *Funny Business* (Soho, 1989), a fascinating and amusing story about a year spent immersed in the group dynamics of Sony.
31. "Culture shock at home: working for a foreign boss," *Business Week,* December 17, 1990, p. 84.
32. "NTT unit to offer data aid to Japanese clients in U.S.," *Wall Street Journal,* February 22, 1990, p. B2.
33. "Japanese-American culture clash," *New York Times,* September 9, 1990, Section 3, Part 2, p. 25.
34. "Culture shock at home: working for a foreign boss," *Business Week,* December 17, 1990, p. 80.
35. "Quasar firing policy gets poor reception," *Washington Post,* December 13, 1990, p. E1.
36. "Japanese firm wins ruling in rights case," *Wall Street Journal,* December 6, 1991, p. A3.
37. "Japanese car makers are coddling their U.S. kids," *Business Week,* March 4, 1991, p. 21.
38. "Fujitsu unit reorganizes, trims staff," *Communications Week,* April 1, 1991, p. 36; "Subaru pulls into the image shop," *Business Week,* August 19, 1991, p. 86; "It's a shakier perch for Toshiba's laptops," *Business Week,* August 5, 1991, p. 62.
39. "Now Akira Yeiri really has to burn rubber," *Business Week,* May 27, 1991, p. 72.
40. "So far, America is a blowout for Bridgestone," *Business Week,* August 6, 1990, p. 82.
41. Roger Goodman, *Japan's International Youth: The Emergence of a New Class of Schoolchildren* (Clarendon Press, 1990), as reviewed in *Japan Times Weekly International Edition,* January 14, 1991, p. 15.
42. "Full of eastern power," *Economist,* June 9, 1990, p. S12.
43. Confidential interview with a New York publisher.
44. "Sony Corp. selects an American to stand for election to board," *Wall Street Journal,* May 28, 1991, p. B8.
45. "Sony Corp. names Michael P. Schulhof to new post," *Wall Street Journal,* March 7, 1990, p. B10; "Media Colossus," *Business Week,* March 25, 1991, p. 67; "Sony selects Ron Sommer, a European, to lead U.S. sales and marketing arm," *Wall Street Journal,* December 13, 1990, p. B10.
46. Sony Third Quarterly Report, December 31, 1991, p. 7; "Sony's holiday films surprise skeptics," *Wall Street Journal,* January 15, 1992, p. B1.
47. "New money comes to Tinsel Town," *Financial Times,* December 10, 1990, p. 14.

48. "Vain man: why Guber-Peters may bomb in Tokyo," *Spy,* April 1990, p. 42; "Canton succeeds Price as chairman of the Columbia Pictures unit of Sony," *Wall Street Journal,* October 4, 1991, p. B4; Edward Klein, "A yen for Hollywood," *Vanity Fair,* September 1991, p. 200.
49. "Adventures in wonderland," *Barron's,* October 7, 1991, p. 8.
50. "Where's Walter?" *Forbes,* January 21, 1991, p. 108; "Norio Ohga's America," *New York Times,* November 25, 1990, Section 3, p. 6.
51. "Sony to list 29% of unit in a bid to reduce debt," *Wall Street Journal,* November 8, 1991, p. B4; "Tokyo traders shun Sony unit's new stock," *Wall Street Journal,* November 25, 1991, p. C2; "Sony to raise up to $3 billion in Japan, U.S.," *Wall Street Journal,* August 6, 1991, p. A3.
52. "Building smaller, buying bigger," *New York Times Magazine,* February 18, 1990, p. 62.
53. "Sony selects Ron Sommer, a European, to lead U.S. sales and marketing arm," *Wall Street Journal,* December 13, 1990, p. B10.
54. "The emergence of a global company," *Financial Times,* October 2, 1989, p. 5.
55. Confidential interview with Sony supplier.
56. Nissan 1990 Annual Report, p. 6.
57. "Sam Kusumoto: this mind of Minolta has an American heart," *Pinnacle,* May–June 1991, p. 8; "Head of Minolta in U.S. gives up president's job," *New York Times,* January 9, 1992, p. D4.
58. "How to grow strong on humble pie," *Economist,* November 23, 1991, p. 94.
59. "Saks management teams with Tobu of Tokyo in bid to buy U.S. retailer," *Wall Street Journal,* March 16, 1990, p. A3.
60. "Incomplete, but being restored," *New York Times,* September 19, 1991, p. R15.
61. "Hollywood is losing some glitter for tinsel-weary Japan investors," *Wall Street Journal,* July 10, 1991, p. A9.
62. "Marks & Sparks' wake-up call," *Financial Times of Canada,* October 28, 1991, p. 10; "The quality imperative," Royal Bank Letter, September/October 1991, p. 8.
63. "Shot-gun approach," *Financial Times,* December 3, 1990, "Japanese Industry," p. iv.
64. "A French Euro-blockage," *Financial Times,* December 18, 1991, p. 12.
65. "At Daewoo, a 'revolution' at the top," *Business Week,* February 18, 1991.
66. "Just as U.S. firms try Japanese management, Honda is centralizing," *New York Times,* April 11, 1991, p. A1; "Honda loses its way," *Economist,* September 14, 1991, p. 79; "A multinational changing gears," *Financial Times,* August 12, 1991, p. 12.

Chapter 5: Ship and Forget

1. Interview with Subaru Public Relations Dept.; "Subaru pulls into the image shop," *Business Week,* August 19, 1991, p. 86; "Japan's auto industry may soon consolidate as competition grows," *Wall Street Journal,* April 24, 1990, p. A1.
2. Interview with Subaru Public Relations Dept.; "Subaru pulls into the image shop," *Business Week,* August 19, 1991, p. 86; "Japan's auto industry may soon consolidate as competition grows," *Wall Street Journal,* April 24, 1990, p. A1.

3. "Japan's HDTV: what's wrong with this picture?" *Business Week*, April 1, 1991, p. 90.
4. "Fujitsu open for business in Canada," *Computerworld*, June 24, 1991, p. 101.
5. "CDC to resell NEC systems," *Computerworld*, January 20, 1992, p. 12.
6. "The rival Japan respects," *Business Week*, November 13, 1989, p. 108.
7. "Mail sort," *Wall Street Journal*, January 10, 1992, p. A8.
8. "Kodak plans to restructure corporate-wide," *Wall Street Journal*, November 11, 1991, p. A4.
9. "IBM agrees to sell notebook-size PCs to Hitachi Ltd. for resale in Japan," *Wall Street Journal*, December 26, 1991, p. B4.
10. "Wang Labs, shifting focus, will sell IBM computers," *Wall Street Journal*, June 19, 1991, p. A3.
11. "When a company promises service, does it mean it?" *New York Times*, November 4, 1990, Section 3, p. 6.
12. "Apple: new team, new strategy," *Business Week*, October 15, 1990, p. 92; "Apple users voice Mac concerns," *Computerworld*, December 17, 1990, p. 10.
13. Dell Computer advertisement, *Wall Street Journal*, July 18, 1991, p. B3.
14. "When a company promises service, does it mean it?" *New York Times*, November 4, 1990, Section 3, p. 6.; CompuAdd advertisement, *Wall Street Journal*, November 13, 1990, p. B3.
15. "Apple gets a little more help from its friends," *Business Week*, October 28, 1991, p. 132.
16. Gordon W. Prangle, *At Dawn We Slept* (Penguin, 1981), p. 11.
17. "Computer race puts old guard to the test," *Globe and Mail*, August 7, 1990, p. B2.
18. "Hitachi's mainframes get jump," *Wall Street Journal*, June 4, 1990.
19. Interview with Hitachi Public Relations Dept.
20. "Supercomputer bout," *Business Tokyo*, April 1990, p. 32.
21. "Nissan gets back in the driving seat," *Financial Times*, December 31, 1990, p. 10; "Nissan Motor takes over control of French dealer," *Financial Times*, April 4, 1991, p. 6.
22. Interview with Bridgestone Public Relations Dept.; "So far, America is a blow-out for Bridgestone," *Business Week*, August 6, 1990, p. 82; "Bridgestone discovers purchase of U.S. firm creates big problems," *Wall Street Journal*, April 1, 1991, p. A1.
23. "Digitised sighs," *Economist*, August 4, 1990, p. 68.
24. "Japanese get first crack at new gadgets," *Wall Street Journal*, December 3, 1990, p. B1.
25. "IBM," *Business Week*, June 17, 1991, p. 30.
26. "Reporter's notebook," *Wall Street Journal*, November 16, 1990, p. B7A.
27. "IBM unveils 486-based portable," *Computer Systems News*, September 30, 1991, p. 10.
28. "Supercomputer bout," *Business Tokyo*, April 1990, p. 32.
29. "Japanese product development," *Journal of Business Strategy*, November/December 1990, p. 31.
30. "Pushing the envelope at Boeing," *New York Times*, November 10, 1991, section 3, page 1.
31. "Meridian Norstar launched in the UK," Northern Telecom press release, January 28, 1991, p. 4.

32. "The geniuses who made VCRs simple enough for a 50-year-old," *Business Week,* December 31, 1990, p. 54.
33. "OutFroxed," *Economist,* October 26, 1991, p. 86.

Chapter 6: Pumping Iron

1. Marie Anchordouguy, *Computers Inc.* (Harvard University Press, 1989), p. 167.
2. Fujitsu 1990 Annual Report, p. 3.
3. "Fujitsu unit reorganizes, trims staff," *Communications Week,* April 1, 1991, p. 36.
4. Confidential interview with Fujitsu executive.
5. "ICL may transfer expertise to Japan," *Computerworld,* December 24, 1990, p. 49.
6. "Japan's less-than-invincible computer makers," *Economist,* January 11, 1992, p. 59.
7. Fujitsu advertisement, *Economist,* January 28, 1992, pp. 72–73; "Fujitsu means business for America," Fujitsu advertising brochure; Fujitsu 1990 Annual Report, inside cover.
8. "Japanese Technology," *Economist,* December 2, 1989, Survey, p. 17.
9. *Business Week Innovation 1990,* p. 39.
10. "Top of the pops," *Economist,* June 23, 1990, p. 59.
11. "Five chip-mates become competitors," *Financial Times,* December 3, 1990, "Japanese Industry," p. 5.
12. "In realm of technology, Japan looms larger," *New York Times,* May 28, 1991, p. C8.
13. "Sony is turning more cautious after reverses," *Wall Street Journal,* January 7, 1992, p. B1.
14. "Japanese Technology," *Economist,* December 2, 1989, Survey, p. 16; "What U.S. scientists discover, the Japanese convert—into profit," *Wall Street Journal,* June 25, 1990, p. 16.
15. "Nissan and Hitachi team up to create a 'mobile office,' " *Wall Street Journal,* December 13, 1990.
16. Canon advertisement, *Business Week,* October 29, 1990, p. 68.
17. "Data General board ousts co-founder," *Wall Street Journal,* May 26, 1990, p. B1.
18. "Xerox tries to shed its has-been image with big new machine," *Wall Street Journal,* September 20, 1990, p. A1.
19. "Discovering the hidden computer," *Computerworld,* November 25, 1991, p. 20.
20. Confidential interview with AT&T executive.
21. Confidential report to an O.E.C.D. government.
22. "How U.S. robots lost the market to Japan in factory automation," *Wall Street Journal,* November 6, 1990, p. A1.
23. "Sony is turning more cautious after reverses," *Wall Street Journal,* January 7, 1992, p. B1.
24. Toshiba *Product Guide,* Fall 1991.
25. "Japan Inc. bows to the customer," *CIO,* August 1990, p. 91.
26. "Thinking Machines thinks big," *Computerworld,* November 4, 1991, p. 12.
27. Interview with Robert Easton, the Wilkerson Group, Inc., New York.

28. DRI/McGraw-Hill estimates that office equipment rose from 3% to 18% of America's investment in plant and equipment from 1980 to 1989, "A lot to learn," *The Economist,* March 3, 1990, p. 65.
29. "Putting computers together again," *Economist,* August 25, 1990, p. 55.
30. For further discussion, see William H. Davidow and Bro Uttal, *Total Customer Service* (Harper & Row, 1989), p. 160.

Chapter 7: Disintegrate Yourself

1. Speech presented by Edmund Fitzgerald to the New York Society of Security Analysts, February 15, 1990; Northern Telecom 1990 Annual Report; interview with Northern Telecom Public Relations Dept.
2. "Olivetti set for a very tough year," *Financial Times,* February 19, 1991, p. 20.
3. "Noted Japanese retailer plans Ritz Tower store," *New York Times,* June 19, 1991, p. D6.
4. "Unisys will cut costs via pact with Motorola," *Wall Street Journal,* January 30, 1992, p. B5.
5. "IBM bends its rules to make a laptop," *Wall Street Journal,* April 15, 1991, p. A9C.
6. "Kodak opts out," Businessland Inc. advertising supplement, *Wall Street Journal,* November 20, 1990.
7. "Outsourcing is it at Diesel Technology," *Computerworld,* May 27, 1991, p. 61.
8. "Conner's drive is getting a bit gummed up," *Business Week,* April 29, 1991, p. 31.
9. "If it ain't broke, fix it anyway," *Financial Times of Canada,* January 21, 1991, p. 13.
10. "Quantum has one tough hurdle to leap," *Business Week,* July 8, 1991, p. 84.
11. "The arrival of haute carture," *Economist,* July 29, 1989, p. 53.
12. Anna Versteeg, "Self-directed work teams yield long-term benefits," *Journal of Business Strategy,* November/December 1990, p. 9.
13. "American Express integrates network," *Computerworld,* June 24, 1991, p. 66.

Chapter 8: Decentralize Yourself

1. "Satisfaction guaranteed for customers and crew," *Wall Street Journal,* January 28, 1991, p. A14.
2. Ray Schultz, "Taking empowerment to the front lines," pp. 2–3 (unpublished essay).
3. Ibid., p. 1
4. "IBM announces details of plan to break its business into more autonomous pieces," *Wall Street Journal,* December 6, 1991, p. B3.
5. "IBM realigns duties of senior executives," *Wall Street Journal,* December 6, 1990, p. B6.
6. "IBM restructuring to shift power from mainframe execs," *Computerworld,* November 25, 1991, p. 1.
7. "Retail follies; auto industry innovation," *Wall Street Journal,* November 15, 1991, p. A14.
8. "Silicon Valley firms moving overseas," *Financial Post,* September 3, 1990, p. 36.

9. "Du Pont weaves pattern to fit in Europe," *Wall Street Journal,* November 12, 1991, p. A5.
10. "A new model for Big Blue," *New York Times,* March 8, 1992, Section 2, p. 2.
11. "Nintendo is ruling out a new home in Seattle," *New York Times,* February 11, 1992, p. D2.
12. Confidential interview with McGraw-Hill executive.
13. "It started with an egg," *Business Week,* December 2, 1991, p. 142.
14. "A car is born," *Economist,* September 29, 1990, p. 76.
15. "A multinational changing gears," *Financial Times,* August 12, 1991, p. 12; "55 miles per gallon: how Honda did it," *Business Week,* September 23, 1991, p. 82.
16. "America's new king of Europe's roads," *Economist,* March 9, 1991, p. 63.
17. "People," *Fortune,* Pacific Rim 1990, p. 91.
18. "One high-tech race where U.S. leads: personal computers," *The Wall Street Journal,* October 31, 1989, p. A1.
19. T. W. Kang, *Gaishi* (Basic Books, 1990), p. 150.
20. "Picking Japan's research brains," *Fortune,* March 25, 1991, p. 92.
21. IBM 1991 Annual Report, pp. 54ff.
22. "IBM," *Business Week,* June 17, 1991, p. 30.
23. "When IBM's big guns won't do," *New York Times,* July 18, 1991, p. D1.
24. "Motorola wants to light up another market," *Business Week,* October 14, 1991, p. 50.
25. "The racy Viper is already a winner for Chrysler," *Business Week,* November 4, 1991, p. 36.
26. "On the shop floor," *Economist,* July 13, 1991, p. 78.
27. "The bad boy of Silicon Valley," *Business Week,* December 9, 1991, p. 64.
28. "But will it wash?" *Economist,* July 13, 1991, p. 70.
29. "Tinkerers versus dreamers," *Economist,* December 23, 1989, p. 73.
30. "Can Dell, CompuAdd broaden niches?" *Wall Street Journal,* February 5, 1990, p. B1; "PC slump? What PC slump?" *Business Week,* July 1, 1991, p. 66.
31. "NEC in the U.S.: a detour on the road to the big time," *Business Week,* August 5, 1991, p. 64.
32. "Rock 'n' roll gadget maker takes on Japan," *Wall Street Journal,* September 10, 1990.
33. "Fujitsu meets Europe," *Communications Week,* August 13, 1990, p. 46.
34. "Competition versus collaboration," *Financial Times,* December 3, 1990, "Japanese Industry," p. 5.
35. "From pyramid to pancake," *Wall Street Journal,* June 4, 1990, p. R37.
36. "GM slices and GM slashes, but the flab survives," *Business Week,* December 23, 1991, p. 27.
37. "From pyramid to pancake," *Wall Street Journal,* June 4, 1990, p. R37.
38. "Corporate decision-making," *Economist,* September 8, 1990.
39. Confidential interview with Storage Technology executive.

Chapter 9: Maximize Customer Contact

1. "How Detroit Diesel, out from under GM, turned around fast," *Wall Street Journal,* August 16, 1991, p. A1.

2. Confidential interview with Detroit Diesel distributor; "How Detroit Diesel, out from under GM, turned around fast," *Wall Street Journal*, August 16, 1991, p. A1.
3. Confidential interview with Detroit Diesel distributor.
4. Interview. Ibid.
5. For a thorough discussion of customer expectations, see William H. Davidow and Bro Uttal, *Total Customer Service* (Harper & Row, 1989).
6. "Red ink flows freely at makers of Unix systems," *Wall Street Journal*, December 6, 1990, p. B1.
7. "IBM's Japan unit to restructure sales, marketing," *Wall Street Journal*, December 17, 1991, p. B4; "IBM: no layoffs anticipated," *Asahi Shimbun Japan Access*, December 23, 1991, p. 5.
8. "McKinney excels as IBM's Europe chief," *Wall Street Journal*, December 4, 1989, p. 9F.
9. "A new, open IBM keeps heavy cargo rolling out," *Computerworld*, December 24, 1990, p. 20.
10. "IBM," *Business Week*, June 17, 1991, p. 27.
11. "Abe Peled's secret start-up at IBM," *New York Times*, December 8, 1991, pp. 3–6.
12. "Who's the most pampered motorist of all?" *Business Week*, June 10, 1991, p. 90.
13. "Competition versus collaboration," *Financial Times*, December 3, 1990, "Japanese Industry," p. 5.
14. "Less is more," *Economist*, May 25, 1991, p. 75.
15. Conner advertisement, *CSN*, April 22, 1991, p. 30.
16. "Coping with local sensitivities," *Financial Times*, October 13, 1989, p. 5.
17. Akio Morita, *Made in Japan* (E. P. Dutton, 1986), p. 157.
18. Ray Schultz, "Taking empowerment to the front lines," pp. 2–3 (unpublished essay).
19. James C. Morgan, *Cracking the Japanese Market* (Free Press, 1991), pp. 123ff.
20. "Tape wars: how Philips beat Sony," *Financial Times of Canada*, February 25, 1991, p. 1.
21. "Matsushita, pitting itself against Sony, agrees to back Philips's digital cassettes," *Wall Street Journal*, July 8, 1991, p. B2.
22. "Fujitsu buying maker of computers in Europe," *New York Times*, May 30, 1991, p. D2.
23. "Fujitsu will invest $40.2 million in Hal Computer, a start-up firm," *New York Times*, August 29, 1991, p. B5; "High-tech thriller," *Denver Business*, April, 1990, p. 22.
24. "Fujitsu open for business in Canada," *Computerworld*, June 24, 1991, p. 101.
25. "Fujitsu, McDonnell-Douglas to unveil alliance in factory automation field," *Wall Street Journal*, January 28, 1991, p. B3.
26. "Can new Macs restore shine to Apple's future?" *Computerworld*, December 24, 1990, p. 22.
27. "Apple and IBM discuss a swap of technologies," *Wall Street Journal*, June 7, 1991, p. B1.
28. "Manufacturers convert dealers into franchisees," *Wall Street Journal*, March 13, 1990, p. B1.
29. "Moving the Pampers faster cuts everyone's costs," *Wall Street Journal*, July 14, 1991, Section 3, p. 5.
30. "Dell: mail order was supposed to fail," *Business Week*, January 20, 1992, p. 89.

31. "Compaq Computer finds itself where it once put IBM," *Wall Street Journal,* January 13, 1992, p. B4.
32. "Digital to cut personal computer prices, begin marketing, mail-order campaign," *Wall Street Journal,* January 13, 1992, p. B2; "IBM to test selling its PCs by mail," *Wall Street Journal,* April 29, 1992, p. B1.
33. "It's a shakier perch for Toshiba's laptops," *Business Week,* August 5, 1991, p. 62.
34. "A quantified success," *INC.,* August 1991, p. 54.

Chapter 10: Sell Peace of Mind

1. Gartner Group, Inc., 1986–88 Annual Reports; "Saatchi & Saatchi to sell Gartner for $70 million," *Wall Street Journal,* July 5, 1990, p. B4; "Gartner Group buyout complete," *Computer Systems News,* October 15, 1990.
2. "Otisline," *INC.,* September 1989, p. 8.
3. "Moving the Pampers faster cuts everyone's costs," *New York Times,* July 14, 1991, p. 5; "Reinventing companies," *Economist,* October 12, 1991, p. 67.
4. "Turning a source of headaches into a source of profits," *New York Times,* January 26, 1991, Section 3, p. 10.
5. "DEC unbundles service fees . . ." *Computer Systems News,* November 5, 1990, p. 3.
6. SNET 1989 Annual Report, p. 4.
7. "Review notebooks," *PC World,* February 1992, p. 123.
8. "Achieving quality is an everyday, all-day process," *IBM Directions,* Fall 1990, p. 6.

Chapter 11: Japan's Wish List for the Year 2000

1. Shintaro Ishihara, *The Japan That Can Say No: Why Japan Will Be First Among Equals* (Simon and Shuster, 1990).
2. Shintaro Ishihara, "Forget Pearl Harbour," *Economist,* November 30, 1991, p. 21.
3. Yoshimichi Yamashita, "Japanese executives face life out of the nest," *Wall Street Journal,* December 16, 1991, p. A14.
4. "All eyes are on MITI's research wish list," *Wall Street Journal,* August 24, 1988, p. 10.
5. "Dogfight in the Pacific," *Business Tokyo,* February 1992, p. 29.
6. "Global dogfight: world's major airlines scramble to get ready for competitive battle," *Wall Street Journal,* January 14, 1992, p. 1.
7. "Dogfight in the Pacific," *Business Tokyo,* February 1992, p. 32.
8. "Building new materials from what's lying around," *Business Week,* November 11, 1991, p. 168.
9. "Sweat and superconductors," *Economist,* July 21, 1990, p. 87.
10. "All eyes are on MITI's research wish list," *Wall Street Journal,* August 24, 1988, p. 10.
11. Koji Kobayashi, *Rising to the Challenge* (Harcourt Brace Jovanovich Japan, 1989), p. 61.
12. "Concerns Seek U.S. aid in race for technology," *Wall Street Journal,* June 18, 1991, p. B5.
13. *The U.S. Computer and Semiconductor Industries: A Partnership for Success* (Semiconductor Industry Association, 1990).

14. "Now software isn't safe from Japan," *Business Week,* February 11, 1991, p. 84.
15. "Can the U.S. stay ahead in software?" *Business Week,* March 11, 1991, p. 98.
16. Ibid.
17. Ibid., p. 104.
18. "U.S. manufacturer to sell equipment for making LCD screens for computers," *Wall Street Journal,* September 12, 1991, p. B4.
19. "Polyvision nips the heels of the LCD," *New York Times,* March 1, 1992, p. F7.
20. "The media mess," *Economist,* February 29, 1992, p. 17.
21. "Blurred borders: industries find growth of digital electronics brings in new competitors," *Wall Street Journal,* February 18, 1992, p. 1.
22. "Throw-away high-tech," *Economist,* February 29, 1992, p. 76.
23. "Prices of HDTV sets sink as Sharp creates a cheaper version," *Wall Street Journal,* February 3, 1992, p. B2.
24. "Cool air, Japanese style," *New York Times,* August 11, 1991, p. 10.
25. "Thinking big, Japanese buy Berlitz," *New York Times,* November 11, 1991, p. D9.
26. "After the credits, the debits," *Economist,* February 29, 1992, p. 73.
27. "America cracks down," *Economist,* January 18, 1992, p. 80.
28. "Under water: Japanese purchases of U.S. real estate fall on hard times," *Wall Street Journal,* February 21, 1992, p. 1.
29. "Japan's sharp turn," *Business Week,* March 2, 1992, p. 32.

Chapter 12: Building the Customer-Driven Organization

1. Milton Friedman, "Gammon's Law points to health-care solution," *Wall Street Journal,* November 12, 1991, p. A20.
2. GM expects to post a 1991 loss of nearly $6 billion," *Wall Street Journal,* February 24, 1992, p. B3.
3. "Winter of despair, spring of hope," *Financial Times,* February 17, 1992, p. 12.

Chapter 14: Japan Tomorrow: The Big Green Tsunami

1. "A greener bank," *Economist,* May 23, 1992, p. 79.
2. "Cleaning up," *Economist,* September 8, 1990, Survey, p. 26.
3. "How Japan became so energy-efficient: it leaned on industry," *Wall Street Journal,* September 10, 1990, p. A1.
4. "New order," *Economist,* August 25, 1990, p. 58.
5. "Japan sets an example for the world," *Japan Times Weekly International Edition,* December 17, 1990, p. 12.
6. NTT advertisement, *Look Japan,* September 1991, inside front cover.
7. "Environmental spending," *Economist,* October 12, 1991, p. 107.
8. In an advertisement, the state of Massachusetts ranked growth rates for four high-tech industries in that state in 1991 as follows: environmental manufacturing (30%), biotechnology (23%), software (19%), environmental services (15%), telecommunications equipment (15%); *New York Times,* May 31, 1992, p. D5.
9. "Cleaning up," *Economist,* September 8, 1990, Survey, p. 5.
10. "The perils of greening business," *Economist,* October 14, 1989, p. 75.

11. "Growth vs. environment," *Business Week,* May 11, 1992, p. 74; "Back to conservation," *Economist,* August 11, 1990, p. 27; "Who dares . . . and loses," *Economist,* September 1, 1990, p. 61.
12. "Energy and the environment," *Economist,* August 31, 1991, Survey, p. 21.
13. "Conservation power," *Business Week,* September 16, 1991, p. 90.
14. "Energy and the environment," *Economist,* August 31, 1991, Survey, pp. 12, 19.
15. "Saving the planet," special *Business Week* advertising supplement, p. 97.
16. "Price tag is producing groans already," *Wall Street Journal,* October 29, 1990, p. A7.
17. *Environmental Investments: The Cost of a Clean Environment,* United States Environmental Protection Agency, December 1990, p. v.
18. "For each dollar spent on clean air someone stands to make a buck," *Wall Street Journal,* October 29, 1990, p. A1.
19. "Corporate legal costs in America," *Economist,* August 17, 1991, p. 57.

BIBLIOGRAPHY

Marie Anchordoguy, *Computers, Inc.* (Harvard University Press, 1989).
A thoroughly researched and well-explained history of Japan's computer industry.

William H. Davidow and Bro Uttal, *Total Customer Service* (Harper & Row, 1989).
A thoughtful and practical guide to building an effective customer service strategy, the "ultimate weapon."

Carol Gluck, *Japan's Modern Myths* (Princeton University Press, 1985).
Professor Gluck describes the ideology Japan used to drive its industrialization into high gear during the critical 1890–1912 period. To a very large extent the myths the Japanese created about themselves during this time are those that drive them to this day. Gluck shows how the Japanese think about themselves and the world around them.

Matthews Masayuki Hamabata, *Crested Kimono* (Cornell University Press, 1990).
This is a study of the interwoven structure of Japanese families and Japanese companies. It complements John Roberts's *Mitsui,* describing the familial nature that pervades all Japanese organizations from the household, or *ie,* to the *keiretsu.* Hamabata shows how power is created and transmitted in Japan's important commercial families.

Gary Katzenstein, *Funny Business* (SoHo Press, 1989).
The amusing story of the ups and downs of an American who spends a year working at Sony in Tokyo.

Koji Kobayashi, *Computers and Communications* (MIT Press, 1986).
Kobayashi spells out clearly, in English, how one of Japan's most eminent portwar industrialists thinks. The insights are invaluable. Nowhere else does

a Japanese industrial leader—Kobayashi ran NEC—describe exactly how he thinks a company should operate, who should report to whom, and why. Kobayashi's highly visual style—he draws pictures of everything—can be difficult to follow at first. But once you get the hang of it, one of Japan's largest firms is laid bare. A unique book and essential to understanding how your Japanese competitors think.

Koji Kobayashi, *Rising to the Challenge* (Harcourt Brace Jovanovich Japan, 1989). This is Kobayashi's autobiography, chronicling the rise of an impoverished child to the first rank of industrial power in Japan. Full of insights on NEC operations and methods.

Konosuke Matsushita, *Quest for Prosperity* (PHP Institute, Inc., 1988). Matsushita's brand names—Panasonic, Quasar, and Technics—are in almost every living room in America. Konosuke Matsushita started life as an orphaned street urchin. From nothing he built Matsushita Electric, which today sells $49 billion in consumer and industrial electrical and electronic products. This story of vision and perseverance against all odds is central to any understanding of modern Japan's powerhouses. Reading it back-to-back with John Roberts's *Mitsui* gives a strong impression of the range and scope of the Japanese industrial character.

John Roberts, *Mitsui* (Weatherhill, 1989). A history of one of Japan's great commercial and industrial houses, *Mitsui* is a must read for anyone trying to understand the past, present, and future of Japan's *keiretsu*. Founded in 1683, Mitsui is possibly the oldest business in the world. *Mitsui* is a study in how Japanese firms weather the enormous changes of the centuries.

George Sansom, *A History of Japan* (Stanford University Press, 1958). Breathtaking in its scope and long regarded as the standard history of Japan in English, Sansom is a cornerstone for anyone trying to understand Japan and its ways. In three volumes, the book looks intimidating. But if you are serious about competing with the Japanese, this serious work is for you.

Ronald P. Toby, *State and Diplomacy in Early Modern Japan* (Princeton University Press, 1984). Toby looks at Japan's relations with the outside world during the two and a half centuries before Admiral Perry's 1853 visit to Tokyo Bay. This period, mistakenly regarded as the time of complete isolation was also Japan's most formative. The nation-state of Japan was created then as were most of the management principles used to govern the country and its corporations. How Japan worked with other countries between 1600 and 1853 is essential to understanding how Japan relates to the outside world today.

Karel van Wolferen, *The Enigma of Japanese Power* (Vintage Books, 1990). A clear and level-headed look at Japan's political, social, and industrial structure by a seasoned Japan hand. We liked it so much that we both read it twice. Very little of note happens in Japan today that van Wolferen hasn't already outlined in this thoroughly engaging, often very funny, and well-researched book.

INDEX